The Critical Reception of Edith Wharton

Studies in American Literature and Culture:
Literary Criticism in Perspective

Literary Criticism in Perspective

James Hardin (*South Carolina*), General Editor

Books in the series *Literary Criticism in Perspective* trace literary scholarship and criticism on major and neglected writers alike, or on a single major work, a group of writers, a literary school or movement. In so doing the authors—authorities on the topic in question who are also well-versed in the principles and history of literary criticism—address a readership consisting of scholars, students of literature at the graduate and undergraduate level, and the general reader. One of the primary purposes of the series is to illuminate the nature of literary criticism itself, to gauge the influence of social and historic currents on aesthetic judgments once thought objective and normative.

Edith Wharton on her patio at Pavillion Colombe,
France, ca. 1920s.

Helen Killoran

The Critical Reception
of Edith Wharton

CAMDEN HOUSE

First published 2001
by Camden House

Camden House is an imprint of Boydell & Brewer Inc.
PO Box 41026, Rochester, NY 14604–4126 USA
and of Boydell & Brewer Limited
PO Box 9, Woodbridge, Suffolk IP12 3DF, UK

ISBN: 1–57113–101–9

Library of Congress Cataloging-in-Publication Data

Killoran, Helen, 1941–
    The Critical Reception of Edith Wharton / Helen Killoran.
      p. cm. — (Studies in American literature and culture)
    Includes bibliographical references (p.) and index.
    ISBN 1-57113-101-9 (alk. paper)
      1. Wharton, Edith, 1862–1937—Criticism and interpretation—History.
    2. Women and literature—United States—History—20th century. I. Title.
    II. Series.

PS3545.H16 Z6868 2001
813'.52—dc21

                                                        2001035774

A catalogue record for this title is available from the British Library.

This publication is printed on acid-free paper.
Printed in the United States of America

To the Magnificent Multitudes
Killorans and Jenkinses

Contents

Preface

EDITH WHARTON MAY BE the greatest American author of the early twentieth century—the greatest author, not the greatest female author. Critics who favor other authors may argue, but Edith Wharton will make them work. Before and since R. W. B. Lewis's Pulitzer Prize-winning biography of Edith Wharton, critics have probed the edges, but have yet to pierce the essence of her philosophy, purpose, and narrative technique. Critics during and after her lifetime have criticized her for the purported influence of Henry James, thereby impugning her originality. They have criticized her neglect of the existence of contemporary cultural and historical currents abroad or at home, then decided she could not know about social matters in the United States because she had lived too long in France and could not know current English. They sighed that she had had "it" once, but now "it" was gone.

Nevertheless, some critics have developed a core consensus about how to interpret her major work. One problem with their critical conversation, however, is the tendency to assume another's errors for instance by repeating that Edith Wharton was the pupil of Henry James. It will become quite apparent that the bias here runs largely (but not entirely—see chapter 8) against that idea. Critics have yet to recognize the full dimensions of Edith Wharton's greatness because they have not yet recognized the knowledge, aesthetics, and magnificent technical innovations at the root of her creative philosophy.

This volume on Edith Wharton, in common with the other volumes in the Camden House Literary Criticism in Perspective series, examines critical trends chronologically, making no attempt at all-inclusiveness, but seeking representation. Chapter 1, "Preview," summarizes the trends in the criticism from 1898 to the present and includes the metamorphosis of "the feminine" into feminism. Readers wishing more sophisticated discussions of that subject, can consult the sections of feminist and other theory in libraries or major bookstores. Chapter 2 discusses the vast criticism on *The House of Mirth* (1905), so vast, in fact, that it was necessary to arrange the material chronologically within major topics. Chapter 3 studies *Ethan Frome* (1911). As those familiar with *Ethan Frome* and *Summer* will understand, these works have been variously called long short stories, novellas, and novels. Merely for convenience, the terminology used here is "novel." Chapters 4, 5, and 6 focus on *The Custom of the Country* (1913), *Summer* (1918), and *The Age of Innocence* (1920), respectively. Then chapter 7 notes the rising critical interest in *Ghosts* (1937). Chapter 8, "Review," sums up the main trends, opinions, fads, and political and social changes, from groundbreaking to downright silly, which have shaped the first one hundred years of Edith Wharton's critical reception. It also lists the basic sources for the study of Edith Wharton and her work. A chronological bibliography and index follow. As always, the author must take complete responsibility for errors, opinions, and choice of emphasis.

Acknowledgments

IMUST EXPRESS MY DEEP SADNESS about the death in 1998 of one of the first great Edith Wharton scholars, James Tuttleton, whose work will nevertheless live on. In fact, his reference, with Kristin O. Lauer and Margaret P. Murray, *Edith Wharton: The Contemporary Reviews* (New York: Cambridge UP, 1992) has been indispensable to use of the early reviews. I acknowledge with deepest appreciation the infinite patience of Camden House editors Jim Hardin and Jim Walker, and the generous financial support of Ohio University-Lancaster.

I deeply value the bolstering of my Dad and other family members, the exceptionally efficient OU-L library staff, especially Julia Robinson. My celestially sent Research Assistant, Patricia DeLong, lifted such tremendous burdens from me that she inspired this refrain as I worked: "Thank heaven for Pat!"

Finally, excerpts from *A Backward Glance* and the photograph of Edith Wharton at Pavillon Colombe are reprinted by permission of the Estate of Edith Wharton and the Watkins/Loomis Agency.

Abbreviations for Citations

BG   Edith Wharton. *A Backward Glance*. New York: Appleton-Century, 1934. Rpt. New York: Scribners, 1985.

CC   Edith Wharton. *The Custom of the Country*. New York: Scribners, 1913.

CR   James W. Tuttleton, Kristin O. Lauer, and Margaret P. Murray, eds. *Edith Wharton: The Contemporary Reviews*. New York: Cambridge UP, 1992.

EF   Edith Wharton. *Ethan Frome*. New York: Scribners, 1911.

G   Edith Wharton. *Ghosts*. New York: Appleton-Century, 1937.

GS   Edith Wharton. *The Ghost Stories of Edith Wharton*. New York: Scribners, 1973.

S   Edith Wharton. *Summer*. New York: Appleton, 1918.

After all, one knows one's weak points so well, that it's rather bewildering to have the critics overlook them and invent others.

—Edith Wharton, 19 November 1907

1: Preview—
The Feminine, the Lull, the Feminist

HERS WAS, AND IS, A PUZZLING GENIUS. During Edith Wharton's lifetime, critics grudgingly admired her craftsmanship, but back-handedly referred to it as too clever and too artificial. Then, as if in an attempt to explain the mystery of such artificially clever fiction, they created a myth that imagined her seated at the feet of the man who became known as "The Master," Henry James. James attracted the praise of conservative critics who liked his focus on morals, ethics, and human behavior. Critics with socialist leanings and interest in the welfare of the "lower classes" were offended by wealth. But although both James and Wharton had some wealth, their incomes, by the standards of the wealthy, were modest. But these critics thought that at the feet of the master Wharton absorbed whatever skill and wisdom it takes to become an author. How else could a woman write so well? Women can only imitate greatness.

She never could shake the shadow of Henry James in the eyes of critics and the public. This great author was her dear friend, but in no way her teacher. As late as 1934 she attempted to break the spell in the "Henry James" chapter of *A Backward Glance*. Essentially, Edith Wharton became a victim of repetition and association and, of course, history. Those academic critics under the thrall of early socialism felt that the accident of Wharton's wealth and connections made her undemocratic and outside the spirit of "realism," the genre of writing associated with William Dean Howells, and the preferred writing style of the time. She was accused of being too rich and aristocratic and, obviously, employing servants, the rich and aristocratic could not also develop a social conscience. In addition, her tendency to cite classical allusions irritated her less educated detractors. In a 1922 essay entitled "The Great American Novel," she felt forced to defend the leisure-class subjects she knew best as being just as human as "the man with the dinner pail" (652). Yet she had not ignored the lower classes as testified by *Ethan Frome* (1911), *The Fruit of the Tree* (1913), *Summer* (1918), and any number of short stories.

After she moved to Europe, Wharton found herself criticized as "not American enough," and people insisted that she had lost touch with the sound of American English. Again a victim of history, her charitable efforts for the French and Belgians during the First World War disrupted the regularity of her fictional output. Furthermore, she was accused again and again of writing works that lacked morality, of creating weak characters, and of stiffness, both personal and literary. As time passed, her late work was dismissed as inferior, written by a woman unable to sustain quality when her emotions subsided, a woman as outdated as the dust of old lavender, a woman slipping into the trap of writing magazine fiction merely for the income. Yet the assumption beneath this criticism is that she had been an artist at least once, when she won the Pulitzer Prize for *The Age of Innocence* in 1921.

After Edith Wharton died in 1937, criticism all but ceased, but people quietly continued to read *The House of Mirth* and *Ethan Frome*. The Second World War forced academic critics to put their energy toward the war effort, and critical conversation all but stopped. Interest was aroused once again when Percy Lubbock's biography appeared in 1947—a flash that quickly died out. But as the country settled down after the war, New Critics of the fifties and sixties such as Blake Nevius, Geoffrey Walton, Irving Howe, and others, began to write about her, although none delved as deeply as he might have. The pause continued until the release of Edith Wharton's private papers in 1968 made possible the advent of R. W. B. Lewis's Pulizer Prize-winning biography in 1975.

The publication of Lewis's biography coincided almost exactly with the rise of the first wave of feminism. A second, feminist, biography by Cynthia Griffin Wolff appeared in 1977. The Edith Wharton Society, formed in 1984, began to publish the *Edith Wharton Review*, and to hold biannual conferences that now attract scholars from all over the world. Another group, The Edith Wharton Restoration, purchased The Mount, the home she designed and loved but which had fallen into serious disrepair. Thanks to the work of people like Scott Marshall, progress toward restoration to its original beauty has already resulted in its designation as a historical landmark. Finally, in the nineties, some critics removed her from the cultural contexts that had prevented true appreciation of her work, and Edith Wharton was resurrected and appreciated as a genius and great literary artist. Her works are being reissued in numerous editions, and her out-of-print novels have again found their way into bookstores. Much of this delayed success can be credited to the rise of feminism, but in addition culture simply changed enough for readers to notice that Edith Wharton's novels and stories are not outdated. As a critical perspective, feminism has its politics, however, as do other critical theories. Each develops its own perspective, both illuminating and limiting. As a result, the critical conversation has become vast and challenging. But whatever the cause, Edith Wharton is finally recognized as a great American author.

Victorian Lavender:
The Reception of Wharton During Her Lifetime

Edith Wharton's early stories began to appear in 1898, the end of the Victorian era. The early reviewers who wrote about her praised her craftsmanship, but those who came later smilingly dismissed her work as something to be put in a drawer with a lavender sachet, to be removed some long time later and read with sighs and sentiment. In general, they held two culturally ingrained prejudices against her. First, she belonged to the "inferior" sex, a society female writer entering a tradition scornfully biased against what Nathaniel Hawthorne called "scribbling women." Second, she had the misfortune of fortune, since she had descended from the Dutch patroons and British landowners, whose wealth constituted the "old money" of Manhattan. The supposition was that such a woman could not understand the average working person. The matter worsened in the 1920s when a form of socialism represented by *The New Republic* became popular in academic circles. Critics, mostly academic middle-class men, scorned the accidents of Edith Wharton's wealth and womanhood, and naturally that affected their evaluations of her work. They confused their invented cliché of the fur-clad, pretentious female snob with the content of her stories and novels. Charges abounded that her upper-class characters, based on the privileged "four hundred," constituted too narrow a subject matter: the highly aristocratic social set of New York at the *fin de siècle*, also called the Gilded Age. Critics automatically categorized Edith Wharton with the women of her set—those not college educated, who learned a little French, music, needlework, and tea-pouring from questionably educated governesses. She also bore the burden of her own family, who hurt her deeply by refusing to speak of her as an author. Because Wharton was related to most of the members of New York society, the wound from her family's ostracism of the most valued part of her life can be more easily understood.

Edith Wharton's superb craftsmanship represented the only matter reviewers and critics consistently agreed upon during her lifetime, although some insisted that with their "brilliancy" and "cleverness," the works must be "too clever," "artificial," "unoriginal," "unimportant," or even "classical" to be realist. At a later period, critics did place Wharton among realists, but when the biographies became available, the truth proved strikingly different from the assumptions and generalities.

The general tenor of the criticism can be found in Carl Van Doren, who in 1923 accuses Wharton of exposing upper-class splendors "merely as noisy brass to the finer metal of the authentic inner circles" (95). He calls her milieu less an "American aristocracy" than an "aboriginal aristocracy," whose characters, straying from custom, "walk through their little drama with the non-adventurous stride of puppets" (97), obviously fearful that any straying from custom would invite disaster. While admitting Wharton's "magnificent irony" (98), Van Doren undermines it by reflecting on its coldness and surmising that "her advance in satire may arise from nothing more significant than her retreat into the past for a subject" (98). Yet in the eleven novels Edith Wharton published between 1900 and 1920, only *The Valley of Decision* (1902) about eighteenth-century Italy, and *The Age of Innocence* about New York in the 1870s mined the past. She would write just one more historical novel, *Old New York*, in 1924. (Another, *The Buccaneers* [1937], set in the 1870s, found incomplete at her death, has since been published.) *The House of Mirth* (1905), *The Custom of the Country* (1913)—and in fact all of her other writings—were contemporary with the times during which they written.

The admired craftsmanship became a complaint: it was *too* good. Vernon L. Parrington's jealous-sounding remarks (1921), responding principally to *The Age of Innocence*, at first concede Wharton's "keen intellect" (151), her cerebral analysis, and the structural ingenuity of her books, but then Parrington makes this often-quoted statement, a fuller version of which can be found in chapter 2: "But when one has said that the craftsmanship is a very great success, why not go further and add that it doesn't make the slightest difference whether one reads the book or not. . . . Her distinction is her limitation. . . . " Then, in 1925, in the first book-length work on Edith Wharton, Robert Morss Lovett, apparently another liberal of those times, struck a similar blow, one that began the slow decline of Edith Wharton's reputation. Meanwhile voices in her defense, buried in small journals, went largely unheard. Lovett claims that "Mrs. Wharton" is not only cold, defensive, and snobbish, but " a novelist of class. . . . [and] her conception of class is limited. The background of the human mass is barely perceptible through her high windows . . ." (75). Lovett's insistence that she was a relic who did not understand evolution or the problems of the masses destroyed any sense of her relevance to modern life: "The unleashing of the cruder forces in the racial and industrial conflict has thrown the world back into a more primitive phase of the evolution struggle. All this has come to pass since Edith Wharton made her appearance in Literature nearly thirty years ago. She cannot claim to have been born out of her due time, but it is among the happy consequences of her persistence in her original well-doing that she remains for us among the voices whispering the last enchantments of the Victorian age" (87).

Contributing to the painfully progressive descent of the author's reputation, Regis Michaud (1928) admits Wharton's "excellent craftsmanship" and deft plot construction, but like Lovett, he compares her to Henry James. He calls her characterizations "objectivity verging on indifference and even on cruelty," her field limited, her psychology flimsy (55), and he pronounces the remainder "antediluvian" (56). He insists, in an odd statement, that her "old-fashioned" (55) Victorian characters "live without a real moral background" (58). Then he repeats the leftist position: "Modern critics. . . . are shocked by her indifference to social or political problems" (55–56). Jacob Zeitlin and Homer Woodbridge (1929) quote George Moore's apology for Lovett's "restricted sociological test"—"Is there, or is there not. . . . always an abundance of new novels available of just the sort which the proletariat likes?" Moore concludes that a "revision rather than a reversal of judgment was in process, a new flexibility of thought about Edith Wharton's work" (712). If so, Lovett did not contribute to it.

Possibly the first critic to note the literary depth of Wharton's work, Katharine Fullerton Gerould, in her review of *The Glimpses of the Moon* (1923), gives the conservative, aesthetic viewpoint of Edith Wharton's talent and places her among both male and female writers: "Her superb gift of narrative, her well-nigh faultless building of a plot, none can question. Architectonicé, as Matthew Arnold calls it, is not usually the gift of the female artist; and perhaps the appearance of Mrs. Wharton's name on nearly all the submitted lists of the 'twelve greatest women' is attributed to her masculine power of handling events. . . . In any given novel of hers . . . you always have to recognize her as a master-builder. She knows, infallibly, how to tell a story." Gerould compares Wharton to Balzac in her ability to show society revolving around questions of money (although her main theme is marriage). She praises Wharton's irony, wit, and gift of laughter. The presence of the Fulmer children at the end of the novel demonstrates the kind of humor that contains the truth that "life is like that." Rather than church divorce laws, this is the "real center of the labyrinth . . . this goes back to something . . . fundamental[, a] feeling of a certain type of human being concerning the marriage relation . . . and the Cave is rebuilt in the depths of the Ritz" (CR 307–10).

Other critics, assuming her minor importance as an American author, began short probes of her novels during the "period of neglect" from 1938 to 1975—that is, after her death, until provisions of her will allowed access to her private papers in 1968, and R. W. B. Lewis had time to research and write his revealing biography.

The Lull: 1938–1975

Between 1938 and 1975, Edith Wharton was not quite neglected. After 1938 critical attention diminished, and most attention focused on *The House of Mirth, The Age of Innocence,* or *Ethan Frome.* Writers on Wharton in these years mostly speculated, repeating much of what had previously been written about: her apparent lack of knowledge about her native country and her failure to "discover" it. She had lived abroad too long to know America, people said, explaining her "inferior" late work. A story goes that the question was anticipated by one particularly naive reporter, who arrived at Hyères to interview Edith Wharton. When the young lady asked how Wharton's English stayed so modern, the author replied that she picked it up by listening to peoples' conversations in elevators. The reporter, it is said, took her quite seriously.

New Critics and formalists made brief incursions into Wharton's novels. What genre did her work represent? Was it psychological, realist, naturalist, internationalist, novel of manners, historical, or simply Jamesian imitation? Only one critic uses the term that Wharton herself used in *The Writing of Fiction,* the "chronicle novel."

At the same time, interest in colonial and Puritan influences on Wharton, partly in the context of the regionalist and local color concepts of genre that focused on morality and value, evolved into discussions of the socio-cultural influences of regionalism, determinism, or social Darwinism. Critics eagerly raised questions of genre, of realism and naturalism, anticipating the appearance of a "Great American Novel" that would encompass the entire nation, similar perhaps to the way Tolstoy's *War and Peace* encompasses Russia.

But in general, after the attack on Pearl Harbor on 7 December 1941, the quantity of literary criticism declined radically. The nation turned nearly all its resources, from paper and ink to many of the literary critics themselves, toward winning the Second World War. The specific result was a virtual silence about Edith Wharton (and others) for the dozen years between 1939 and 1951. Even so, serious voices here and there began to repeat the title of an essay by Edmund Wilson (1938), "Justice to Edith Wharton." Wilson provides some biography and a survey of the writings, with a backhanded assertion (to greatly paraphrase) that she was good while she was here, but now she's gone. He refers to her books as dealing with the "artificial moral problems of Bourget" developed in James's least satisfactory manner, having "the character of expensive upholstery" (19). He also calls her a "passionate social prophet" and "at her strongest and most characteristic, she is a brilliant example of the writer who relieves an emotional strain by denouncing his generation" (20). He concludes that she was a "child of a political movement played out, yet passes on something of its impetus to the emergence of the society of the future" (31). But in 1939 Ludwig Lewissohn could still write about Wharton as a Victorian, stressing her status as the social aristocrat related to the Rhinelanders, Roosevelts, Astors, and the rest of the "four-hundred," members of old families on the famous list that Mrs. William Backhouse Astor based on how many people could fit into her ballroom.

In 1947 Yvor Winters included Wharton in his book, but only in the context of a discussion of Henry James. There he argues that the New England moral sense was merely an intensification of that of New York (305). He strangely considers *The Bunner Sisters* her best short novel (307), but redeeming that, gives Wharton serious credit, for at her best she "gives greater precision to her moral issues than James is able to achieve" (310). In addition, the advent of Percy Lubbock's biography (1947), *Portrait of Edith Wharton*, produced an interesting effect, not only letting people feel a false sense of "knowing" the truth about the author, but also encouraging continued interest in her work.

The Feminine

Waves of women's movements have swelled and waned since before the Victorian era and such sea changes are reflected in much early Whartonian criticism. The common assumption, accepted by most men and women, was that literature written by women could not be seriously "literary" because female qualities such as sentiment destroyed the effort. Few would write as Hamilton Wright Mabie (1902) did in discussing *The Valley of Decision* that "Mrs. Wharton is the accomplished artist, to whom the art of writing is an end in itself." Familiar cultural prejudices constantly interfered with a fair evaluation of her work, and when it was more or less fairly evaluated, the automatic second assumption was that a man must be helping out somewhere. Men, and many women, believed that the only way to explain a female writer's serious success was either to find "masculine qualities" in her person or her writing, or to attribute her writing to a man behind the scenes—in this case Henry James. Otherwise, a woman's writing was merely a feminine diversion—a hobby like making riddle books.

As it happened, Wharton's first collection of short stories, *The Greater Inclination* (1898), appeared during an ongoing debate about the value of Henry James's novels. Both wrote in the manner of realism, that is, in a manner meant to evoke life as actually lived, and both emphasized the human damage caused by warped moral values. As a result, Wharton instantly found herself cast in James's shadow. In addition to its innate sexual prejudice, this pairing resulted from a political attempt to place Wharton in the neohumanist literary camp of morality-conscious James supporters and against the socially conscious liberal detractors of James's writing. Furthermore, James served to supply "the man behind the woman" needed to justify any praise awarded to a female writer. The most generous technique of accomplishing this detraction often involved discussing supposedly masculine dimensions of her work, like "cold intellect," as Hildegard Hawthorne does in 1908:

> Some one has said, "Never make a general statement about women, because at most you know a hundred or two, and the other millions probably don't in the least resemble any of your particular collection." But one may perhaps venture on a generalisation of Mrs. Wharton's women, the women she is making familiar to us in one book after another; the women she has drawn with a fine point, decisively, yet with an extraordinary lack of sympathy. These women are creatures of the intellect, and the passions which disturb the current of their cold-flowing lives are of the mind, not of the heart. . . . These women express not excess, but emptiness. (216–17)

"Masculine" qualities such as intellect were nearly attributed to her by men such as Henry Dwight Sedgwick (1908), even as he attempted to defend her femininity:

> When a woman writes a novel such as "Jane Eyre" or "Adam Bede" there is a general masculine agreement that the talents and capacities which created the novel are of a particularly masculine order. In Mrs. Wharton's case men are debarred from any such self-complacent theory, for her talents and capacities are not only intrinsically feminine, but also, despite her cleverness which, general speaking, is a neutral trait, they are superficially feminine. This fundamental fact of Mrs. Wharton's femininity is conspicuous in many ways. . . . There is also in the stories what one may call a certain feminine capriciousness or arbitrariness, even beyond the autocracy of the story-teller,—a method of deciding upon instinct rather than upon reflection. (59–61)

Women writers like Edith Wharton found themselves in a Catch-22: a logical, reasoning woman was accused of frigidity and of writing like a man, but defense of any feminine qualities simply made matters worse, indicating a woman drawing on some unnamed instinct rather than reason. Nevertheless, there is some validity to the observation of Wharton's inability to render strong emotion in her early work, particularly in the earliest stories, in *The Valley of Decision,* and even in *The House of Mirth,* all of which seem to have been written in intellectual overdrive. Yet by the time she had written *Ethan Frome* (1911), she had conquered that weakness. Reviews of *The Greater Inclination,* a collection of stories, illustrate critical attitudes that, although the shading changed, remained fairly constant during Wharton's lifetime. The most popular technique of explaining a successful female writer (beyond quoting Samuel Johnson's comment that the surprise is not in her doing it well, but in her doing it at all) involved aligning her with a successful man like Henry James.

While little disagreement about the quality of her craftsmanship occurred among reviewers and critics of either gender, it required only the coupling of the two names, James and Wharton, to point out a perceived emotional frigidity (which Wharton would probably have called "restraint") a perception that in retrospect seems exaggerated when her work is compared, first to the usually sentimental writing then expected from women, and second to the most famous modernist writers. "Mrs. Wharton writes with the finished ease of the skilled craftsman, and with the feeling and distinction of the artist," writes an anonymous reviewer of *The Greater Inclination* (1899).

But as technical superiority automatically meant that the machinery must be compared to a refrigerator rather than, say, Henry Adams's dynamo, which most readers familiar with Edith Wharton's biography might find more appropriate, the perception of her coldness expanded to criticism of her characters: "Artistry first of all. In technique and finish all she has touched is distinctive. . . . To compare [the novels] to the work of Henry James is conventional, but it is also unavoidable. . . . *The House of Mirth* impress[es] without being impressed with its atmosphere of artificiality. In technique it is near perfection but one cannot breathe. . . . All her women are parasites, cruel as leeches and as soulless" (251). And according to the reviewer for *Munsey's Magazine* (1901), "Her men are subtle and complex ladies wearing mustaches." The question of Wharton's "ineffective" male characters continues today. (See for instance, David Holbrook, *Edith Wharton and the Unsatisfactory Man*). The assumption is that Wharton could not portray a "strong" male character, not that she that deliberately drew these characters in shades of weakness. Some might argue for Ethan Frome's endurance as strength or that Vance Weston and Frenside of *Hudson*

River Bracketed (1929) are, or develop into, strong characters. Even so, the observation seems largely correct. Although weak or strong, if the characters play their parts, the question seems unimportant except for those who want to find "weak men" to emphasize powerful women.

The "emotional frigidity" of which Edith Wharton was constantly accused does allow restraint, a positive quality in most writing. Even so, that skill was presented negatively, as in the *Independent* (1904): "Moral defeat is the sum total of every situation portrayed. . . . and no one except perhaps Mr. Henry James can present a revolting scene with more social delicacy." R. W. B. Lewis reports, however, that Wharton wrote W. C. Brownell, her editor at Scribners, after receiving copies of some reviews he had sent her, that she felt discouraged by "the continued cry that I am an echo of Mr. James (whose books of the last ten years I can't read, much as I delight in the man)" (131).

Unknown to today's critics is the fact that Edith Wharton attempted a response to a review by John D. Barry. In *Literary World* (April, 1899) Barry writes, "I recall reading the first story, 'The Muse's Tragedy,' in *Scribner's Magazine* and being impressed by its fine quality and by its resemblance to the work of Mr. Henry James. The author, Miss Edith Wharton, has evidently studied Henry James very closely. . . ." Miss Wharton apparently does not believe in the principle that a writer should always begin his story or his article with a short phrase. . . . a shrewd bit of advice given many years ago by Col. Thomas Wentworth Higginson to Miss Louisa Alcott [was] always to begin her stories with conversation. . . . Miss Wharton has not as yet mastered her technique . . ." (CR 105–6). And in his May 1899 column, Barry's having heard from Edith Wharton either directly or indirectly, did not improve matters, for at the end of his next column Barry becomes decidedly catty: "She is said . . . not to relish the frequent references made by her readers to her indebtedness to Henry James, so her next book will probably not be marked by a slavish adherence to the methods of a very questionable literary model" (CR 152–53). Barry's comparison annoyed Wharton so unforgettably that she alludes to it thirty-five years later in *A Backward Glance* (1934), using the opportunity cunningly to disassociate herself from Henry James by following her comments with credit to another close friend, Walter Berry:

> "When Mrs. Wharton," the condescending critic wrote, "has learned the rudiments of her art, she will know that a short story should always begin with dialogue."
> "Always"? I rubbed my eyes. Here was a professional critic who seemed to think that works of art should be produced by rule of thumb, that there could be a fixed formula for the design of every

short story ever written or to be written. . . . I had pondered [the principles of my craft] deeply, and this egregious commentary did me the immense service of giving my ponderings an axiomatic form. Every short story, I now saw, like every other work of art, contains within itself the germ of its own particular form and dimensions, and *ab ovo* is the artist's only rule. In an instant I was free forever from the bogey of the omniscient reviewer, and though I was always interested in what was said of my books, and sometimes (though rarely) helped by the comments of the professional critics, never did they influence me against my judgment, or deflect me by a hair's-breadth from what I know to be "the real right" way. . . .

  In this I was much helped by Walter Berry. (BG 114)

As Lewis puts it: "By 1899 it was already too late . . . for so resolute a writer as Edith Wharton to be anybody's *élève*" (131). But no denial would stop an anonymous reviewer for *Critic* (1899) from egregiously accusing her of plagiarizing from Henry James: "The pointing out of plagiarism, or unconscious adaptation or imitation, is a task neither pleasant nor difficult nor lofty. . . . [but it] becomes more imperative in proportion as the work considered is more clever. It is Miss Wharton's cleverness that betrays her and assigns her to her place" (CR 24). Edith Wharton's response to having been falsely put in her "place" among plagiarists is, unlike the unpleasantness with John D. Barry, unrecorded, but her response to having "masculine" qualities was pride. She enjoyed having her writing thought "masculine" because at the time that adjective indicated quality.

  The excerpts that follow should provide a sense of the thinking about "the feminine" in literature in the early part of the century. Again, in 1908, Hildegard Hawthorne, as a female critic, was backhandedly generous, alluding to the criticism of Wharton's frigidity: "Mrs. Wharton writes with a . . . deliberate art, with a satisfying finish. She is wholly devoid of humour, but humour as an asset in the world amid which her creations move would be absolutely undesirable. These people must take each other and be taken with the utmost seriousness. One whole-hearted laugh would melt their icicle existences entirely away" (215). Also in 1908, Henry Dwight Sedgwick's comments contain some contemporary entertainment: "There is . . . in the stories what one might call a certain feminine capriciousness or arbitrariness, even beyond the ordinary autocracy of the story-teller,—a method of deciding upon instinct rather than upon reflection. Take the union of episodes. Mrs. Wharton sees her story in episodes; or rather she sees episodes and puts them together. . . . A man would acknowledge their independence, and leave them apart; but Mrs. Wharton, insisting on her autocratic prerogative, forcibly unites them" (61).

On the other hand, in his 1930 book Fred L. Pattee praises *The Valley of Decision* in a chapter entitled "The Feminine Novel": "She started on her wingings full-fledged: she needs blush at no surviving awkwardness. Again it is noteworthy that her first major novel was an attempt to catch the trade winds of a popular fictional movement. . . . The historical fiction movement produced nothing better done" (250). Then in 1935 Harlan Hatcher, responding to *The Age of Innocence*, praises her in the true patronizing spirit of "The Feminine." The book announced that:

> [T]he most distinguished woman of letters of her generation had felt the strong current of the new day, and that she could remain abreast of it in spirit without losing her established bearings or the delicate odor of Victorian lavender. . . . She had remained the cultivated and decorous lady, fastidious in taste, restrained in irony and in wit. She had preserved her cool detachment from the specimens under her edged scalpel, and under the assault of modernism she had not relaxed her firm grasp on her own materials and her individual methods in creating her art. (90)

Another female critic, Margaret Lawrence, wrote in *The School of Feminity* (1936) of "helpmeets," whom she defines this way: "The helpmeet women are not all gentlewomen in actuality. But they are intrinsically, for they have all the qualities of the gentlewoman. They are self-effacing, faithful and, in the old sense of the word, womanly, which is to be interpreted now, unambitious for themselves" (249). Of Edith Wharton's fiction she remarks, "She places her sympathy, though very delicately, with the men. This does not set her outside the helpmeet class of writer. On the contrary, it encloses her completely within it. For the helpmeet is essentially a man's woman." She goes on to discuss May of *The Age of Innocence* as "the conventionalized presentation of femininity" and an example of "the design for femininity against which the feminist movement was a revolt. . . . Edith Wharton is a romantic and a gentlewoman [who, as a helpmeet writer] believes that somehow this thing between men and women should get settled with dignity and happiness" (258–59).

"The Feminist Takeover of Edith Wharton"

When feminism replaced "the feminine" as a concept after the gap of about a generation, it came in two waves. The first focused on social prejudice against women, which in the main came from the concept of women's repression by a "patriarchal culture." Considering the critical abuse that she had received from men and women such as those quoted above, Edith Wharton appeared on the surface to fit nicely into this category. Feminism's premises included the ideas that women were consistently used for the sexual pleasure of men, forced into marriage, vilified in divorce, pressured out of the professions, denied equal education, equal pay for equal work, and equal participation in politics. On these premises feminists built the concept of the social construction of sexual identity. They agreed that female sexuality is suppressed by men, and also that women have internalized or "reified" men's "patriarchal" idea of women as "Other." In short, women were forced to believe men's lies. Feminists theorized that for the most part sexual identity was not a result of biological factors, but of a social hegemony (a psychological infusion of male-founded state and cultural concepts) designed to deprive women of power. Why men would wish to control in this way has been explained mainly in terms of their desire for sexual dominance, though the biological source of desire for dominance seems at least partly to contradict the concept of social construction. But as will become evident, biological theories emerged as well.

The critical evolution of Edith Wharton into a feminist began cautiously enough. Against stronger voices, Peter Conn (1983) regarded Wharton as having come only halfway to feminism. While "her loyalty was always to stability and tradition," she was also "the victim of traditional codes and customs" and consequently "a profoundly divided woman" (173).

The "first phase" of feminism began with Virginia Woolf's ideas as expressed in *A Room of One's Own* (1929) and *Three Guineas* (1938) and ended, most probably, with *The Second Sex* by Simone de Beauvoir (1949). First-phase feminists emerging in the seventies attempted to show that as a divorced, childless woman living alone in Europe, Edith Wharton had carved a niche in the male profession of authorship. This, they reasoned, showed her sympathy to feminists who rallied for male/female parity. Margaret McDowell (1974), writing five years before the publication of *The Madwoman in the Attic*, a seminal critical work of feminism, attempts to align Edith Wharton with feminism by building ironies around stereotypes: "Repeatedly she questioned the validity of a woman's submitting to the restrictions imposed upon her in a male-oriented society." She further points out that the subject of a third of Wharton's novels and stories is "the marriage question." Wharton exposes the "penalties experienced by women as they confronted such common realities as abortion, illegitimacy, economic dependence, and the double standard of sexual morality" (520). McDowell cites *The Fruit of the Tree* (1907) as a feminist novel because its protagonist is a professional nurse. She says carefully, however, that "the exact nature of Edith Wharton's feminism resists easy definition," but that "it is possible to deduce from her work her feminist concerns, which thus tend to be cumulative and implicit rather than explicit" (523). Cynthia Griffin Wolff felt bolder. She used Erikson's psychological theory of adult development combined with a feminist approach, writing Edith Wharton's biography to interpret many of her works in *A Feast of Words: The Triumph of Edith Wharton* (1977). Wolff and McDowell proved to be the vanguard of this "first phase" of feminism regarding Edith Wharton. In 1980 Elizabeth Ammons attempted to show that Wharton's "fiction records her public argument with America on the issue of freedom for women . . . [and] is both a record of one brilliant and intellectually independent woman's thinking about women and a map of feminism's ferment and failure in America in the decades surrounding the Great War" (ix).

Subsequently, second-phase feminism developed into two branches. This phase was rooted in Betty Friedan's *The Feminine Mystique* (1963), a popular book based on the idea that bored, frustrated middle-class American women felt trapped in intellectually stifling domesticity. Second-phase feminist criticism looks most closely at female biology as a source of positive creativity in life and art, regarding it as a difference to celebrate. It sees women's experiences as differing from men's, but notes oppression by a male-dominated language intended to exclude women. If women are limited by words like "chairman" and "postman" and otherwise excluded from the language, how can they become writers, let alone postal workers? Feminists also began to examine the unconscious, beginning to use the Lacanian theories derived from Freudian and Kristevian theories. They pointed to social and economic conditions, the inadequacy and absence of institutions helpful to women, and women's financial victimization by a patriarchal economic system. This criticism began to absorb the literary Marxism and socialism that had excluded Edith Wharton (and Henry James) in the thirties because of their relative wealth and their subject matter related to the social upper classes.

Alexandra Collins (1982) provides an example of second-phase feminist criticism when she compares Edith Wharton's *The Reef* to Virginia Woolf's *Mrs. Dalloway*. Her conclusion is primarily a reiteration of the 1930s' Marxist ideals:

> [T]hey reveal similar views toward the future of civilization. In their writing, they show a certain disdain for democracy. Both fear the chaotic force of humanity as a whole, unable to understand what Wharton called "the man with the dinner pail" and "promiscuous contacts" with "agglutinated humanity" (*The Reef*, p. 10) and what Woolf de-

scribed in her letters as "The London poor, half-drunk and very sentimental or completely stolid with their hideous voices and clothes and bad teeth," and that for both art is the "key element in the . . . creation of a more ideal world." (56–7)

A second branch of second-phase feminist theories led to a less exclusively American and European view, to include third-world enslavement under postcolonial regimes. Many critics felt that the first branch of the second phase breaks down too simply into a binary opposition that omits many diverse elements of race and class. Second-phase, second-branch feminism is a more activist movement than the others, as shown by Kate Millett's angry *Sexual Politics* (1969). That powerful book distinguished between sex and gender, regarding the patriarchy as viewing the female as an inferior male. At nearly the same time, Shulamith Firestone wrote *The Dialectic of Sex* (1970), which attempted to substitute sex for class as the prime historical determinant. Germain Greer's *The Female Eunuch* (1970) shows the neutralization of women's power by a patriarchal society, while Sheila Rowbotham's *Hidden from History* (1973) discusses how Marxist theory ignores women and how Marxist feminists' main task should be to study relations between gender and the economy. In *Women's Consciousness, Man's World* (1973) Rowbotham points out the double oppression of the sexual division of labor of women at work and in the home. Subsequent Marxist-feminists showed a particular interest in *The House of Mirth* and *The Custom of the Country* because of these novels' subjects—women trying to improve their social and personal status by marrying wealthy men, apparently having no other choice. Yet further examples seemed hard to obtain.

Soon Elaine Showalter created "gynocriticism," an alternate canon of "suppressed" women's literature and culture, for feminists tended to attribute the literary quality and equality of the traditional "white male" canon to suppositions based on the ideas of deconstruction. Criticizing the "narrow literariness" of the early work of Gilbert and Gubar, feminist theorists of this second phase-second branch adapted the deconstructionist theories of Derrida and others for their purposes because they purport to show that texts have no fixed meaning. "Texts" is used as a democratic word meant to equalize, for instance, the works of Shakespeare with matchbook covers, or of Tolstoy with candy wrappers, for if texts have no fixed meaning, no fixed value can be placed upon them. But as James Tuttleton so aptly phrases it, based on aesthetics, "these writers [Augusta Jane Evans Wilson, Harriet Beecher Stowe, Fanny Fern, and Mrs. E.D.E.N. Southworth] were being held out to us, with a straight face, as neglected geniuses worthy of comparison with Hawthorne, Melville, and Henry James" (8).

Pushing feminist ideas even further, and into problematic areas for critics who wish to support Edith Wharton—who had been so often accused of literary frigidity—the gender theories of Helene Cixous and Luce Irigaray stress the "writing effect of the text" and "writing the body," encouraging women to allow their sexual energy to flow into their writing as men presumably do. They should find and overcome or remove the "phallocentrism" of literary and social constructs. Lesbian feminists such as Mary Daly in *Gyn/Ecology* (1978) chart male sexual violence in all cultures and history, and suggest a new "gynomorphic" vocabulary with which to counter male mythology. The poet Adrienne Rich wrote her influential essay, "Compulsory Heterosexuality and Lesbian Existence" (1980) to theorize that by way of an invisible "lesbian continuum" all women are innately lesbian or "abnormal," allowing them to share their own history and culture outside of the "rapacious power" of a heterosexual patriarchal culture.

Most feminist criticism of Edith Wharton and her work remains within the first phase or the first branch of the second phase, presumably because her subject matter and characters do not lend themselves well to second-phase, second-branch investigation. There are, for instance, no African-American characters or easily recognizable homosexual characters. Some attempts have been made to establish or refute Wharton's prejudice against Jews by using Simon Rosedale from *The House of Mirth* as a prime example, supplemented by a few offhand remarks in some letters, but those essays are at best "slippery," as deconstructionists view language.

An examination of the criticism reveals that, for the most part, two types of feminists write about Edith Wharton: radical and moderate. The radicals generally study feminism rather than Edith Wharton. These women often attempt to prove a feminist theory by using examples from an author's work. By the laws of logic, however, examples chosen because they prove the theory are fallacies of hasty generalization, and such critics rarely appear more than once in Wharton's bibliographical literature. The other group consists of women and some empathetic men who primarily study Edith Wharton, but who also espouse feminism. These critics range from those who use variations of feminist theories to illuminate Edith Wharton and her work, to those who in varying degrees are likely to include some close reading and use feminist theories moderately in their subjects and conclusions. Voices of dissent and a few simple abstainers also exist, but generally find their ideas drowned out by the very volume of feminist points of view.

Julie Olin-Ammentorp issued a caution in 1988: "Most feminist critics seem to imply that Wharton, though never one to ally herself with the feminist movements of her day, was a kind of inherent feminist" (237). Rather, she argues, Wharton was a "special woman who accepts her own success as something due to her, something she has earned" (242). "Edith Wharton's challenge to feminist criticism is the challenge created by historical distance and by shifting definitions of feminism itself." She continues by saying that in shaping a "Wharton who conforms to . . . expectations . . . [feminist critics] have oversimplified the complexities of Wharton's personality and times," and that although they have respected her genius, "they have detached it from the woman as a whole" (243).

Olin-Ammentorp's voice was joined by that of James Tuttleton in a controversial essay entitled "The Feminist Takeover of Edith Wharton" (1989). He describes a conference where "speaker after speaker assumed as a given that Mrs. Wharton had languished in obscurity, stifled by the critical prejudice of the patriarchy, until the present generation of feminist critics had rescued her from oblivion." He continues: "All of this suggested to me a complete unfamiliarity with the massive bibliography of Wharton studies before the 1970s" (8). Having written several annotated bibliographies of Edith Wharton, he formed a background from which to make that statement. He mentions that the "thirty-year ban on the inspection of her private papers delayed . . . biography and other kinds of cognate criticism" (9) and goes on to discuss the fiction and how it "does not serve very well to buttress the ideology of a feminism engaged in an attack on men, their domination and cruelty, on marriage as such, or on the so-called patriarchy" (11).

This side of the argument is beautifully summed up by Elsa Nettles (1997):

> [Edith Wharton] did not conceive of the writers she revered as belonging to a masculine tradition inherently hostile to women. It is true, she was sensitive to the prejudice against women writers; she attacked [a literary] double standard. . . . But she did not seek to create or validate a woman's tradition implicit in the idea of a masculine tradition to which women are alien. Unlike Virginia Woolf, she did not regard the language of English literature as the creation of men, its syntax ill-suited to the needs of the female writer. She did not view the English language itself as an instrument of male domination or feel the need to create a new sentence or a new language. Paradoxically, the fashionable society which marginalized writers, denied her literary companionship and never acknowledged her importance as a writer, in at least one way made men and women equal. In upholding as a part of its code of manners a standard of speech to which both men and

women were taught to conform, her society made its language the
possession and privilege of both its male and female members. (87)

According to Tuttleton, "One could, without embarrassment or hy-
perbole, intelligently compare [Edith Wharton] with Howells and
James, Scott Fitzgerald and Sinclair Lewis, and others" (8).

Earlier critics, assuming her minor importance as an American author,
began a short probe of her novels during the "period of neglect" from
1938 to 1975, after her death and before the provisions of her will allowed access to her private papers. One exception was James Gray
(1946) who argues that with, among other things, her talent for
"making epigrams . . . she greatly affected the novel in our time" (85)
but after *The Age of Innocence* she fell into the trivial and tawdry. Then
in 1947 Lubbock's influential but snide *Portrait of Edith Wharton* appeared, creating a short spark of public interest. After the war, as criticism gradually reappeared, Anne Freemantle (1951) takes an entirely
different approach. She notes the "moral truth" defended by the col-
lective conscience, but also indicates that

> Mrs. Wharton, in brief, has been far too much the professional
> novelist to sustain the qualities which first and very justly brought her
> fame. These were . . . an unflagging distinction of manner and a very
> high and very penetrating wit. Nor was this all. Her people were very
> much alive and several of her earlier books at least had that virtue so
> immensely rare in our letters: architectonic beauty, beauty of inner
> structure. Yet her work is fading and crumbling and will be almost
> forgotten until a time so detached from the present arises that people
> can go back to a little of it as to something quaint and sweet and
> lavendered, wondering that . . . Edith Wharton could have taken seri-
> ously the conventions of a small and unimportant social group, could
> have in ultimate judgment identified herself with these futile and fugi-
> tive notions and confronted the moral world with the standards of a
> silly and cruel game. Yet that is what from first to last she has done.
> (466)

However, Blake Nevius (1953) offers three reasons why Wharton
should have a permanent claim on critical attention: she successfully
chronicled the twilight of old New York, she was second only to Henry
James as a novelist of manners, and she "overcomes . . . the narrowing
influence of her subject matter by her exploitation of two great and in-
terlocking themes" (9). The themes are "the spectacle of a large and
generous nature . . . trapped by circumstances ironically of its own de-
vising into consanguinity with a meaner nature," and a definition of
"the nature and limits of individual responsibility" (10).

The notable difference in tone between Freemantle and Nevius deserves comment. Freemantle represents, along with "moralism," Marxism, and several other movements, "impressionist criticism," one of the forms against which the New Critics of the forties responded in protest. Impressionist critics judged a book by the feelings they experienced while reading it, and while Freemantle also notes Edith Wharton's ability to structure a novel, most of the comments quoted above represent an emotional reaction. Another pressure against which New Critics reacted, while at the same time trying to adopt some of its principles, was science. After the Second World War, Hiroshima and Nagasaki, and volatile industrialization, science became the glamorous subject in the universities at the expense of the humanities. Literary critics both hated it and attempted to emulate it. So even though the New Criticism was declared "dead" about 1950, it and its structured "scientific" methods of reacting to literature stayed alive at least until the seventies, and in fact, vestiges of it can still be found. According to Vincent B. Leitch, the major critics associated with New Criticism by the late 1940s were T.S. Eliot, I. A. Richards, William Empson, John Crowe Ransom, Alan Tate, R. P. Blackmur, Cleanth Brooks, René Wellek, W. K. Wimsatt and, to some extent, Kenneth Burke, F. R. Leavis, and Yvor Winters (24), names that occur throughout these pages. The original ideals of New Criticism were to expunge politics and purify the aesthetics of criticism, but of course, like most criticism, it spread in many directions and took on as many new purposes. Unlike criticism that preceded it, it refused to die when it was "dead."

Louis Auchincloss, interpreting setting (part of the purview of New Criticism), wrote a survey of Wharton's work (1961) in which he notes insightfully that "perfection irritates as well as it attracts" (21) to explain some people's aversion to Edith Wharton. He calls her "not only the pioneer but the poet of interior decoration," referring to her precise descriptions of interiors. Irving Howe's introduction to *Edith Wharton* (*Twentieth Century Views*) opens with the frequently echoed phrase of Edmund Wilson's, "Justice to Edith Wharton," but devotes itself to "the problems faced by Mrs. Wharton's critics" (2)—whether she actually was the heiress of Henry James, and whether she adequately addressed "the world and its change." It suggests exploring Wharton's "dark personal vision," an apparent reference to questions of morality-religion-determinism-naturalism, as well as the psychological dimension, which also became one of the topics of New Criticism. Michael Millgate (1964) remarks that James's failure to "depict the American money-maker in action" is highlighted by Edith Wharton's success with *The Custom of the Country,* and proclaims that Wharton "occupies an extremely important intermediary position between [the generations of] James and Fitzgerald" (63). He remarks (without examples) that *The Custom of the Country's* characters and situations can be found in originals in the novels of Howells or James (64), but he notes that "the achievement of Edith Wharton still remains insufficiently recognized" (66).

Gary Lindberg (1975) cites Edith Wharton as a writer of the novel of manners. Not only does he put her in the company of Austen, Balzac, Stendhal, and Tolstoy, but also he recognizes, as Hatcher put it in 1935, that "she wrote of a time when social assumptions tried to survive under a historical change from a mercantile to an industrial economy, the enormous gap separating [her] world . . . from that of the great and growing industrial democracy." Because of this, in Wharton's novels, unmannered "Goth invaders" disregard manners useless in their view of the "continuity of human affairs." Lindberg reasons that Wharton and the limitations of characterization under the constraints of this form should be assessed in the context of American literature, for "she is, curiously enough, as self-conscious about manners and social structures as Emerson or Mark Twain . . . in her constant urge to explain the network of manners" (173).

But the book that changed (and perhaps charged) everything, was the Pulitzer Prize-winning *Edith Wharton: A Biography* by R. W. B. Lewis, which was published on the cusp of the rise of feminism. It revealed several surprises about the writer. Most startling to those who had come to perceive Edith Wharton as a frigid Victorian was Lewis's discovery that she had had a passionate extramarital affair with Morton Fullerton and had left behind the pornographic fragment, "Beatrice Palmato," concerning father-daughter incest, apparently intended as background to a short story. Lewis traces (and dispels) rumors that Wharton was the illegitimate daughter of one of her brothers' tutors and reveals a "nervous breakdown" (probably a severe case of clinical depression) about 1898 and he finds no basis for the assumption that James had been her mentor. To his amazement, Lewis also discovers that Wharton had attempted to exert deliberate control over any future biography by leaving a packet of papers labeled "For My Biographer" (xi). A person could conclude that she was arrogant, or that she simply knew, as she might know any fact, that the value of what she had accomplished would eventually surface. Lewis terms her "shrewd" and "one of the most intelligent women who ever lived" (xii). Such details jumped off his pages and into the gristmill of feminist criticism.

Only two years later a second, quite different biography appeared, by Cynthia Griffin Wolff. Whereas Lewis had used traditional historical biographical techniques with some use of Erikson, Wolff preferred to apply Eriksonian psychological theory to Wharton's life, interpreting it as the victory of a woman over patriarchal oppression. She analyzed Wharton's fiction through the lens of Eriksonian stages of life to show the psychological changes and growth that led to her conquering most social obstacles.

Thus, the foundation for feminist interpretations of Edith Wharton's life and work had now been laid. Both biographies reveal a woman of compassion and of passion, of long and loyal friendships, a person who treated her lifelong servants as family, but whose defensive shyness made her appear stiff and formidable in public. Because of her perfectionism she could be difficult, and because of her quick wit and strong opinions, she occasionally hurt peoples' feelings. She had some incompletely explained fallings out with members of her family. Overall she emerges as a person of compassion, humor and vast interests. Unfortunately, Wharton's disapproval of Lubbock's marriages probably led to his untrustworthy biography.

Lubbock's biography, first accepted as a "charming" and "true portrait" of the author now appears more and more unreliable—even devious—in light of the work of Lewis and Wolff. No longer were critics forced to depend on Lubbock's innuendoes and circumlocutions, and Wharton's evasive memoir, *A Backward Glance* (1934). Lewis's biography mostly summarizes rather than analyzes Wharton's work, but points to the promise of the neglected short stories, while Wolff's biography provides painstaking feminist readings of much of Wharton's writing, all worth careful consideration. Like two meteorites hitting the earth on the same day, the publication of these revealing biographies coincided with and fed feminist theories, the side effect of which has been the increase in speed and volume of articles and books about her.

It seems that whatever issues reviewers and critics have raised—Wharton's "Jamesianism," her craftsmanship, the influence of sexual roles, class bias, her triumph after the Pulitzer Prize and her honorary doctorate at Yale, her "frigid" or "detached" attitude, her lack of psychological insight, or her failure to create sympathetic characters—critics generally (with some notable exceptions) took the kernel of truth in the wrong direction until after the publication of the Lewis and Wolff biographies. Eventually, however, critics began to correct course as will become apparent beginning with *The House of Mirth.*

Works Consulted

Ammons, Elizabeth. *Edith Wharton's Argument with America*. Athens, GA: U Georgia P, 1980.

Auchincloss, Louis. *Pioneers and Caretakers: A Study of 9 Women Novelists*. Minneapolis, MN: U of Minnesota P, 1961.

Barry, John D. "New York Letter." *Literary World* (1 April 1899): 105.

———. "New York Letter." *Literary World* (13 May 1899): 152–53.

Collins, Alexandra. "The Art of Self-Perception in Virginia Woolf's *Mrs. Dalloway* and Edith Wharton's *The Reef*." *Atlantis* 7.2 (Spring 1982): 47–58.

Conn, Peter. *The Divided Mind: Ideology and Imagination in America 1898–1917*. New York: Cambridge UP, 172–96.

Daly, Mary. *Gyn/Ecology: The Metaethics of Radical Feminism*. Boston, MA: Beacon, 1978.

de Beauvoir, Simone, *The Second Sex*. 1949. Ed. and trans. H. M. Parshley. New York: Vintage, 1974.

Firestone, Shulamith. *The Dialectic of Sex: The Case for Feminist Revolution*. New York: William Morrow, 1970.

Freemantle, Anne. "Edith Wharton: Values and Vulgarity." H. C. Gardiner, S. J. (ed.), *Fifty Years of the American Novel: A Christian Appraisal*. New York: Scribners, 1951.

Gerould, Katharine Fullerton. "Mrs. Wharton's New *House of Mirth*." *New York Times Book Review* (23 July 1922): 1, 2.

Gilbert, Sandra M. and Susan Gubar. *The Madwoman in the Attic: The Woman Writer and the Nineteenth-Century Literary Imagination*. New Haven, CT: Yale UP, 1979.

Gray, James. *On Second Thought*. Minneapolis, MN: U of Minnesota P, 1946.

Greer, Germain. *The Female Eunuch*. London: MacGibbon & Kee, 1970.

Hatcher, Harlan. *Creating the Modern American Novel*. Murray Hill, New York: Farrar & Rinehart, 1935. 28–89.

Hawthorne, Hildegarde. *Women and Other Women: Essays in Wisdom*. New York: Duffield, 1908. 212–31.

Holbrook, David. *Edith Wharton and the Unsatisfactory Man*. New York: St. Martin's, 1991.

Lawrence, Margaret. *The School of Femininity*. New York: Stokes, 1936. 248–64.

Lawson, Richard H. *Edith Wharton*. New York: Ungar, 1977.

Leitch, Vincent B. *American Literary Criticism from the 30s to the 80s.* New York: Columbia UP, 1988. 24–59.

Lewis, R. W. B. *Edith Wharton: A Biography.* New York: Harper & Row, 1975.

Lindberg, Gary H. *Edith Wharton and the Novel of Manners.* Charlottesville, VA: UP of Virginia, 1975.

Lovett, Robert Morss. *Edith Wharton.* New York: McBride, 1925.

Lubbock, Percy. *Portrait of Edith Wharton.* New York: Appleton-Century-Crofts, 1947.

Mabie, Hamilton Wright. "Mr. Mabie's Literary Talks." Rev. of *The Valley of Decision. Ladies Home Journal* 19 (May 1902): 17.

McDowell, Margaret. "Viewing the Custom of her Country: Edith Wharton's Feminism." *Contemporary Literature* 15 (1974): 521–38.

Michaud, Regis. *The American Novel To-Day: A Social and Psychological Study.* Trans. of *Le roman Americain d'aujourdhui.* Paris: Boivin, 1926. Boston, MA: Little, Brown, 1928.

Millett, Kate. *Sexual Politics.* 1969. New York: Avon, 1970.

Millgate, Michael. "The Novelist and Other Businessmen: Henry James, Edith Wharton, Frank Norris." *American Social Fiction: James to Cozzens.* New York: Barnes and Noble, 1964.

"Mrs. Wharton's Nativity: The Clever and Subtle Disciple of Henry James a Native of the American Metropolis." Rev. of *Crucial Instances* by Edith Wharton. *Munsey's Magazine* (June 1901): 435–36.

Nettles, Elsa. *Language and Gender in American Fiction: Howells, James, Wharton and Cather.* Charlottesville, VA: UP of Virginia, 1997.

Nevius, Blake. *Edith Wharton: A Study of Her Fiction.* 1953. Berkeley, CA: U of California P, 1961.

Olin-Ammentorp, Julie. "Edith Wharton's Challenge to Feminist Criticism." *Studies in American Fiction* 16.2 (Autumn 1988): 237–44.

Parrington, Vernon L. "Our Literary Aristocrat." *Pacific Review* 2 (June 1921): 157–60. Rpt. in *Edith Wharton: A Collection of Critical Essays.* Ed. Irving Howe. Englewood Cliffs, NJ: Prentice-Hall, 1962. 1151–54.

Pattee, Fred L. *The New American Literature 1890–1930.* New York: Century, 1930. 245–54.

"Review of *The Descent of Man and Other Stories.*" *Independent* 56 (June 1904): 1334–35.

"Review of *The Greater Inclination.*" *Academy* 57 (8 July 1899): 40.

Rich, Adrienne. "Compulsory Heterosexuality and Lesbian Existence." *Signs: Journal of Women in Society and Culture* 5.4 (1980) Rpt. in *Compulsory Heterosexuality and Lesbian Existence*. Denver, CO: Antelope, 1980. 3–32.

Rowbotham, Sheila. *Hidden from History: 300 Years of Women's Oppression and the Fight Against It*. London: Pluto, 1973.

———. *Women's Consciousness, Man's World*. London: Penguin, 1973.

Sedgwick, Henry Dwight. *The New American Type and Other Essays*. Boston, MA: Houghton-Mifflin, 1908. 53–95.

Tuttleton, James W. "The Feminist Takeover of Edith Wharton." *The New Criterion* (March 1989): 6–14.

———. *The Novel of Manners in America*. Chapel Hill, NC: U of North Carolina P, 1972.

Tuttleton, James W., Kristin O. Lauer, and Margaret P. Murray. *Edith Wharton: The Contemporary Reviews*. New York: Cambridge UP, 1992.

Van Doren, Carl. *Contemporary American Novelists: 1900–1920*. New York: Macmillan, 1923.

Wharton, Edith. *A Backward Glance*. New York: Appleton-Century, 1934. Rpt. New York: Scribners, 1985.

———. "The Great American Novel," *Yale Review* 16 (April-July 1927): 646–55.

Wilson, Edmund. "Justice to Edith Wharton." 1941. Rpt. in Irving Howe, ed., *Edith Wharton*. Englewood Cliffs, NJ: Prentice-Hall, 1962. 19–31.

Winters, Yvor. *In Defense of Reason*. New York: Swallow P. and William Morrow, 1947.

Wolff, Cynthia Griffin. *A Feast of Words: The Triumph of Edith Wharton*. New York: Oxford UP, 1977.

Zeitlin, Jacob and Homer Woodbridge. *Stuart Pratt Sherman: Life and Letters*. 2 Vols. New York: Farrar & Rinehart, 1929.

2: *The House of Mirth—* From Morality to Taxidermy

A CINDERELLA STORY IN REVERSE, *The House of Mirth* (1905) concerns an orphan, Lily Bart, who becomes the restless flower of New York high society. She knows that her literal survival depends upon marriage to any man who can provide the appropriate money and family status. But Lily's reservations involve a complex of conscience, prejudice, love for Lawrence Selden, and her inability to visualize herself married. Every moment calculated to result in an engagement finds Lily distracted elsewhere. Believing a relatively small allowance from her Aunt Peniston inadequate, Lily supports her search for a wealthy husband by acting as secretary to her hostesses and accepting gifts of last year's gowns. Her one moment of triumph occurs in a scene in the center of the novel in which she poses as *Mrs. Lloyd*, the subject and title of Sir Joshua Reynolds' painting, in a *tableaux vivants* entertainment designed to launch the Wellington Brys into high society. While some appreciate the artistry of her effort, a number of the men feel that the diaphanous draperies of the painting purposely advertise her sexual wares. When Lily also succumbs to the temptation to gamble, a losing streak prompts her to accept Gus Trenor's offer to "invest" her remaining funds in the stock market. She naively fails to realize that for Trenor the resulting "dividends" are intended to purchase her favors. When Bertha Dorset, Lily's best friend, hears of this, she transforms into Lily's worst enemy, successfully contriving to throw Lily out of high society. Lawrence Selden comes to her rescue, but too late. Lily tries to work for a living, fails, and accidentally-on-purpose (the story is purposefully vague) dies alone in a cheap boarding house after taking an overdose of chloral hydrate, a sleeping potion.

Questions of Morality

At its publication, reactions were for the most part either scathing or ecstatic, depending to a great extent on whether the reviewers caught the novel's irony. Either way, the conclusions of many reviewers depended on how they perceived Edith Wharton's treatment of morality. They easily recognized the source of the title in Ecclesiastes: "The heart of the wise is in the house of mourning; but the heart of fools is in the house of mirth" (Eccl 7:4), but they wondered whether it was absolutely necessary for Wharton to allow the heroine die in order to make her moral point. In the air still lingered the belief, going at least as far back as Dr. Samuel Johnson, that what people read would affect their morals.

An anonymous reviewer for the *Independent* excoriates the book for its indulgence of immoral modern fashions. Reviewers in the *Nation*, *Bookman*, *Literary Digest* and others tend to agree. Charles Eliot Norton, the father of Edith's good friend Sara (Sally) Norton and soon-to-be President of Harvard, in a view widely shared, "huffed a little and laid it down that no woman not spotlessly virtuous (which ruled out Lily Bart) could be the heroine of a truly serious novel" (Lewis 152). On the other side, the *Outlook* reviewer, no whit less moralistic, finds that a "story of such integrity of insight and workmanship is an achievement of high importance in American life" (CR 113), and, according to James McArthur in *Harper's Weekly*, "Never was a society summoned to a sterner tribunal than in this book" (CR 118).

Edith Wharton's friend, Paul Bourget, in the preface to his French translation of the novel, *Chez les heureux du monde* (1908), naturally praises the novel as "a masterpiece of . . . the [novel of manners] genre." But others who did not know her, including many famous authors and publishers, also acclaim it, including Hamlin Garland, the *Century's* R. W. Gilder, and Mary Cholmondely. Thomas Wentworth Higginson (who first published Emily Dickinson) considers the novel "to stand at the head of all American fiction, save Hawthorne alone" (Lewis 152). Henry James, who had famously urged Edith Wharton to remain "tethered to native pastures," seems of two opinions, on the one hand admiring the book, but on the other finding it "two books and too confused," as well as "better written than composed." However, he blames the "deadly difficulties" of writing a novel of manners about America (Lewis 153). In a new generation, critics like Nancy Topping Bazin (1983) and Margaret McDowell (1990) weigh questions of morality quite differently. Bazin describes three ethics at work in the novel, Christian, capitalist, and male chauvinist, each of which requires that Lily "compromise her dignity and self-respect" (97); she concludes that the novel is weakened by Wharton's "sentimentalization of the domestic ideal, the working class, the early pieties, and death" (107). But McDowell proposes that a main theme of the novel is Lily's moral victory in a directionless society. By destroying the letters she could have used as blackmail to ensure her readmission to it, she returns good for evil.

Structure and Theme

As a result of the predominately high praise, the illustrated hardback of *The House of Mirth* sold 140,000 copies in its first year at $1.50 per copy, and it remained a bestseller through 1906 (Lewis 151). Not surprisingly, its success firmly established Edith Wharton's reputation as a novelist, and brought her serious critical attention.

Unlike those critics who feel that the characters and scenes lack contrast, the editor and critic, Robert Brownell, lauds the novel's "grand construction" (Lewis, 154). Several years later, Carl Van Doren (1923) acknowledges its beauty of structure but finds the work "fading and crumbling." The tragedy of Lily Bart in *The House of Mirth* he says, is not "that of a woman crushed by the trivial notions of trivial people; Lily is shown as one whose weakness it was that she could not win upon the contemptible terms of their idiotic game" (466–67).

Irving Howe's 1952 essay, "A Reading of *The House of Mirth*," expresses reservations about Wharton's tone and style, especially her "ladies' magazine rhetoric," and he is troubled by the detachment of the plot from "moral positives." But he examines the novel's structure perceptively, tracing Lily's literal step-by-step descent into social oblivion (129). The question of the novel's structure, or lack of it, continues to occupy many critics. Lawrence J. Dessner (1983) finds that it "lacks crucial aspects of overall design" (57), but Judith Fryer (1986) convincingly maps the major scenes in the novel showing how they descend through stages of increasing disorder until the death scene in which Lily carefully orders her few remaining possessions. Other critics carry the concept of symbolic structure even further. Annette Larson Benert (1990) claims that the structure of the novel is not linear but spatial, and that the carefully designed interior spaces contain a "web of signification" (28) linking outer and inner worlds in a geography that "gradually excludes Lily . . . from human society" by relegating her to the street (35). Eileen Connell (1997), in a welcome historical approach, concludes that perhaps Nettie's small apartment hovering on the "margins of safe regions . . . symbolically bridges some of the various cultures and literary divisions in the novel" (590).

Questions of Social Responsibility

Questions of social responsibility were raised by leftists annoyed that Edith Wharton was born wealthy and wrote about what she knew: life among the wealthy. One way to deal with this was to predict the demise of her work. Ludwig Lewissohn (1932) states outright, in a much quoted line, that Edith Wharton's "work is fading and crumbling and will probably be almost forgotten until a time so detached from the present that people can go back to a little of it as to something quaint and sweet and lavendered . . ." (466). Others, however, perceive an "enormous gap" between Wharton's world and that of the "great and growing industrial democracy" (Hatcher 1935, 30), which blinded her to the sordid and brutal aspects of working-class life. Socialists like Vernon Parrington (1921) deride her: "She is too well bred to be a snob, but she escapes it only by sheer intelligence. The background of her mind, the furniture of her habits, are packed with a potential snobbery, and it is only by scrupulous care that it is held in leash. She is unconsciously shut in behind plate glass, where butlers serve formal dinners, and white shoulders go up at the mere suggestion of everyday gingham" (153). Later, during the depression, Edmund Wilson, a self-proclaimed communist, cautiously defends Wharton's contribution to American literature in "Justice to Edith Wharton" (1938), even while judging the "language and some of the machinery" of *The House of Mirth* outdated and melodramatic (21). Her best work, he feels, was written in the twenty years between *The House of Mirth* (1905) and *The Age of Innocence* (1920), possibly excepting *The Fruit of the Tree* (1907), while her later work declines in quality. But Wilson unexpectedly and fairly adds that several of her novels set in New England prove that Wharton was indeed sympathetic to the lower classes.

Tethered to Henry James

Most early critics (for the most part neo-humanists, and New Critics writing out of universities) continued to pair Wharton and James without actual evidence, as if the matter were indisputable. The assumptions rested on a general knowledge of the authors' friendship. Of course the two wrote about similar subjects, knew many of the same people, the same social structures, and the same places such as old New York and Boston, and both were expatriates.

In addition, as feminists have frequently noted, because female American novelists had not yet risen to the status of a Henry James, the largely male critical establishment assumed that women were incapable of succeeding except by imitation of men. Furthermore, circumstances of women's lives, and the assumptions about them by men at the time, made it unusually difficult for a woman to rise to literary acceptance. Even Emily Dickinson's poetry remained undiscovered until the 1920s, and after that it took serious editing and a number of years before it could be fully appreciated. While at the time Ellen Glasgow, Sarah

Orne Jewett, and Mary Wilkins Freeman enjoyed minor reputations, their work seemed inconsistent and "regionalist" compared to most of Edith Wharton's. True, after Wharton's 1921 Pulitzer Prize for *The Age of Innocence*, many critics accused her of abandoning art for popularity and the income provided by slick magazines, but recent criticism has demonstrated much literary excellence in her late work.

Joseph Warren Beach (1932) defends Wharton against the influence of James by examining their comparative narrative techniques, but the consensus seems to run the other way. Walter Fuller Taylor (1936), as Robert Morss Lovett did in 1925, places her directly at the feet of the master as his most proficient and illustrious disciple. But Edmund Wilson (1938) does recognize the important distinctions in the work of Wharton and James—"James's interests were predominantly esthetic: he is never a passionate social prophet" (20). He goes on to say that her "culture . . . was remarkably solid for an American woman." Such backhanded compliments easily account for much of the feminist revolt of the seventies.

Of course literary politics were ever at play in the shifting critical fortunes of both writers. James himself becomes more and more difficult to read after *The Portrait of a Lady*. The pro-James camp (conservatives, in general) finds his late work artful, intriguing, and psychologically faithful to human life, while the anti-James camp considers it too obtuse to be worth the effort and furthermore (undemocratically) unavailable to the average reader. Unknown until later was the fact that Edith Wharton had written in a letter to Sara (Sally) Norton in 1901 a comment that James's *The Sacred Fount* was a waste of a great talent (Lewis and Lewis 45). In another letter, this one to William Brownell in 1902, she expressed disappointment with *The Wings of the Dove* (Lewis and Lewis 71). Not only had Wharton become disenchanted with James's novels, she had taken his advice before he offered it. For when, after reading *The Valley of Decision* (1901) James wrote Wharton's sister-in-law that the main flaw of *The Valley of Decision* is its wooden characterizations, he otherwise praised the book, but he stated with an emphasis that critics have repeated to death that Edith Wharton must be "tethered to native pastures." The message was meant to reach her, but the fallacy of cause and effect seems to support the idea that she had taken his advice in writing *The House of Mirth*. In fact, the novel was already in progress at the time James wrote his letter (Lewis 153).

Percy Lubbock's 1947 biography continues the habit of connecting Wharton to James, as does an otherwise wonderful book by Millicent Bell (1965). Though this assumption was to be challenged by Lewis's

biography in 1975, and by feminist critics generally, it causes no aston-
ishment that Wharton's protest to John D. Barry's reviews (1899)
comparing her to Henry James went unremarked.

Questions of Genre

Lagging critical interest revived considerably after the release of Wharton's private papers in 1968. One of the first major issues to emerge
was that of genre, especially naturalism. Critics have always had a difficult time agreeing about whether *The House of Mirth* qualifies as an
American novel of manners, a naturalist novel like Theodore Dreiser's
Sister Carrie, a realist, sentimental, or determinist novel, a tragedy, or
something else. Blake Nevius (1953) gives the novel a mixed analysis,
finding Lily to be the product of heredity and environment, with
Wharton using deterministic analogies from nature to create an "un-
mistakably pessimistic tone" (58) while laboring vainly to control its
episodic structure. Nevertheless, he assumes that Wharton's manners
were European, and since she seemed incapable of dropping them, she
could not convincingly conceive an "'American' culture" (66). This
point emphasizes a sub-theme running through early Whartonian criticism, namely, that Edith Wharton was not "American enough." The
objection seems odd since she was living in New York and Lenox, Massachusetts, at the time she wrote *The House of Mirth*. Such remarks become more understandable after *The Custom of the Country* appeared in
1913, the year that the author moved permanently to Paris.

   The genre debate began, ironically, without the critics' knowledge
of Henry James's as yet unpublished comment (in 1905) that *The
House of Mirth* was not one, but two books. Louis Auchincloss (1961)
takes a biographical approach that depends on the dubious Lubbock
biography and Wharton's reticent *A Backward Glance* (1934), and he
goes so far as to compare her writing to Proust's. In 1962, Marie Bristol became the first of many to gloss the novel using Thorstein Veblen's *Theory of the Leisure Class.* She denies Wharton's discipleship to
Henry James, and also that *The House of Mirth* is a novel of naturalism
or realism; but, moving close to Marxist-economic criticism, she proposes that it be called a novel of dialectics because it "converses" between both devices. James Tuttleton (1966), however, argues for its
Balzacian realism, and in his 1972 book on the subject, as specifically
an *American* novel of manners. In addition, since the novel seems to
put its heroine at the mercy of apparently determinist or naturalist
forces, a long and inconclusive critical debate raged over these genres.
Other critics of the seventies explored the conflict between possible

sentimental and melodramatic genres. Questions of genre temporarily fade after the seventies, replaced by questions of feminism and racism, only to re-emerge in the nineties, incorporated into discussions of Wharton's work as modernist or feminist. Almost all criticism after the middle-seventies built upon the foundation laid by feminist theory. Probably the most influential essays of the seventies were those by Cynthia Griffin Wolff, and later Elaine Showalter, Joan Lidoff, and Wai-Chee Dimock.

Even so, Michael J. O'Neal turned to an examination of narrative voice distinguishing grammatical constructions in the narration of various characters to prove that narrative is as important as the drama of the plot. A case in point is Bruce Michelson's "Edith Wharton's House Divided" (1984), which concerns itself with the genre of drama *in* the novel. Michelson discovers borrowings from the Romantic stage in *The House of Mirth* (See also Wolff [1994]) and finds structures of both the sentimental drama and of a novel about drama emphasized by Lily's acting ability. However, a paradox develops because the "well-made play" moralizes, while the well-made novel normally effaces moralizing. But *The House of Mirth* employs both realism and naturalism along with the dramatic conventions, thereby indicating the complexity of the genre of realism (201). That the question of realism posed by the novel "both mocks and makes earnest use" of conventions (213) points up the novel's intricacy and ambition.

Besides dramatic convention, the influence of the popular novel is the subject of a much-republished feminist essay by Elaine Showalter (1985). According to Showalter, the popular novels of the period seemed to imply that women had no lives after the age of thirty and that the only lives they could live before thirty focused on marriage as work. Wharton's development of *The House of Mirth* also helped define her, "the Perfect Lady" as novelist, in that Lily's plight follows Wharton's own career. The novel concerns the transformation of the beautiful woman into an object for the satisfaction of men. Such a "Lady" must die to make room for modern women like Edith Wharton who can then live, work, and create a language of feminine growth. The novel accomplishes that in part by satirizing popular women's novels. However, Wharton does not focus simply on women. She points out the difficulties of men through her male characters, many of whose problems parallel those of the women. Apparently, effective change can come only from outsiders like the Jewish Simon Rosedale. Finally, Lily discovers a sense of community with working women like Gertie Ferish, so that *The House of Mirth* also becomes a transition to a new type of fiction. "The death of the lady is thus also the death of the lady novelist, the dutiful daughter who struggles to subdue her most powerful imaginative impulses" (22). Lily Bart gives way to the presence of a new generation of women.

The question of genre arises again in 1987 when Carol Miller looks at Wharton's technique of irony as "a deliberate strategy linking writer and audience" (82). In its blend of romanticism and determinism for ironic effect, the novel becomes far more than the naturalist story of an anti-heroine. By contrast, Amy Kaplan (1988) compares Wharton's realism with that of William Dean Howells. Her modernist argument is that realism "explores the relation between two conflicting meanings of 'society'" mediated through spectatorship as Lily travels from one interior to another receiving her identity from the eyes of the ever-present crowds. At the end, when she is no longer in anyone's line of vision, she loses herself completely and dies.

Jeanne Boydston (1988) points out that although Wharton professed exasperation with the popular novels that preceded her, criticizing the works of Louisa May Alcott and others, she was actually indebted to a number of them, including Lydia Maria Child's *The Rebels*, Susan Warner's *The Wide, Wide World*, and even Alcott's *Work*, all traditional domestic novels.

Taking on the critics who, as they characterize Wharton as an anti-modernist "literary aristocrat," find themselves unable to explain her popular following, Catherine Quoyeser (1989) summarizes the varying narrative voices as well as conflicting plot genres: the business plot, naturalistic plot, sentimental and melodramatic plots, ironic plot, and realistic plot. An intricate argument leads to the conclusion that these "residual" genres work together in a prophetic manner that explains how the novel's popular appeal may have resulted from the intense "crisis of bourgeois individualism [heightening] the cathartic effect of its conclusion" (78).

Nancy Bentley (1995) asks whether Lily is a "drawing room naturalist" who seeks to affix permanent identity. She examines the problem of "the real Lily," leading to "the specialized realism of the taxidermist" (191). Bentley anticipates a contemporary issue by noting that an "anthropological paradigm . . . informs" the novel (194).

Donald Pizer (1995) on the other hand, tests the assumption that *The House of Mirth* is an example of social determinism rather than naturalism. Because the final scene contains religious notes and because other characters seem as determined as Lily manage to free themselves, Wharton enforces the idea that the premise is not the complete story. Possibly "men and women also gain strength and derive meaning from their desires, hopes, and faiths" (247).

Richard A. Kaye (1994) asks the genre question once more. Is *The House of Mirth* a naturalist and Darwinian determinist novel or realist novel, or both? He compares alterations to the galleys with Edith Wharton's original synopsis, to conclude that "Scribner's revisions suggest Wharton's attempt at forging a synthesis of realist and naturalist philosophical premises in fiction" (72). In 1995, Kaye expands on his ideas, emphasizing the importance of the context of textual history as a locus of authorial intention. He discovers that Wharton had changed Selden's personality from a melodramatic, bitter, but empathetic character who openly does not love Lily (who pathetically implores him to marry her) to the existing character. He also finds that at first Lily "expresses in summary fashion the social-Darwinist precepts central to many naturalist texts."

Finally, tying naturalism to gender and consumerism, Lori Merish (1996) contends that "naturalist texts enact gendered fantasies of surveillance that work to contain the radical potential of feminine consumer desire, and to redefine the female consumer subject as commodity *object*" because "it deals with the problem of the feminine consumer at precisely the moment when American culture was beginning to see itself as more dependent on consumption than on a form of production that could be understood as masculine in character" (323–24).

Questions of Language and Theory

Questions of language can range broadly from examinations of active verbs to literary deconstruction and complex theories by Marx, Barthes, Bakhtin, Lacan, Freud, Veblen and others impossible to synthesize, but essential to show the direction of recent criticism. Deconstruction uses polarities to show how the words in the text destabilize one another essentially by canceling each other's meanings, leaving them indeterminate. Mary Ellis Gibson (1985) begins the examination of language used in Wharton's novels of old New York: *The Custom of the Country* and *The Age of Innocence,* as well as *The House of Mirth.* She finds language and other ambivalence toward complexities of changing social codes and their meanings in Wharton's New York society. In another view of language, Patricia Meyer Spacks (1985) investigates the type of gossip that serves financial ends through speculation about money and the public world. Here, language "supplies the currency" of speculation in the marriage market as a social force in *The House of Mirth;* gossip "speculates" about people as representative of social position, becoming a power that can destroy personal reality. Roslyn Dixon (1987) discusses a different way of using language: She evaluates Wharton's use of multiple points of view as a means expressing her opinion that Darwinian principles rather than Christian values "inform" the American social framework.

Returning to feminism, Frances Restuccia (1987) stresses that *The House of Mirth* is about two feminisms. To simplify a complex argument that includes Roland Barthes' theories of language, one "feminism" treats Lily as art object and victim; the second sees her as a manipulator of patriarchal language, an interesting contradiction. At about the same time, Dale M. Bauer (1988) uses Bakhtinian theories of heteroglossia (layered voices) to explore how Lily Bart misreads the "monologic" and "dialogic" language of culture. She is unable to speak outside of the conventional politicized language available to her because her inner voice conflicts with the "outer" voices of family, pastor, and the social injunction against divorce. Lily becomes the victim of gossiping voices, and in the end she fails to find the word that would "make all clear."

Expanding from one to many words, Louise Barnett (1989) treats *The House of Mirth* as a "speech act drama" in which high society is a fully realized character. In this speech act drama, however, no language exists for personal discourse, only for social discourse dominated by the linguistic strategies of men. While Wharton creates a language of "feminine growth" for herself, that language is not present in the novel. Consequently, the "word that would save both Lily and Selden . . . remains unuttered and unutterable" (61). Ellie Ragland Sullivan reaches similar conclusions from a Lacanian psychoanalytic perspective. Lacan defines hysteria as the "lack of a signifier or representation of being as a woman" (464). To Lacan, the hysteric's discourse "speaks" to the subconscious from a position of absence, loss, and deprivation. As a victim of this hysteria, Edith Wharton was driven to learn how to "be" as a woman and subliminated this drive into her writing. Consequently, she creates a Lily who deteriorates into silence, emptiness, and ultimately, lifelessness.

Ellen J. Goldner (1992) plays upon the pun "that associates the indirect act of speech with the horizontal position of the body" namely *lie* (285). In this novel, women, especially Lily and Bertha, tell lies as a means of protecting their sexual reputations, and Lily lies to herself about the real meaning of Gus Trenor's "loan" and the large "dividends" she receives from non-existent sources. Lies make their tellers visible as causes of "social anxiety" because, as tellers move from small private to larger public spheres, untruths threaten to expose social inequities. Critical explanations become more and more dense: "The lies temper the powerful closing image [of Lily as Sleeping Beauty] with a warning that causation might be displaced from broader social processes in which the woman's lying body has been caught" (303).

Like Wolff, Gilbert and Gubar, and others, Ruth Bernard Yeazell (1992) combines language with economics when drawing upon Thorstein Veblen, in particular his phrases "conspicuous consumption," and "conspicuous waste," to discuss how "Wharton represents a world in which people acquire and maintain status by openly displaying how much they can afford to waste" (714). The women in the world of this novel create the impressions by which people judge social position, and it is important that these impressions reveal no sign that labor produced the impressions of the required audience. "The position of leisure-marker is the only one [Lily] knows how to fill" (719) and she is incapable of labor. Beginning with the "intimations" of a "transformative word in the text," Janet Gabler-Hover and Kathleen Plate (1993) focus on the interpretation of "Beyond!" as "the word which made all clear," and "the talisman of feminist metaphysics in the novel" (358). They conclude that drawing upon Freud's *Beyond the Pleasure Principle,* Nietzsche's *Beyond Good and Evil,* and Heidegger, the word "beyond" "signifies beyond patriarchy" (359), since "art is a configuration of will to power." Lily is the only creator of her own art, but "by lifting the veil of illusion to reveal herself as the tableau, she complicates the possibilities of female freedom." Because a veil "perpetually defers the question of truth" (363), the tableau makes Lily a Signifier. But she exists *only* as Signifier with whom "no sexual relation is possible" (364), so "Beyond!" means "beyond consciousness, beyond language" (367).

Using Bakhtin's "ideological discourse" Carol Baker Sapora (1993) discusses Lily Bart as divided or "doubled" in an essay strong on the background of the double in fiction. Here the question of Lily Bart's double raises the early twentieth century's "Woman Question." Sapora believes that doubling helps women deal with forbidden independence and other gender issues, and that Wharton uses the technique to deliver encoded or double messages.

Grace Ann Hovet and Theodore R. Hovet (1993) return to the subject of the *tableaux vivants,* adding the language of novels by Warner, Alcott, and Stowe to their considerations of how the "rhetoric of vision empowers the 'male gaze'" (335) and affects the woman's identity. In the case of *The House of Mirth,* Lily fails to establish the dialogue that could break the male gaze, but the possibility of doing so is raised in the other novels.

Economics

Diana Trilling's well-known essay, "*The House of Mirth* Revisited" (1962), argues for Wharton as a mainstream American author by attempting to remove the 1930s' Marxist prejudice against her "snobbery" as "a society lady become society author" (103) and shows instead how she used class structure to center her novel on moral and social commentary. In 1965 Auchincloss adds that Lily belongs by birth to "old New York" but by preference to "the invaders" (an anachronistic reading of characters who first appear in *The Custom of the Country*) "who had been so fabulously enriched by the business growth following the Civil War" (25–26).

Employing the language of the marketplace, the first Marxist essay appeared in 1985 written by Wai-chee Dimock: "As a controlling logic, a mode of human conduct and human association, the marketplace is everywhere and nowhere, ubiquitous and invisible" (123). Words like "cost," "payment," and "speculation" (as a pun on Selden as spectator) support plot details of sex in exchange for money or power. "Power resides in the ability to define the terms of exchange" (126), and this ability may also belong to women. Contracts are often unspoken, clear to those with wealth, like Mrs. Peniston or Gus Trenor, but unclear to those without it, like Lily Bart, who ironically is essentially for sale but must pay for that privilege. Dimock concludes that, "private morality is finally defenseless against an exchange system that dissolves the language of morality into its own harsh, brassy parlance" (135).

Now other new themes of the marketplace emerge. One is the concept of Edith Wharton as a professional author in a world of men. Wharton's apprenticeship as an author is a concern of Amy Kaplan (1986), particularly as the female apprentice preparing for the financial market. Kaplan contends that Wharton writes herself "out of the private domestic sphere and [inscribes] a public identity in the marketplace" (434), ultimately concluding that Edith Wharton is not a traditionalist, but a modernist dealing with the realities of contemporary consumer culture.

The subject of *The House of Mirth* lends itself particularly well not only to Veblenesque, but also to Marxist approaches as Dimock earlier demonstrates. Robert Shulman (1987) adds psychology to the mix to show that Lily Bart's "divided self" is an "example of the power of the market society to divide people internally and to separate them from a community" (268). To him, Wharton shows "cultural hegemony" (the assumptions of government and the general public) at work on a "sensitive woman" of the highest social position in the American class system (283).

In an article concerned with structure and chance, Mark Seltzer (1987) writes about "the network of relations establish[ed] among . . . texts" (89). Two other critics show how narrative dissolves into economics. Lillian S. Robinson (1994) discusses how *The House of Mirth* translates "the new fortunes of the marketplace" into a traffic in women that expresses culture, while Marilyn Maness Mehaffy (1994) writes about "polarized metaphors of female desire driven by the turn-of-the-century American bourgeois-capitalist prerogative." In the "network" of personal relations, including female desire, Clare Colquitt (1991) addresses the blackmail scene to show that Wharton wished to define an "economy of desire" in the "social, economic and moral realities of passionate exchange" (155).

To Margit Stange (1998), Lily depicts the "status of the female body as the substrate of value—and the object of debasement—in the discursive economies of consumer culture, sexual selection, and the literary marketplace." Lily gains self only at the moment of "modification" by the consumer's perception of her value, like that represented by the *tableaux vivants* scene. But Elaine Orr (1997) shows that the novel is about contractual negotiation and relational negotiation rather than bargain and trade, and to her that helps open up the novel's "enigmatic" ending. She points out that Lily has many non-economic desires in the novel, such as love and friendship. Consequently, to her, the unspoken word that made all clear at the conclusion of *The House of Mirth* is "the word of friendship."

Gender, Race and Class

A number of recent studies of *The House of Mirth*, not surprisingly, focus on the key postmodernist issues of gender, race, and class, and also not surprisingly, take strikingly different approaches. For instance, Linda Dittmar (1991) compares Wharton's concept of the woman artist with that in Nella Larsen's *Quicksand* (1928) to illuminate a connection between the artist's powerlessness and her ultimate objectification as a "blank page" for "fantasies of gender, class, and race." Christopher Gair (1997) compares *The House of Mirth* to *The Custom of the Country* to "examine . . . representations of the relationship between self, ethnic, and national identities in and immediately preceding the Progressive Era in the New York sections" of these novels (350).

Two authors, Christian Riegel (1992) and Irene Goldman (1993), treat anti-Semitism in *The House of Mirth* through the character of

Simon Rosedale. Riegel reads the subject in the historical context of old New York's attitudes without necessarily attributing them to the author. But Goldman does look at Wharton's own views on the subject, and in so doing provides a useful history of Jewish immigration in New York at the turn of the century. "Racial ideologies were growing in importance as a way of understanding history, designing political policy, and perhaps reinforcing the wavering sense of superiority of the Anglo-Dutch upper class" (28). Wharton may have acquired her own ideas from reading Hippolyte Taine and William Lecky, and through them come to believe that everyone had a racial inheritance that influenced not only physical attributes but also "intellectual, linguistic, moral and spiritual characteristics" (30). To Wharton and her friends, Jews were "at best distasteful, although . . . on an individual basis they could be quite presentable." While Goldman recognizes the "dark" critical readings of Wharton's attitudes toward Jews, she points out that Rosedale's character exceeds the stereotype, that he gradually becomes a real person who "sins," not against morality, but against taste. The complex stereotyping of the period makes it too simple to characterize Edith Wharton as anti-Semitic in spite of some indisputably unpleasant comments in one or two of her letters, which in any case should be balanced by her lifetime friendships with Jews like Bernard Berenson.

Finally, Jennie A. Kassanoff (2000) introduces a theory based on a public interest in eugenics and taxidermy at the turn of the nineteenth century: The "patrician impulse to glorify racial culture and the taxidermic quest to capture eugenic nature shared a common desire—to secure an American identity impervious to hybridization and change—" (64). Kassaoff argues that Wharton's early fiction is profoundly invested in race, class, and nationalism (61). Lily represents the "anxiety" that the masses might take over culture, while the oligarchic Anglo-Dutch would fail to reproduce, thereby committing racial suicide. Kassanoff states that Wharton implicitly believes in "a genealogical conception of American citizenship . . . and class decline into an anthropology of racial extinction" (61).

Drama and the Arts

Judith Fryer (1986) discusses the type of cultural work accomplished by the novel's *tableaux vivants* scene when enlightened by an "Emblem" from Wharton's allegorical "The Valley of Childish Things." Providing an excellent background history of the *tableaux vivants* and frequently adapted paintings, Fryer explains the often risqué and spectacular nature of this theater-related entertainment. As she reads the story, at stake in the "emblem" is skin, the exterior covering of the woman, the body that exposes the woman as "commodity, object, Other, to the observing male." Further at stake is how "women represent themselves as the cultural constructions they have assimilated" (45). Lily constructs herself from her body, foreshadowing her final tableau, the *tableau mordant.*

Using an unusual method of considering structure and genre, Wendy Steiner (1989) defines "ekphrasis" as one art contemplating another. In *The House of Mirth* she finds this contemplation in opposed plot structures, one a Horatio Alger capitalist plot, and the other a chivalric romance. A long argument leads to examples of Lily's "self-picturing" in her *tableau vivant,* and its romantic effect on Selden.

Cynthia Griffin Wolff (1995) demonstrates the novel's structural affinity with, and many allusions to, Edwardian drama. Maureen Howard points out a "game of hide and seek" between Lily and Selden and posits that Wharton believed that "each amusing detail must carry more than its apparent weight," so that we find Lily attracted or repelled by décor throughout the novel. Revisiting the subject of interiors (See Fryer [1986]), John Clubbe (1996) feels that *The House of Mirth* chronicles Lily Bart's attempt to move from the interiors available to a single woman lacking money to create her own ideal interior (542). She cannot be deterministic as many feminist critics have contended because the author clearly provides many opportunities for Lily to "take charge of her life." But Lily prefers to live a fantasy (543). Wharton shows that failure to "read" interiors in relation to their inhabitants "signifies" a failure of imagination. Clubbe traces Lily's lack of appropriate emotional response (in reference to Ruskin and Downing) through each of the interior backgrounds of the novel to find that interiors "function as waiting-rooms before the inevitability of death," and he notes that how people arrange this waiting-room says much about them. Lily's tidy, orderly boarding house room indicates her acceptance of responsibility for her life.

Comparisons and Contrasts

Many critics choose a comparison-contrast approach. In Kate Chopin's *The Awakening* and in *The House of Mirth,* C. J. Wershoven (1987) sees interiors as social cages that imprison women. Each heroine has a moment of awakening, each begins but does not complete a change, and of course, each commits suicide. In 1989 Sandra Gilbert and Susan Gubar compare the novel to *The Awakening* (and other novels), finding that Lily's "awakening," the insomnia that leads to her death, makes Edna Pontellier's sexual awakening seem "easy."

Kristina Brooks (1996) compares *The House of Mirth* to Pauline Hopkins' novel, *Contending Forces: A Romance Illustrative of Negro Life North and South* (1899), as turn-of-the-century naturalist novels of the fallen woman. Henry James had illustrated the importance of George Eliot to Edith Wharton's writing by comparing Eliot's *Daniel Deronda* to *The House of Mirth* while Stuart Hutchinson (1997) also finds a number of parallels between those novels. Both Gwendolyn Harleth and Lily Bart are financially insolvent, both perform in a *tableau vivant*, both feel the presence of the Furies, and both are "advised" by a man who might have been a lover.

Citing a different author, Linda Costanzo Cahir (1999) writes of Lily Bart as the "sociable isolato" who succumbs to risks and impulses that result in her isolation from society. "Like the biblical Ishmael, Lily is disinherited . . . and orphaned." Cahir finds *The House of Mirth*'s social world "corrupt and self-serving," parallel, in fact, to scenes in "The Try-Works" chapter of Melville's *Moby Dick* and "The Paradise of Bachelors and the Tartarus of Maids," which also involve corrupt, self-serving societies. (See also Colquitt above.)

The variety, the entire array of methods of approaching *The House of Mirth*, and the many conclusions reached about it can only mean one thing: Edith Wharton has written a novel that breathes, a novel that lives with all the complexity of psychology, structure, and humanity of a great work of art. Something new can always be said; something old can always be said in a new way. Yet *The House of Mirth* is probably not Edith Wharton's greatest novel. Probably it is merely her most accessible as the first novel by Edith Wharton that most students, and therefore most theorists, read. They are captivated by it, and apply theories of narrative form, structure, gender, race, class—Marxist, Bakhtinian, Derridian, Lacanian—any number of combinations and permutations of those, any number of feminist approaches, all of which seem to bear fruit. The quality of that fruit may range from the gnarled but sweet apples to the paper pills of thought that Sherwood Anderson describes in *Winesburg, Ohio*. Or it may range widely as the nearly poor George Willard does—the young journalist stepping on the train, lighting out for the territory of his life. Intriguingly, no critic since the thirties has mentioned the absence of "the man with the dinner pail" as Edith Wharton complained in her essay, "The Great American Novel" (652). The debate over the genre of *The House of Mirth* has proved especially interesting in that realists initially seemed to win it. But once again naturalism has become a favorite topic of discussion. Edith Wharton once mentioned that one of her favorite novels was *Summer*, a novel of the lower classes. But many critics have instead argued that—and it is difficult to disagree—her best novel is *Ethan Frome*, a work as different from *The House of Mirth* as possible. Yet, neither *Summer* nor *Ethan Frome* has been discussed in terms of naturalism.

Works Consulted

Abbott, Reginald. "'A Moment's Ornament': Wharton's Lily Bart and Art Nouveau." *Mosaic* 24.2 (Spring 1991): 73–91.

"The Abode of the Fool's Heart." Rev. of *The House of Mirth* by Edith Wharton. *Literary Digest* 31 (December 1905): 886.

Ammons, Elizabeth. *Edith Wharton's Argument with America*. Athens, GA: U Georgia P, 1980. 25–42.

Auchincloss, Louis. *Pioneers & Caretakers: A Study of 9 American Women Novelists*. Minneapolis, MN: U of Minnesota P, 1961.

———. "Edith Wharton." *Seven Modern Novelists*. 1970. Ed. William Van O'Connor. London: Fairleigh Dickinson UP, 1982. 11–45.

Barnett, Louise K. "Language, Gender and Society in *The House of Mirth*." *Connecticut Review* 11.2 (Summer 1989): 54–63.

Barry, John D. "New York Letter." *Literary World* (1 April 1899): 105–6.

———. "New York Letter." *Literary World* (13 May 1899): 152–53.

Bauer, Dale. "The Failure of the Republic." *Feminist Dialogics: A Theory of Failed Community*. Albany, NY: State U of New York P, 1988. 89–127.

Bazin, Nancy Topping. "The Destruction of Lily Bart: Capitalism, Christianity, and Male Chauvinism." *Denver Quarterly* 17.4 (Winter 1983): 97–108.

Beach, Joseph Warren. *The Twentieth Century Novel: Studies in Technique*. New York: Appleton-Century-Crofts, 1932. 291–93.

Beaty, Robin. "Lilies that Fester: Sentimentality in *The House of Mirth*." *College Literature* 14.3 (Fall 1987): 263–75.

Bell, Millicent. *Edith Wharton and Henry James: The Story of Their Friendship*. London: Peter Owen, 1965.

Benert, Annette Larson. "Geography of Gender in *The House of Mirth*." *Studies in the Novel* 22.1 (Spring 1990): 26–42.

Benstock, Shari. "'The word which made all clear': The Silent Close of *The House of Mirth*." *Famous Last Words: Changes in Gender and Narrative Closure*. Ed. Allison Booth. Charlottesville, VA: UP of Virginia, 1993. 230–58.

Bentley, Nancy. *The Ethnography of Manners: Hawthorne, James, Wharton.* New York: Cambridge UP, 1995. 160–211.

Blackall, Jean Frantz. "The Intrusive Voice: Telegrams in *The House of Mirth* and *The Age of Innocence.*" *Women's Studies* 20 (1991): 163–68.

Bourget, Paul. "Preface" to *Chez les heureux du monde* (1908). Trans. Charles Du Bos. *Edith Wharton Review* (Spring 1991): 19–22.

Boutell, Alice. Rev. of *The House of Mirth* by Edith Wharton. *Critic.* 48 (March 1906): 249–50.

Boydston, Jeanne. "'Grave Endearing Traditions': Edith Wharton and the Domestic Novel." *Faith of a (Woman) Writer.* Eds. Alice Kessler-Harris and William McBrien. New York: Greenwood P, 1988. 31–40.

Bristol, Marie. "Life Among the Ungentle Genteel: Edith Wharton's *The House of Mirth* Revisited." *Western Humanities Review* 16.1 (Autumn 1962): 371–74.

Brooks, Kristina. "New Woman, Fallen Woman: The Crisis of Reputation in Turn-of-the-Century Novels by Pauline Hopkins and Edith Wharton." *Legacy* 13.2 (1996): 91–112.

Cahir, Linda Costanzo. "The Sociable Isolato." *Solitude and Society in the Works of Herman Melville and Edith Wharton.* Westport, CT: Greenwood P, 1999. 99–105.

Clubbe, John. "Interiors and the Interior Life in Edith Wharton's *The House of Mirth.*" *Studies in the Novel* 28.4 (Winter 1996): 543–64.

Colquitt, Clare. "Succumbing to the 'Literary Style': Arrested Desire in *The House of Mirth.*" *Women's Studies* 20.2 (1991): 153–62.

Conn, Peter. *The Divided Mind: Ideology and Imagination in America, 1898–1917.* Cambridge: Cambridge UP, 1983. 172–96.

Connell, Eileen. "Edith Wharton Joins the Working Class: *The House of Mirth* and the New York City Working Girls' Clubs." *Women's Studies* 2.6 (1997): 557–604.

Cuddy, Lois A. "Triangles of Defeat and Liberation: The Quest for Power in Edith Wharton's Fiction." *Contemporary Literature* 8 (1982): 18–26.

Dessner, Lawrence. "Edith Wharton and the Problem of Form." *Forum* 24.3 (1983): 54–63.

Dimock, Wai-chee. "Debasing Exchange: Edith Wharton's *The House of Mirth.*" *PMLA* (October 1982): 783–92. Rpt. in *Edith Wharton: Modern Critical Views.* Ed. Harold Bloom. New York: Chelsea House, 1986. 123–38.

Dittmar, Linda. "When Privilege is No Protection: The Woman Artist in *Quicksand* and *The House of Mirth*." *Writing the Woman Artist: Essays in Poetics, Politics, and Portraiture*. Ed. Suzanne W. Jones. Philadelphia, PA: U of Pennsylvania P, 1991. 133–54.

Dixon, Roslyn. "Reflecting Vision in *The House of Mirth*." *Twentieth Century Literature* 33.2 (Summer 1987): 211–22.

Friman, Anne. "Determinism and Point of View in *The House of Mirth*." *Papers on Language and Literature* 2.2 (Spring 1966): 175–78.

Fryer, Judith. *Felicitous Space: The Imaginative Structures of Edith Wharton and Willa Cather*. Chapel Hill, NC: U of North Carolina P, 1986. 75–95.

———. "Reading *Mrs. Lloyd*." *Edith Wharton: New Critical Essays*. Eds. Alfred Bendixen and Annette Zilversmit. New York: Garland P, 1992. 27–55.

Gabler-Hover, Janet and Kathleen Plate. "*The House of Mirth* and Edith Wharton's 'Beyond!'" *Philological Quarterly* 72.3 (Summer 1993): 357–78.

Gair, Christopher. "The Crumbling Structure of 'Appearances': Representation and Authenticity in *The House of Mirth* and *The Custom of the Country*." *Modern Fiction Studies* 43.2 (Summer 1997): 349–73.

Gilbert, Sandra M. and Susan Gubar. "Angel of Devastation: Edith Wharton on the Arts of the Enslaved." *No Man's Land: The Place of the Woman Writer in the Twentieth Century*. Vol. 2: *Sexchanges*. New Haven, CT: Yale UP, 1989. 123–68.

———. *Madwoman in the Attic*. New Haven, CT: Yale UP, 1979.

Gibson, Mary Ellis. "Edith Wharton and the Ethnography of *Old New York*." *Studies in American Fiction* 13.1 (Spring 1985): 57–69.

Goldman, Irene C. "The *Perfect* Jew and *The House of Mirth*: A Study in Point of View." *Modern Language Studies* 23.2 (Spring 1993): 25–36.

Goldner, Ellen J. "The Lying Woman and the Cause of Social Anxiety: Interdependence and the Woman's Body in *The House of Mirth*." *Women's Studies* 21 (1992): 285–305.

Hale, E. E., Jr. "*The House of Mirth*." Rev. of *The House of Mirth* by Edith Wharton. *Bookman* 22 (December 1905): 364–66.

Hatcher, Harlan. *Creating the Modern American Novel*. New York: Farrar & Rinehart, 1935.

Hays, Peter L. "Bearding the Lily: Wharton's Names." *American Notes & Queries* 18.5 (January 1980): 75–76.

Hochman, Barbara. "The Rewards of Representation: Edith Wharton, Lily Bart and the Writer/Reader Interchange." *Novel: A Forum on Fiction* 24.2 (Winter 1991): 147–61.

———. "*The Awakening* and *The House of Mirth*: Plotting Experience and Experiencing Plot." *The Cambridge Companion to American Realism and Naturalism*. Ed. Donald Pizer. New York: Cambridge UP, 1995. 211–35.

"*The House of Mirth* and Other Novels." Rev. of *The House of Mirth* by Edith Wharton. *Nation* 81 (20 November 1905): 44–47.

Hoeller, Hildegard. "'The Impossible Rosedale': Race and the Reading of Edith Wharton's *The House of Mirth*." *Studies in Jewish Literature* 13 (1994): 14–20.

Hovet, Grace Ann, and Theodore R. Hovet. "*Tableaux Vivants*: Masculine Vision and Feminine Reflections in Novels by Warner, Alcott, Stowe, and Wharton." *American Transcendental Quarterly* 7.4 (December 1993): 335–56.

Howard, Maureen. "'The Bachelor and the Baby': *The House of Mirth*" in *The Cambridge Companion to Edith Wharton*. Ed. Millicent Bell. New York: Cambridge UP, 1995. 137–56.

Howe, Irving. "A Reading of *The House of Mirth*." From Irving Howe's Introduction to *The House of Mirth* by Edith Wharton. 1962. Rpt. in *Edith Wharton: A Collection of Critical Essays*. Ed. Irving Howe. Englewood Cliffs, NJ: Prentice-Hall, 1962. 119–29.

Hutchinson, Stuart. "From *Daniel Deronda* to *The House of Mirth*." *Essays in Criticism* 47.4 (October 1997): 315–31.

Kaplan, Amy. "Edith Wharton's Profession of Authorship." *English Literary History* 53.2 (Summer 1986): 433–57.

———. "Crowded Spaces in *The House of Mirth*." *The Social Construction of American Realism*. Chicago, IL: U Chicago P, 1988. 88–103.

Karcher, Carolyn L. "Male Vision and Female Revision in James's *The Wings of the Dove* and Wharton's *The House of Mirth*." *Women's Studies* 10 (1984): 227–44.

Kassanoff, Jennie A. "Extinction, Taxidermy, *Tableaux Vivants*: Staging Race and Class in *The House of Mirth*." *PMLA* 115 (January 2000): 60–74.

Kaye, Richard A. "Literary Naturalism and the Passive Male: Edith Wharton's Revisions of *The House of Mirth*." *The Princeton University Library Chronicle* 56.1 (Autumn 1994): 46–72.

———. "Textual Hermeneutics and Belated Male Heroism: Edith Wharton's Revisions of *The House of Mirth* and the Resistance to American Literary Naturalism." *Arizona Quarterly* 52.3 (Autumn 1995): 87–116.

Koprince, Susan. "Edith Wharton's Hotels." *Massachusetts Studies in English* 10.1 (Spring 1985): 12–23.

Lawson, Richard H. *Edith Wharton*. New York: Fredrick Ungar, 1977. 29–39.

Lewis, R. W. B. *Edith Wharton: A Biography*. New York: Harper & Row, 1975.

Lewis, R. W. B. and Nancy Lewis. *The Letters of Edith Wharton*. New York: Scribners, 1988.

Lewissohn, Ludwig. *Expression in America*. New York: Harper & Bros., 1932. 464–69.

Lidoff, Joan. "Another Sleeping Beauty: Narcissism in *The House of Mirth*." *American Realism*. Ed. Eric J. Sundquist. Baltimore, MD: Johns Hopkins UP, 1982. Rpt. in *American Quarterly* 32.5 (1980): 519–39.

Lindberg, Gary H. *Edith Wharton and the Novel of Manners*. Charlottesville, VA: UP of Virginia, 1975. 87–93.

Link, Franz. "A Note on 'The Apparition of These Faces . . .' in *The House of Mirth* and 'In a Station at the Metro.'" *Paideuma* 10.2 (Fall 1981): 327.

Lovett, Robert Morss. *Edith Wharton*. New York: Robert M. McBride, 1925.

Lubbock, Percy. *Portrait of Edith Wharton*. New York: D. Appleton, 1947.

MacMaster, Anne. "Virginia Woolf and the Female Moderns." *Virginia Woolf: Texts and Contexts*. Eds. Beth Rigel Daugherty and Eileen Barrett. Westerville, OH: Pace UP, 1996. 216–22.

McArthur, James. "Books and Bookmen." *Harper's Weekly*. 49 (2 December 1905): 1750.

McDowell, Margaret B. "'Sharpening of the Moral Vision': *The House of Mirth*." *Edith Wharton*. Boston: G. K. Hall, 1976. Revised 1991. 43–52.

McIlvaine, Robert. "Edith Wharton's American Beauty Rose." *American Studies* 7.2 (August 1973): 183–85.

Mehaffy, Marilyn Maness. "Manipulating the Metaphors: *The House of Mirth* and 'the Volcanic Nether-Side' of 'Sexuality.'" *College Literature* 21.2 (June 1994): 47–62.

Merish, Lori. "Engendering Naturalism: Narrative Form and Commodity Spectacle in U.S. Naturalist Fiction." *Novel: A Forum on Fiction* 29.3 (Spring 1996): 319–45.

Michelson, Bruce. "Edith Wharton's House Divided." *Studies in American Fiction* 12.2 (Autumn 1984): 199–215.

Miller, Carol. "'Natural Magic': Irony as Unifying Strategy in *The House of Mirth*." *South Central Review* 4.1 (Spring 1987): 82–91.

Moddelmog, William E. "Disowning 'Personality': Privacy and Subjectivity in *The House of Mirth*." *American Literature* 70.2 (June 1998): 337–63.

"Mrs. Wharton's Latest Novel." Rev. of *The House of Mirth* by Edith Wharton. *Independent* 59 (20 July 1905): 150–51.

Nettles, Elsa. *Language and Gender in American Fiction: Howells, James, Wharton and Cather*. Charlottesville, VA: UP of Virginia. 86–120.

Nevius, Blake. *Edith Wharton: A Study of Her Fiction*. 1953. Berkeley, CA: U of California P, 1961. 53–77.

"New Novels." Rev. of *The House of Mirth* by Edith Wharton. *Athenaeum* [England] 4074 (24 November 1905): 718.

Norris, Margot. "Death by Speculation: Deconstructing *The House of Mirth*." *Edith Wharton: "The House of Mirth."* Ed. Shari Benstock. Boston, MA: Bedford, 1994. 431–46.

"A Notable Novel." Rev. of *The House of Mirth* by Edith Wharton. *Outlook* 81 (21 October): 404–6.

Olin-Ammentorp, Julie. "Edith Wharton's Challenge to Feminist Criticism." *Studies in American Fiction* 16.2 (Autumn 1988): 237–44.

O'Neal, Michael J. "Point of View and Narrative Technique in the Fiction of Edith Wharton." *Style* 17.2 (Spring 1983): 270–89.

Orr, Elaine Neil. "Contractual Law, Relational Whisper: A Reading of Edith Wharton's *The House of Mirth*." *Modern Language Quarterly* 52.1 (March 1991): 53–70.

———. "Negotiation [*sic*] Our Text: The Search for Accommodations in Edith Wharton's *The House of Mirth*." *Subject to Negotiation: Reading Feminist Criticism and American Women's Fictions*. Charlottesville. VA: UP of Virginia, 1997. 27–45.

Ouzgane, Lahoucine. "Mimesis and Moral Agency in Wharton's *The House of Mirth*." *Anthropoetics* 3.2 (Fall 1997/Winter 1998): 1–8.

Papke, Mary E. "Edith Wharton's Social Fiction." *Verging on the Abyss: The Social Fiction of Kate Chopin and Edith Wharton*. New York: Greenwood P, 1990. 89–101; 103–128.

Pizer, Donald. "The Naturalism of Edith Wharton's *The House of Mirth*." *Twentieth Century Literature* 41.2 (June 1995): 241–48.

Poirier, Richard. *A World Elsewhere*. New York: Oxford UP, 1966.

Price, Alan. "Lily Bart and Carrie Meeber: Cultural Sisters." *American Literary Realism* 13.2 (Autumn 1980): 238–45.

Quoyeser, Catherine. "The Antimodernist Unconscious: Genre and Ideology in *The House of Mirth*." *Arizona Quarterly* 44.4 (Winter 1989): 55–79.

Radden, Jennifer. "Defining Self-Deception." *Dialogue: Canadian Philosophical Review* 23.1 (March 1984): 103–120.

Raphael, Lev. *Edith Wharton's Prisoners of Shame: A New Perspective on Her Neglected Fiction*. New York: St. Martin's P, 1991. 255–74.

Restuccia, Frances L. "The Name of the Lily: Edith Wharton's Feminism(s)." *Contemporary Literature* 28.2 (Summer 1987): 223–38.

Riegel, Christian. "Rosedale and Anti-Semitism in *The House of Mirth.*" *Studies in American Fiction* 20.2 (Autumn 1992): 219–24.

Robinson, Lillian S. "The Traffic in Women: A Cultural Critique of *The House of Mirth.*" *Edith Wharton's "The House of Mirth."* Ed. Shari Benstock. Boston, MA: Bedford, 1994. 340–58.

Sapora, Carol Baker. "Female Doubling: The Other Lily Bart in Edith Wharton's *The House of Mirth.*" *Papers on Language and Literature* 29.4 (Fall 1993): 371–94.

Saunders, Catherine. *Writing the Margins: Edith Wharton, Ellen Glasgow and the Literary Tradition of the Ruined Woman.* Cambridge, MA: Harvard U, 1987. 7–33.

Schriber, Mary Suzanne. "Convention in the Fiction of Edith Wharton." *Studies in American Fiction* 11.2 (Autumn 1983): 189–201.

Seltzer, Mark. "Statistical Persons." *Diacritics* 17.3 (Fall 1987): 82–98.

Showalter, Elaine. "The Death of the Lady (Novelist): Wharton's *House of Mirth.*" *Representations* 9 (Winter 1985): 133–49. Rpt. in *American Women Fiction Writers, 1900–1960*: Vol. 3. Ed. Harold Bloom. Philadelphia, PA: Chelsea House, 1997. 216–19; and in *Edith Wharton: New Critical Essays.* Eds. Alfred Bendixen and Annette Zilversmit. New York: Garland, 1992. 3–26.

Shulman, Robert. "Divided Selves and the Market Society: Politics and Psychology in *The House of Mirth.*" *Perspectives on Contemporary Literature* 11 (1985): 10–19. Rpt. as "*The House of Mirth*: The Political Psychology of Capitalism." Robert Schulman, *Social Criticism and Nineteenth-Century American Fiction.* Columbia, MO: U of Missouri P, 1987. 268–83.

Spacks, Patricia Meyer. *Gossip.* New York: Alfred A. Knopf, 1985. 171–81.

Stange, Margit. "Edith Wharton and the Problem of the Woman Author." *Personal Property: Wives, White Slaves, and the Market in Women.* Baltimore, MD: The Johns Hopkins UP, 1998. 36–71.

Steiner, Wendy. "The Causes of Effect: Edith Wharton and the Economics of Ekphrasis." *Poetics Today* 10.2 (Summer 1989): 279–97.

Sullivan, Ellie Ragland. "The Daughter's Dilemma: Psychoanalytic Interpretation and Edith Wharton's *The House of Mirth.*" *Edith Wharton: "The House of Mirth."* Ed. Shari Benstock. New York: Bedford, 1994. 464–81.

Taylor, Walter Fuller. *History of American Letters.* Boston, MA: American Book Co., 1936. 350–56.

Tintner, Adeline R. "Two Novels of 'The Relatively Poor': *New Grub Street* and *The House of Mirth.*" *Notes on Modern American Literature* 6.2 (Autumn 1982): Item 12.

Trilling, Diana. "*The House of Mirth* Revisited." *Harper's Bazaar* 81 (1974). Rpt. in *Edith Wharton: A Collection of Essays*. Ed. Irving Howe. Englewood Cliffs, NJ: Prentice-Hall, 1962. 103–118.

Tuttleton, James W. "Henry James and Edith Wharton: Fiction as the House of Fame." *Midcontinent American Studies Journal* 7.1 (Spring 1966): 25–36.

———. *The Novel of Manners in America*. Chapel Hill, NC: U of North Carolina P, 1972. 122–40.

———. "Edith Wharton" *American Women Writers: Bibliographical Essays*. Eds. Maurice Duke , Jackson R. Bryer, and M. Thomas Inge. Westwood, CT: Greenwood P, 1983.

Tuttleton, James W., Kristin O. Lauer, and Margaret P. Murray. *Edith Wharton: The Contemporary Reviews*. New York: Cambridge UP, 1992.

Van Doren, Carl. *Contemporary American Novelists 1900–1920*. New York: Macmillan, 1923. 95–104.

Wagner-Martin, Linda. *The House of Mirth: A Novel of Admonition*. Boston, MA: G. K. Hall, 1990.

Waid, Candace. "Building *The House of Mirth*." *Biographies of Books: The Compositional Histories of Notable American Writings*. Eds. James Barbour and Tom Quirk. Columbia, MO: U of Missouri P, 1996. 161–86.

Walton, Geoffrey. *Edith Wharton: A Critical Interpretation*. 1970. Rutherford: Fairleigh Dickinson UP, 1982. 137–46.

Wershoven, C. J. "*The Awakening* and *The House of Mirth*: Studies of Arrested Development." *American Literary Realism* 19.3 (Spring 1987): 27–41.

Wharton, Edith. *A Backward Glance*. New York: Appleton-Century, 1934.

———. *The House of Mirth*. New York: Scribners, 1905.

———. "The Great American Novel." *Yale Review* 16 (April-July): 644–55.

Wilson, Edmund. "Justice to Edith Wharton." *New Republic* 95 (29 June 1938): 209–13. Rpt. in *Edith Wharton: A Collection of Critical Essays*. Ed. Irving Howe. Englewood Cliffs, NJ: Prentice-Hall, 1962. 19–31.

Wolff, Cynthia Griffin. *A Feast of Words: The Triumph of Edith Wharton*. New York: Oxford UP, 1977. 109–133.

———. "Lily Bart and the Drama of Femininity." *American Literary History* 6.1 (Spring 1994): 71–87.

———. "Lily Bart and Masquerade Inscribed in the Female Mode." *Wretched Exotic: Edith Wharton in Europe*. Eds. Katherine Joslin and Alan Price. New York: Peter Lang, 1993. 259–94.

Yeazell, Ruth Bernard. "The Conspicuous Wasting of Lily Bart." *English Literary History* 59.3 (Fall 1992): 713–34.

3: *Ethan Frome—*
The Murder of a Masterpiece

N O WORK COULD BE LESS LIKE *The House of Mirth*, or anything written by Henry James, than *Ethan Frome* (1911). Its reception has included ideas flowing with no predictability from comparisons to Greek tragedy, to evocation of the influence of Henry James, to the strange contradiction of lauding it as a masterpiece, while calling it "relentless" and "cruel," followed by a trend toward socialist readings, then near silence.

The silence resulted from charges by a famous British critic that *Ethan Frome* is amoral. Lionel Trilling, well respected in academia, tagged *Ethan Frome* a "dead book" because he found it morally inert. Trilling alone nearly killed the novel critically from 1956 until about 1977, a generation during which as few as ten publications about the novel appeared. Those, written from New Critical concepts, included a few intrepid debates against Trilling's Aristotelian analysis, but most critics writing before the seventies would have hesitated before attacking morality. After 1977, a trickle of New Critical essays on structure and symbolism indirectly supported Trilling by pointing out the story's several inconsistencies, but they roused no response to him until Killoran's in 2000.

But the 1977 psychobiographical reading by Cynthia Griffin Wolff and the 1979 mythological reading by Elizabeth Ammons directly renewed critical interest in the novel as they opened lines of biographical and feminist thought. To them the woes suffered by Mattie, Zenobia, and Ethan's mother must contain allegories of Wharton's life and result from a social patriarchy that seeks to repress women. One of the most interesting recent trends in thought about *Ethan Frome* appears to be a return to ideas first mentioned in the forties and again in the sixties— Puritanism, local color, and regionalism, but from a feminist view. Even so, relative to *The House of Mirth*, critical treatments of *Ethan Frome* have been sparse.

The story of *Ethan Frome* is set not merely in winter, but in the unyielding, colorless cold of a frigid winter in the Berkshire Mountains of Western Massachusetts. The narrator, an outsider, gathers bits of detail from the villagers of Starkfield to puzzle out the events of a generation earlier. He arrives at this story: Ethan, a promising young man with training as an engineer, is forced to leave college to return to the farm because of his father's death. When his mother falls ill, Ethan's cousin, Zenobia Pierce, arrives to nurse her, and after his mother's death, Ethan marries "Zeena." She creates financial problems, however, by spending their limited resources on quack cures for symptoms of hypochondria. Because she feels ill, Zeena claims to need household help, so her cousin, the attractive Mattie Silver, arrives to exchange housework for room and board. Ethan and Mattie fall in love. When Zenobia realizes this, she banishes Mattie. Ethan feels helpless, but insists on taking Mattie to the train. On the way, the two decide to go sledding, but even after the exhilaration of "the coast," their passion seems hopeless. They make a suicide pact, then point the sled down a steep incline directly toward a large tree. Ironically or tragically, both survive: Ethan permanently crippled, Mattie paralyzed. Zeena takes Mattie back, and the three live claustrophobically on the impoverished and rapidly deteriorating farm. In the story's present, the narrator observes unimaginable physical and psychological horrors.

The "Greek Tragedy"

The early reviewers of 1911 tried to characterize *Ethan Frome* as an agonizing Greek play placed in a Hawthornian New England setting. They respond to it as if it were drama rather than narrative. The *New York Times Book Review* remarks about the book's "remorseless spirit of the Greek tragic muse," its "frozen horror," and how the "rigidity of the bleak Puritan outlook" survives in spite of the "relentless Fates" (CR 181). The reviewer calls it "a cruel . . . compelling and haunting story" that Edith Wharton had "built of small, crude things and a rude and violent event, a structure whose purpose is the infinite refinement of torture." He concludes that *Ethan Frome* may not be a great novel, but it is an "impressive tragedy" (CR 182). The *Nation* (1911) contended that the "repugnant" Zeena represents Fate in this "drama," inspiring fear and loathing in Ethan. His "submission to obligation" is a remnant of the Puritan "spiritual inheritance. . . . The wonder is that the spectacle of so much pain can be made to yield so much beauty," for under the "wringing torment" is the "conception which the Greeks expressed in the medusa [*sic*] head" (CR 184–85). Meanwhile, the *Saturday Review* claimed that its unusually beautiful writing errs at the end because of "things too terrible in their failure to be told humanly by creature to creature" (CR 185). A story of lovers made to live and suffer indefinitely cannot measure up to Greek drama because "we do not cover the eyes at the spectacle of a really great tragedy" (CR 186).

Yet Frederic Taber Cooper of the *Bookman,* who finds it "hard to forgive" the author's "utter remorselessness" and "blank despair," still comments that "Art for art's sake" justifies its perfect technique (CR 186). The reviewer for the *Bookman* [England] (1912) describes the book as "beautiful, sad, but intensely human . . . its final conclusion" having the "inevitability of a great Greek tragedy" (CR 187).

Edwin A. Bjorkman (1913), however, moves away from the idea of a Greek tragedy and instead sounds the early but now familiar note based on the then developing liberal socialist trend: "The tragedy unveiled to us is social rather than personal. . . . *Ethan Frome* is . . . a judgment on that system which fails to redeem such villages as Mrs. Wharton's Starkfield . . ." (296–97). She "has passed from individual to social art; from the art that excites to that which incites" (299). However, Elizabeth Shepley Sergeant (1915) creates a debate between herself and a companion who upholds the Greek tragedy concept. "What a supremely cruel book!" she remarks. But her interlocutor uses familiar words calling it a "tragic masterpiece" of iron New England fiction, peopled with Euripidean figures. As her companion slowly loses the argument, Sergeant compares Edith Wharton to Mary Wilkins Freeman and Sarah Orne Jewett (names echoed in the criticism again and again) whose novels include "consoling" pussy willows. She also foreshadows Trilling's objections by concluding that, "the real New England tragedy . . . is not that something happens but that nothing does." Sergeant spends most of the article discussing specific works of Freeman and Jewett in comparison to *The House of Mirth,* which she enjoyed, and to *Ethan Frome,* which she finds too realistic and ugly. She ends by predicting that books like Jewett's *The Queen's Twin* will survive when "'Ethan Frome' [is] rotting in his grave."

As with John D. Barry's response to *The House of Mirth,* modern critics who have often quoted the "rose colored glasses" section of *A Backward Glance* have not realized that Edith Wharton was reacting to Sergeant's review in *The New Republic.* Her response defends its realism and attempts to draw attention away from Greek tragedy:

> The book to the making of which I brought the greatest joy and the fullest ease was *Ethan Frome.* For years I had wanted to draw life as it really was in the derelict mountain villages of New England, a life even in my time, and a thousandfold more a generation earlier, utterly unlike that seen through the rose-coloured spectacles of my predecessors, Mary Wilkins and Sarah Orne Jewett. . . . Emily Brontë would have found as savage tragedies in our remoter valleys as on her Yorkshire moors. . . . *Ethan Frome* shocked my readers less than *Summer;* but it

was frequently criticized as "painful," and at first had much less success than my previous books. (BG 293–95)

The usual struggle ensued. As Robert Morss Lovett would later, William Lyon Phelps (1916) dismissed the possibility that Wharton could
be a major living novelist, conceding only *Ethan Frome* as a "masterpiece." He quotes Carl Van Doren in the *Nation* (12 January 1921):
"Not since Hawthorne has a novelist built on the New England soil a
tragedy of such elevation of mood as this." Lovett (1925) declares it a
novel of far more enduring quality than *The House of Mirth*. Reading
Ethan Frome today "the lines are as firm and the colors as clear and
unfaded as on the first reading. . . ."

Representative of the disjunction in the critical thinking about the
novel—a masterpiece, yet too realistically shocking to read and therefore not a masterpiece—Russell Blankenship (1931) calls *Ethan Frome*
"by general acclamation" a masterpiece of grim terror, but one "to be
read, not discussed" (507). Grant C. Knight (1931) agrees, calling the
work "an American classic" of "poignant nudity" (334). Finally, in
1932, Warren Beach, a major and well-known practitioner of the New
Critical school, echoes in his own way the importance of point of view
and narration, all in comparison to Henry James. Because of reviews
like these, Edith Wharton's reputation as a literary writer rested on *The
House of Mirth* until 1921, when *The Age of Innocence* won the Pulitzer
Prize. Yet while *The House of Mirth* and *The Age of Innocence* were
never completely ignored, between the two, *Ethan Frome* emerged after her death as the acknowledged classic.

Henry James

Meanwhile, Edith Wharton had been tolerating her name in the same
sentences as Henry James's since 1899, when her first volume of short
stories appeared. This time, however, it seemed that there could be no
possible sense of him in a novel of hill-people. Reviewers found it anyway. In 1911 the *Nation* undermines both Edith Wharton and Henry
James by calling Wharton "the greatest pupil of a little master" until
"the appearance of *Ethan Frome*." But since James had admitted debt
to Balzac, the *Nation* reasons that the influence of Balzac seems evident in *Ethan Frome*'s "inception and execution." When Edith Wharton wrote a rare preface for the 1922 edition, it possibly responded to
the *Nation's* anonymous critic by citing Balzac's "*Le grande Brèteche*"
as an example of the type of narration she used.

When the Great Depression of the thirties stimulated intellectual
interest in varieties of socialism, it became tempting either to try turn-

ing *Ethan Frome* into a social commentary against the viciousness of poverty, or to rail that Wharton knew nothing about what she had written. Ralph Phillip Boas and Katherine Burton (1933) maintain that Wharton writes merely as an onlooker because of her wealth. Tragedy "lies, where so many theorists have maintained that it cannot lie, in the monotonous hard compulsions of the poor" (264). They also agree that poverty can be found in New England rural districts (265). Adding great weight to the belief that Wharton could be only an onlooker, the great American poet, John Crowe Ransom (1936) censures Wharton's concept (supposedly acquired under James's tutelage) of choosing a narrator whose background might be considered similar to her own. Further, he comments that this type of narration is overdone: "Everybody in fiction nowadays employs him" (284). Odd structural patterns and unsatisfactory detail indicate to him that the narration poses serious difficulty because ideally Ethan would tell his own story. Or Wharton could tell it, but if she did, her cultured upper-class voice would prove incongruent; therefore, the outside narrator represents a compromise, the effect being that the narrator simply invented the story (273). To reinforce his point, Ransom quotes Wharton's own statement that when "an air of artificiality is lent to a tale of complex and sophisticated people which the novelist causes to be guessed at and interpreted by any mere looker-on, there need be no such drawback if the looker-on is sophisticated, and the people he interprets are simple" [EF viii]). Ransom finds it impossible to accept the argument in Wharton's preface (287). He further takes issue with Wharton's "peculiar chronological method" (273), a matter that remains the subject of critical commentary.

The Mere Looker-On

The matter of narrative technique aside, Wharton was accused of not knowing what she was talking about. Although she could not have read them, the 1942 remarks of Alfred Kazin sum up the rancor of many leftist critics:

> [*Ethan Frome*] was not a New England story and certainly not the granite "folk tale" of New England *in esse* its admirers have claimed it to be. She knew little of the New England common world, and perhaps cared even less. . . . The world of the Frome tragedy is abstract. She never knew how the poor lived in . . . New England villages where she spent an occasional summer. There is indeed nothing in any of her work . . . to indicate that she had any conception of the tensions and responsibilities of even the most genteel middle-class pov-

erty. . . . She thought of the poor not as a class but as a condition; the qualities she automatically ascribed to the poor—drabness, meanness, anguish—became another manifestation of the futility of human effort. (60)

Earlier censure of this type had evoked an angry response from the author:

> In an article by an American literary critic, I saw "Ethan Frome" cited as an interesting example of a successful New England story written by someone who knew nothing of New England! "Ethan Frome" was written after I had spent ten years in the hill-region where the scene is laid, during which years I had come to know well the aspect, dialect, and mental and moral attitude of the hill-people. The fact that "Summer" deals with the same class and type as those portrayed in "Ethan Frome," and have the same setting, might have sufficed to disprove the legend—but once such a legend is started it echoes on as long as its subject survives. (BG 296)

During the ten years she "summered" (about six months) in Lenox, Wharton volunteered at the Lenox library, participated in the flower shows, worked with the humane society, and was otherwise socially active among the residents, as well as among the rich inhabitants of the great castles called "summer cottages" (See Lewis [1975], Blackall [1984], and Marshall [1993]).

To add to the injury, a well-known critic, Q. D. Leavis, sledge-hammers the notion of Wharton's debt to James into both public and academic minds simply by the title of her essay: "Henry James's Heiress: The Importance of Edith Wharton." She makes the case for Edith Wharton as a serious novelist by relating the background that qualified her to write Jane Austen-like New York novels (76, 85). But, she says, "we do not know how she acquired the material for that moving study of the sufferings of the respectable poor." Leavis notes that the author "solves the problem of tone by ignoring the reader altogether," and that Wharton was "first to outrage the accepted pretense of seeing the New England countryside idyllically. Hers was informed realism" (83). Leavis gets many things right in this 1938 essay, but her superior tone seems to undo any good she might have done for Wharton's reputation.

But Wharton also had a reputation among editors as "difficult." Ellery Sedgwick, unaware that to Wharton punctuation was as important as word choice (see Blackall 147–63), writes about his editorial altercations with her. He tried to convince her to change her British spelling and punctuation to conform to his magazine's format, but the (to him) unbearably fussy Edith Wharton prevailed in her "Jamesian standards," leaving Sedgwick fearing blame for careless editing. He finally solved the problem by means of a polite footnote denying responsibility. Still, while Sedgwick appears to agree with those who deny Wharton's knowledge of New England, he does not deny the reality of her sources. He remarks that he had grown up in New England where Ethan Frome dwelt and marveled about where Wharton had found the material for this stark and terrible history. "Yankees on the remote farms are a dour race, consenting under duress to a Calvinistic Providence. . . . But the Yankees I knew were in their spiritual inheritance Scotch, and Ethan Frome was an Aeschylean," he writes, alluding to one of the ever-haunting Greek playwrights. He wrote to the author to inquire, and "she bade me turn to Henry James. Somewhere in America Revisited, I think, runs the passage: 'Trim New England farm houses with their green blinds and Cenci-like interiors'" (xxiv-xxv). (Sedgwick means *The American Scene*, 47.)

But Edith Wharton, apparently having given up defending herself against the James "legend," undoubtedly meant Sedgwick to note as well that she had been the Chekhovian lady with the lapdog touring New England with Henry James, and touring, of course, is a means of learning. Sedgwick apparently missed it. He admits quoting from vague memory, but confesses that it caused him to recall a forgotten incident that ironically proves Wharton's power: "Wandering one day among the outbuildings of a ramshackle farm, I was startled by a piercing shriek coming from a wood shed. I flung open the door and there chained to an upright joist, with a chair to sit on, bread and water by her side, was a hag with streaming hair, horribly insane" (xxv).

But from the far left, Alfred Kazin's 1942 remarks in *On Native Ground* gave rise to dialogue. His book, a survey of American literature that includes a generally negative discussion of Edith Wharton and her work, claims that the author specializes in "tales of victimization" (56) rather than Greek "fate." Blake Nevius (1953) believes Alfred Kazin's argument that *Ethan Frome* could be reconciled with *The House of Mirth* by demonstrating "the spiritual value of failure" (197). Critics still refer to Nevius's book which states that as with many of Wharton's novels, the real theme is "the baffling, wasteful submission of a superior nature [Ethan] to an inferior one [Zeena]" (198). According to him, then, both Lily Bart and Ethan represent spiritual waste, not Furies or Fate, and not class victimization.

The Murder of a Masterpiece

Although J. D. Thomas (1953) concludes that the novel is full of mistakes, the final blow to the reputation of *Ethan Frome* as a "masterpiece" probably resulted from Lionel Trilling's important essay, "A Morality of Inertia" (1956). Trilling calls the novel "factitious" and revives the word "cruel": "Whenever the characters of a story suffer, they do so at the behest of their author—the author is responsible for their suffering and must justify his cruelty by the seriousness of his moral intention" (138). He refers to *Ethan Frome* as "a dead book" with no "moral reverberation" occurring during the reading. Instead, it makes the reader participate in the cathartic pleasure that "derives from observing the pain of others" (140). We should "observe something more than mere passivity"—some "meaning, some show of rationality" (141). As Aristotle taught, literature must instruct. Because Ethan does nothing "by moral election" (144), Trilling all but describes it as sinful to enjoy this novel, and he blames Edith Wharton for her "limitation of heart." Trilling's essay virtually halted further critical commentary on *Ethan Frome* until 1961. The first true Wharton scholar, James Tuttleton, notes that that essay was "one of the great failures of this great critic's career" (See Tuttleton, 100). The few essays written during the following seven years either side with Trilling or feebly defend Wharton against him.

However, in 1957 Nancy Leach had turned from moral commentary to apply New Critical techniques to three of Wharton's incomplete manuscripts, concluding that to the author New England represents lack of culture and thwarted human potential. This article helps readers appreciate the craftsmanship praised by the earliest reviewers, by pointing out "the compatibility of setting and character, the uses of light and dark, and the sexual symbolism," as well as the plethora of images of people "caught, bound, trapped" and imprisoned. It demonstrates how white, black, red, and gray imagery play against one another. It concludes that Ethan Frome is "a negative person," and that his tragedy is entirely of his own making. That analysis contradicts the "cruel," unendurable quality to which critics like Trilling had earlier objected.

Another close reading by Joseph X. Brennan (1961) sets out to return the volume to classic status. In an interesting echo of earlier criticism, he remarks that "the narrator has liberally endowed [Ethan] with much the same sensitivity he himself possesses" (349). He contrasts indoor and outdoor scenes, finds the inside of the farmhouse symbolizing morality and constraint, while the outdoors symbolizes natural freedom. Brennan associates Ethan with the Romantic sensibility of nature.

Over time topics had switched from Greek tragedy, to socialist intentions against poverty, to morality, and finally to a kind of Emersonian Romanticism. Still, a relatively large chronological gap in the criticism occurs between 1961 and the mid-seventies. The inevitable exception is provided by Pucknat and Pucknat (1969), who note deep affinities between *Ethan Frome* and Gottfried Keller's *Romeo und Julia auf dem Dorft [A Village Romeo and Juliet]*. In 1974 Richard Lawson expands the subject to the larger topic of German literature in several articles and ultimately in a book of some note.

How Ethan Reflects Edith

1977 did produce three essays, however. That by David Eggenschwiler illustrates their combined points. He debates both Trilling and Kenneth Bernard (1961), proposing that Trilling's accusation of moral passivity in the face of a cruel universe and Bernard's concept that Ethan causes his own suffering are simultaneously possible because the novel is so classically complex that it can contain opposing ideas without destroying its coherence.

Also in 1977, Cynthia Griffin Wolff's critical biography attempts to place each of Wharton's works into the context of her continuing psychological development. Wolff reads *Ethan Frome* as a figment of the narrator's imagination, the same conclusion John Crowe Ransom had drawn. The novel itself is a "vision" pieced together from fragments of gossip, within which Ethan also has a vision, a story that "becomes a veritable dance around the notion of vision" (179). To Wolff the story is not about Ethan at all, but subtly explicates Wharton's "private nightmare" of crossing the threshold from an emotionally starved adolescence to discovery of creative and sexual fulfillment as a mature woman. Wolff further suggests the novel's relationships to Robert Browning's *The Ring and the Book*, Honoré de Balzac's "*Le grand Bretêche*," Herman Melville's "Bartleby the Scrivener," and Emily Brontë's *Wuthering Heights*. The novel's scenery not only recalls Hawthorne's *Blithedale Romance*, but also "Ethan Brand" (163). Wolff concludes that the novel is not actually about Ethan at all, but about the isolation of the narrator, for it "focuses on the narrator's problem: the tension between his public self and his shadow self, his terror of a seductive and enveloping void" (184).

The same year Elizabeth Ammons indirectly concedes the influence of Trilling by summarizing the debates against him. Her feminist approach to *Ethan Frome* describes the novel as a deliberately inverted "Snow White." She cites physical descriptions and typical fairy tale numbers to support the concept that the isolated woman, Zeena, becomes the stereotypical witch in Ethan's eyes, in turn dramatizing a "deeply rooted, male fear of woman" (128). The argument contends that "Zeena's identity and fate stalk Mattie until . . . she too becomes a witch" (132). Ammons's mythological analysis adds a compelling aspect to the canon of critical response that punctuates the great change in Wharton studies instigated by Lewis and Wolff. For *Ethan Frome*, that change turned largely toward psychological and biographical criticism—attempts to draw analogies between the writer's life and her fiction.

Since the late seventies critical output on *Ethan Frome* has decreased to an average of about one article per year possibly because, except for feminist theories, *Ethan Frome* fails to respond to many of the currently prevailing critical approaches. But such trends rarely develop unwaveringly, and in a traditional mode that predominantly agrees with Trilling, Edward Sagarin (1981) reads *Ethan Frome* as "punishment without crime . . . [and] suffering without hope of alleviation" and no possible redemption (97). Wharton, he says, deliberately wrote a unique triangular tragedy that she recognized as "the universal history of mankind" (109).

Two years later, a study by Orlene Murad adds to biographical readings, supposing that the author could identify so well with Ethan because she was "experiencing Ethan's dilemma in a miserable marriage" also caused by a sickly spouse (95). Another biographical connection was found by Jean Frantz Blackall (1984), who uses the literary historical technique to reveal that when Wharton volunteered at the Lenox library, she worked alongside a young woman, Kate Spenser, who had been permanently disfigured by taking the full force of exactly the type of sledding accident that occurs in the novel. In fact, *The Berkshire Evening Eagle* (1904) describes it. Blackall certainly located the source of the crucial scene, if not of the story itself. Scott Marshall would add to this information in 1993 by quoting from Edith Wharton's letters to Kate Spenser.

By the eighties the feminist, psychological, and biographical ideologies, and combinations of them, predominate in studies of *Ethan Frome* to the point that one critic, R. B. Hovey (1986), bravely criticizes the predominating methods, naming Ammons and Wolff in particular for "'creativity'. . . . [that] reshape[s] Wharton's art almost beyond recognition" (4). He fears that their approach will "ossify into the ideological" a work "predominantly realistic" (12), although he finds a recognizably Freudian victory (17). Wolff simply responds by writing another of the essays that attempt to find sources, *romans à clef,* and parallel themes in Edith Wharton's life and work. This time Wolff formulates a metaphorical comparison of the story's themes to problems in Edith's marriage to Teddy Wharton. Her love affair with Morton Fullerton represents "grotesque mirror-images of love deformed" (236). In the cases of Teddy Wharton and Henry James, Wharton's dedication to "*ses deux malades*" [her ailing husband and friend] creates (echoing Trilling) a "lodestone of inertia" around the passionate, energetic woman's neck to parallel Ethan's "lodestone" consisting of Zeena and Mattie. Overall, Wolff contends that the most telling similarities between Wharton's life and art in *Ethan Frome* can be found in her marriage.

Considerations of Sources, Genre, and Religion

The critical reception of the nineties seems to indicate another era of diminished interest in *Ethan Frome,* although it continues to be taught, and few have suggested that it is any less the masterpiece people thought prior to the Trilling attack. Blackall (1992) describes in detail how Emily Brontë's *Wuthering Heights* strongly suggests that the story is essentially a descendant, or even an adaptation, of Brontë's novel. Marlene Springer (1993) reads *Ethan Frome* as "a nightmare of need," adding to Wolff's interpretation by again comparing the barren emotional circumstances of Wharton's life to the starkness of the novel. Zeena had become "a mysterious alien presence, an evil energy . . ." (51). Symbols reveal the tragic web in which the novel's characters find themselves inexorably trapped (94). Springer adds that the novel's philosophy reflects an indifferent universe, the conflict between duty and happiness, the influence of heredity and environment on moral choices, and that, as Trilling had implied, characters "live in the moral universe of the Book of Job" (97).

In contrast (to simplify a long and learned argument) Carol Singley (1995) argues that *Ethan Frome* is both Calvinistic and the result of complex personal and literary forces that affected the author throughout her life. She finds that "Wharton's most Calvinist novel, *Ethan Frome,* posits an unredeemed and unredeemable universe" (107). Donna Campbell (1997), however, returns to Sara Orne Jewett and Mary E. Wilkins Freeman, with whom many critics have grouped Edith Wharton in the regionalist or local colorist genre. But Campbell constructs an argument based on the novel's structure and narration, contending that Wharton distances herself from, for one thing, "the local color use of the female narrator by rejecting a convention common to local color fiction . . ." (163).

So the reception of *Ethan Frome* has moved jerkily through several phases of critical interpretation and back again. Readers have found it too grim to be a true Greek tragedy, and have questioned Edith Wharton's knowledge of New England. They have argued whether it qualifies as a "masterpiece" or as leftist social criticism, found it influenced by local color and regional landscape, as well as strict Calvinist concepts of plain living. Much of the criticism agrees that something must account for the story's horror. Lionel Trilling's immensely influential essay dismissed it as having "moral inertia." After discussions about whether or not it qualifies as a masterpiece halt completely, the word "masterpiece" seems never to have resurfaced. Then, throughout most of its reception, the question became not whether Henry James influenced the novel, but how. The next major turn in the thinking about the novel occurred after the Lewis and Wolff biographies, so full of surprises that they renewed interest in much of Edith Wharton's work. At that point feminist, feminist-psychological, and feminist-biographical readings predominated, their authors fond of finding parallels between Wharton's life, work, and stories that stereotype and degrade women. Oddly out of chronology, at the end of the eighties and nineties New Critics produced bits and pieces of literary historical information. In 2000, religious and regionalist considerations are reemerging, this time tied to feminist ideals. Still no one has solved the puzzle as to why, as Trilling pointed out, a novel in which "nothing happens," produces such indescribable horror.

Edith Wharton's next major novel, *The Custom of the Country*, could not be more different from *Ethan Frome*, returning as it does to high society, yet it has its own horror, the indescribably monstrous Undine Spragg.

Works Consulted

Ammons, Elizabeth. "Edith Wharton's *Ethan Frome* and the Question of Meaning." *Studies in American Fiction* 7 (1979): 127–40.

Beach, Joseph Warren. *The Twentieth Century Novel: Studies in Technique.* New York: Century, 1932.

Bernard, Kenneth. "Imagery and Symbolism in *Ethan Frome*." *College English* 23 (December 1961): 171–84.

Bjorkman, Edwin A. "The Greater Edith Wharton." *Voices of Tomorrow: Critical Studies of the New Spirit in Literature.* New York: Mitchell Kennerley, 1913. 290–304.

Blackall, Jean Frantz. "Edith Wharton's Art of Ellipsis." *Journal of Narrative Technique* 17 (Spring 1987): 145–62.

———. "Imaginative Encounter: Edith Wharton and Emily Brontë." *Edith Wharton Review* 9.1 (Spring 1992): 9–11, 27.

———. "The Sledding Accident in *Ethan Frome.*" *Studies in Short Fiction* 21.2 (Spring 1984): 145–46.

Blankenship, Russell. *American Literature as an Expression of the American Mind.* New York: Holt, 1931.

Boas, Ralph Phillip, and Katherine Burton. *Social Backgrounds of American Literature.* Boston, MA: Little, Brown, 1933. 263–65.

Brennan, Joseph X. "*Ethan Frome*: Structure and Metaphor." *Modern Fiction Studies* 3 (Winter 1961): 347–56.

Cooper, Frederic Taber. "*Ethan Frome.*" Rev. of *Ethan Frome* by Edith Wharton. *Bookman* 34 (November 1911): 312.

———. "Current Fiction: *Ethan Frome.*" Rev. of *Ethan Frome* by Edith Wharton. *Nation* 93 (26 October 1911): 396–97.

Eggenschwiler, David. "The Ordered Disorder of *Ethan Frome.*" *Studies in the Novel* 9 (1977): 237–46.

"*Ethan Frome.*" Rev. of *Ethan Frome* by Edith Wharton. *Saturday Review* [England] 112 (18 November 1911): 650.

Hays, Peter. "Wharton's Splintered Realism." *Edith Wharton Newsletter* 2.1 (Spring 1985): 6.

Hovey, R. B. "*Ethan Frome.* A Controversy about Modernizing It." *American Literary Realism* 19.1 (Fall 1986): 4–20.

James, Henry. *The American Scene.* Bloomington, IN: U of Indiana P, 1968. 47.

Kazin, Alfred. "Edith Wharton." *Edith Wharton: A Collection of Critical Essays.* Ed. Irving Howe. Englewood Cliffs, NJ: Prentice Hall, 1962. 89 94.

Killoran, Helen. "Under the Granite Outcroppings of *Ethan Frome.*" *Literary Imagination* 2.3 (Fall 2000): 32–34.

Knight, Grant C. *The Novel in English.* New York: Richard B. Smith, 1931.

Lawson, Richard. *Edith Wharton and German Literature.* Bonn: Bouvier Verlag Herbert Grundmann, 1974.

Leach, Nancy. "New England in the Stories of Edith Wharton." *New England Quarterly* 30 (March 1957): 90–98.

Leavis, Q. D. "Henry James's Heiress: The Importance of Edith Wharton." *Scrutiny* (December, 1938). Rpt. in *Edith Wharton: A Collection of Critical Essays.* Ed. Irving Howe. Englewood Cliffs, NJ: Prentice-Hall, 1962. 73–88.

Lewis, R. W. B. *Edith Wharton: A Biography.* New York: Harper & Row, 1975.

Lovett, Robert Morss. *Edith Wharton.* New York: Robert D. McBride, 1925.

Marshall, Scott. "Edith Wharton, Kate Spenser, and *Ethan Frome.*" *Edith Wharton Review* 10.1 (Spring 1993): 20–21.

Murad, Orlene. "Edith Wharton and *Ethan Frome.*" *Modern Language Studies* 13 (Summer 1983): 90–103.

Nevius, Blake. *Edith Wharton: A Study of Her Fiction.* 1953. Berkeley, CA: U of California P, 1961.

———. "'Ethan Frome' and the Themes of Edith Wharton's Fiction." *The New England Quarterly Review* 24 (June 1951): 197–207.

Pattee, Fred L. *The New American Literature 1890–1930.* New York: Century, 1930.

Phelps, William Lyon. "The Advance of the English Novel, X." *Bookman* 43 (July 1916): 515–24. Rpt. in *The Advance of the English Novel.* New York: Dodd Mead, 1916.

Pucknat, E. M., and S. B. Pucknat. "Edith Wharton and Gottfried Keller." *Comparative Literature* 21 (Summer 1969): 245–54.

Ransom, John Crowe. "Characters and Character: A Note on Fiction." *The American Review* 6 (January 1936): 271–88.

Review of *Ethan Frome* by Edith Wharton. *The Berkshire Evening Eagle.* [Pittsfield, Mass.] (12 March 1904): 1+.

"Review of *Ethan Frome.*" Rev. of *Ethan Frome* by Edith Wharton. *Bookman.* [England] 41 (January 1912): 216.

Sagarin, Edward. "*Ethan Frome*: Atonement Endures Until Darkness Descends." *Raskolnikov and Others: Literary Images of Crime, Punishment, Redemption and Atonement.* Ed. Edward Sagarin. New York: St. Martin's P, 1981.

Sedgwick, Ellery. Introduction. *Atlantic Harvest.* Boston, MA: Little, Brown, 1947.

Sergeant, Elizabeth Shepley. "Idealized New England." Review of *Ethan Frome* by Edith Wharton. *The New Republic* 3 (May 8, 1915): 20–21.

Springer, Marlene. *Ethan Frome: A Nightmare of Need.* New York: G. K. Hall, 1993.

Thomas, J. D. "Marginalia on *Ethan Frome.*" *American Literature* 27 (November 1953): 405–9.

"Three Lives in Supreme Torture: Mrs. Wharton's *Ethan Frome* a Cruel, Compelling, Haunting Story of New England." Rev. of *Ethan Frome* by Edith Wharton. *New York Times Book Review* (8 October 1911): 603.

Trilling, Lionel. "The Morality of Inertia." *Ethan Frome: A Collection of Critical Essays*. Ed. Irving Howe. Englewood Cliffs, NJ: Prentice-Hall, 1962. 137–46.

Tuttleton, James W. *American Women Writers: Bibliographical Essays*. Westport, CT: Greenwood P, 1983. 100.

Tuttleton, James W., Kristin O. Lauer, and Margaret P. Murray. *Edith Wharton: The Contemporary Reviews*. New York: Cambridge UP, 1992.

Van Doren, Carl. "Contemporary American Novelists." *Nation* 112 (12 January 1921): 40–41. Rpt. in *Contemporary American Novelists 1900–1920*. New York: Macmillan, 1923.

Wharton, Edith. *A Backward Glance*. New York: Appleton-Century, 1934. Rpt. New York: Scribners, 1985. 293–95.

Wolff, Cynthia Griffin. *A Feast of Words: The Triumph of Edith Wharton*. New York: Oxford UP, 1977.

———. "Cold Ethan and 'Hot Ethan.'" *College Literature* 14.3 (1987): 230–45. Rpt. in *Edith Wharton: New Critical Essays*. Eds. Alfred Bendixen and Annette Zilversmit. New York: Garland, 1992.

4: *The Custom of the Country—*
Monstrous Undine

WHILE THACKERAY'S BECKY SHARPE is a character readers love to hate, Undine Spragg has evoked utter distaste among the many critics for whom her ruthless socio-pathology, in combination with Wharton's strident satire, proved "unpleasant." When *The Custom of the Country* appeared in 1913, the first reviewers, late neo-humanists, tried faithfully to find some sustaining moral in the beautifully structured novel, other than its obvious criticism of divorce. Comparisons to *Vanity Fair* and *The House of Mirth* were almost unavoidable and reviewers also felt baffled by the weakness of old New York in the face of the Midwestern "invaders." Later, New Critics lightly touched on the book's minor characters, structure, and genre, but not until the revolutionary 1970s, when feminists shifted the locus of attention, did *The Custom of the Country* and Undine receive their due.

The only surviving child of three, the much-spoiled Undine Spragg convinces her parents to move to New York from the Midwest to advance her social career. Her parents agree because the relocation also removes her from the uncouth influence of Elmer Moffatt, with whom Undine had been infatuated. The Spraggs expect Undine's red-haired beauty and her father's money to grant them entrance into high society, but the three languish at the Hotel Stentorian until Undine accidentally meets Ralph Marvell, a young man from an old New York family, and launches her victorious campaign to marry him. Much in the manner of the picaresque, the novel records the couple's unsuccessful honeymoon, and the birth and neglect of their son, until Undine runs away to live with a richer man, Peter Van Degen. Divorce follows. Van Degen, who might have married Undine, learns that she had refused to visit Ralph during his life-threatening illness. He abandons her when he realizes that she would treat him exactly the same way. Undaunted, Undine contrives to meet Raymond de Chelles, the even richer scion of an old French family. However, de Chelles, as a Roman Catholic, cannot marry a divorced woman. Needing money to bribe Vatican officials into granting her an annulment, Undine threatens Ralph with the loss of custody of their son. When Ralph cannot raise the money, he commits suicide. Undine is now a widow, free to marry de Chelles, and again in custody of her son. She eagerly anticipates stardom in the glittering social life of the Continent. Instead, she finds herself trapped in the traditional role of the "childless" French wife, living with her mother-in-law who, by French custom, rules the house and a husband who, also by French custom, controls the money. When she revolts, de Chelles refuses to father a son, the only means by which Undine can gain social acceptance by the old French families. In revenge, she sells a priceless family heirloom, a Boucher tapestry. The purchaser is none other than the now incredibly wealthy Elmer Moffatt. Undine naturally divorces Raymond de Chelles to marry Moffatt. Ironically, she has arrived back where she started, since before leaving the Midwest, she had already married Moffatt in secret.

Undine has apparently reached her goal, married to a man who shares her love of wealth. She owns mansions, wears fabulous jewels, and travels constantly with people to care for her son so she does not need to bother with him. Then Undine learns that an even more prestigious position exists: wife of an ambassador. Maneuvering Moffatt into an ambassadorship would be possible, but the wife of an ambassador cannot be divorced. The novel leaves Undine, still beautiful, but no longer young and slender, in a state of perfect frustration, but beginning again to calculate.

Only one critical commentary (apart from the initial reviews) appeared in the forty years after the book's publication. Then in the seventies and eighties feminist theories of women as victims of the patriarchy resurrected not only this novel (in which the situation is actually reversed) but also much of Wharton's remaining work. Feminists then turned their attention to the subjects of marriage and divorce as business. A few deconstructed the novel in the process, while others explored the possibility of the novel as an analogy or metaphor for social maladies. Attention next turned to how male discourse affects women's sense of self and how language and writing represent male power over women. Because, like *The House of Mirth*, *The Custom of the Country* focuses on greed and wealth, it lends itself well to Marxist points of view, while a few other critics have looked at it through ethnographic and mythological lenses.

"A Monstrously Perfect Result of the System"

The issue that immediately broke out among reviewers of *The Custom of the Country* derived from Wharton's unusually sharp satire of the protagonist, the glittery, greedy, soulless Undine. The absence of a sympathetic heroine from whom the reader might learn a moral lesson proved the primary early concern. The *New York Sun* (1913) writes that Wharton has created "an ideal monster" with no human feeling, who is "absolutely unmoral," not a real person but an "abstract type," resulting in a "distinct loss of art" (CR 203). The *Saturday Review* returns to the general opinion that Undine had "not a single redeeming moral feature." Henry W. Boynton in the *Nation* accuses Edith Wharton of creating caricatures rather than characters. He criticizes her "sharply satirical tone" as a "dubious sign in a writer who has passed a certain age" (CR 209) and who is losing her position as one of America's most distinguished writers. The *Bookman* [England] (1914) finds no moral but says that the novel is its own warning. In a far more positive review, F. M. Colby claims for the author the right not to be criticized for "excluding reminders of the beauty of human nature," while the *Independent* remarks that Undine has "the mushy moral construction of a sea anemone" (CR 210, 212).

Comparisons with its predecessor, *The House of Mirth,* (and with Thackeray's *Vanity Fair*) were inevitable. Frederick Taber Cooper in the *Bookman* (1913) regards *The Custom of the Country* as a "splendid and memorable piece of work, a portrait to form a worthy contrast to the equally unforgettable one of Lily Bart" (CR 211). The *New York Times Review of Books* (1913) adds, quoting the novel, that Undine is a "monstrously perfect result" of a system of "contemptuous indulgence" of women. L. M. F. of the *New York Review of Books* notes that the novel resembles *The House of Mirth* but that Undine has none of Lily Bart's redeeming characteristics. She is simply "greed personified—without conscience, heart, sense of honor, or sense of humor." The theme of the spoilt, utterly selfish woman has "rarely been developed in a manner so skillful, so delicate, and so completely ruthless" (CR 206). The *Saturday Review* calls Undine "cold, greedy, heartless, and wayward, without a soul and with no realisation of anything but the outward glitter and tinsel of life, she has only one passion, and that is for endless amusement" (CR 210). The reader describes a brilliantly written exposé of the "scandals of divorce" that "should read as a parable" (CR 211).

In creative contrast, the *Athenaeum* [England] (1913) praises Edith Wharton for making Undine a sentimental heroine: "It is, of course, a monstrous record from the sentimental standpoint. But Mrs. Wharton, by avoiding the least hint of sentiment, and laying stress upon the sequence of environment, upbringing, character, has made her heroine a natural and pathetic figure. She succeeds in winning for a cold and selfish character the kindly sympathy, which comes of understanding . . ." (209). However, Percy Lubbock in the *Quarterly Review* (1915) writes that *The Custom of the Country* is an excellent book, yet he regards Wharton's characterizations as failures. He wonders how "Undine, as a mere bubble of rainbow tints, may possibly have substance enough to wound and destroy," and in uncanny anticipation of feminist critics adds that "Undine, being nothing but an exquisite object, should surely have been treated exclusively as an object." He does acknowledge Wharton's having conquered a new problem, that of a stage setting as wide as Lily Bart's but much deeper, one which "absorbs the gaze with its deep layers of distinction and monotony . . . of immemorial ignorance of the world . . ." (52).

However, *The Nation* (1913) reasons that the spoiling of Undine is the result of rapid social changes rather than "contemptuous indulgence" of women. The social changes refer to the pioneer status by which women shared equally in wealth-building toil that suddenly disappeared leaving them trapped in a new stereotype, the "spending woman," awarded that privilege by men as "compensation for what she has suffered and achieved in the past." R. W. B. Lewis (1975) reinforces this concept, remarking that the "great strength of the novel derives from Edith Wharton's understanding of what was *happening,* historically, to the American and French aristocracies in the first decade of the twentieth century. Both were giving way before the two major forces of the historic moment—sexual power and financial aggressiveness" (349). He ends by conjecturing that Undine undoubtedly represented everything Edith Wharton despised in the new American woman (350).

The Ubiquitous Henry James

The inevitable pairing of Edith Wharton's name with that of Henry James occurs again in *The North American Review,* which remarks that the novel owes some interest to "what Henry James calls the 'social scene,'" but adds contrarily that the book has nothing other than a moral lesson (294–99). Henry James, who did seem to want to help Edith Wharton uncouple their names, inadvertently made matters worse. In his favorable review for the *Times Literary Supplement* (England), he hints strongly, in his uniquely convoluted way, of the importance of the novel's allusiveness. He discusses finding "the moral of the treasure of amusement sitting in the lap of [satirical] method with a felicity peculiarly [Edith Wharton's] own" (217). The coupling continues when in 1964 Michael Millgate insists, "it is beyond argument that *The Custom of the Country* itself could not have been written without the whole body of James's achievement behind it" (63).

For forty years after the initial reviews, however, the novel sat patiently in dusty library stacks. The only commentary it received came from a British critic, James Huneker (1915). But even in appreciation of the novel, he belittles it by asking party questions: "What is the name of your favourite heroine? Whom should you like to meet in that long corridor of time leading to eternity . . .?" He answers that he is more intrigued by "disagreeable girls like Hedda Gabbler, Mildred Lawson and Undine Spragg" than by sentimental heroines (314). He finds in "Undine—shades of La Motte Fouqué—quite the most disagreeable girl in our fiction. . . . a much more viable creature than . . . Lily Bart . . ." (324). He goes on to characterize Undine as the greediest of them (327), as temperamental, and as having a poorly furnished mind. He insists that she is not wicked, because "it takes brains to be wicked in the grand manner" (328). Richard Lawson later explores Undine's character in relation to the 1811 novella, *Undine,* by the German writer La Motte Fouqué (Lawson, 1974).

Questions of Genre

The Custom of the Country did not attract as much genre criticism as *The House of Mirth,* but Blake Nevius (1953) comments on it: *The Custom of the Country* is a "fusion of the novel of manners with the picaresque" in order to enhance social comedy (159). Undine follows the classic pattern of the *picaro* happiest in the underworld (157), the huntress taking advantage of an unstable society by emerging wealthily from pioneer status. The novel is arranged in "pecuniary order," with unstable society as Undine's hunting ground. In 1968 James E. Miller, Jr. makes a point relevant both to genre and to the first wave of feminism: character typing. Characters come from the "entire social world . . . the divorcée, the poet, the stupid rich and the wise poor, the sexually restless and the delicate, the sensitive and the insensitive. . . ." He also senses "the uncomfortable presence of sinister elements not clearly visible . . ." (86). Some of the sinister elements appear in Nancy Morrow's 1984 description of the novel as a series of unpredictable games. She concludes that the novel's game-playing "moral landscape . . . is barren and sterile, the tone harsh and angry," and that no moral center exists in the novel (38). Several critics point to the novel as a social allegory or metaphor, or microcosm, as in the case of Joseph A. Ward (1988), who notes that "to James 'the amazing hotel world' is simply a microcosm of America itself" (151), representative of an immoral passion for great wealth. Ward develops the historical growth of the hotel business to conclude that Wharton presents the hotel in *The Custom of the Country* as the vulgar habitation of the nouveau riche. The subject is part of Wharton's view of Americans as rootless wanderers: "It was natural that the Americans, who had no homes, who were born and died in hotels, should have contracted nomadic habits . . ." (CC 512).

Several commentators also have noted Wharton's deep sense of history. The important critic Margaret McDowell (1976) records that Wharton "conveys a sense of depth and abundance; and she reveals a sophisticated artistry and breadth of social knowledge . . . a stirring recreation of the pre-World War I milieu in America and France." Unlike most of the early reviewers, McDowell does find a "firm and commanding" moral stance in Wharton's story (56).

Energy Unleashed

Naturally biographers will search for autobiographical material in the novel. Lewis notes that the novel gave Edith Wharton a good chance to use her enormous knowledge of American and European social history (348). In addition, the four main characters each reveal part of her complex psychology. But most of Edith Wharton is revealed in the characterization of Undine that Lewis casts as "Edith Wharton's antiself; and like all anti-selves, a figure that explains much about its opposite" (349).

Cynthia Griffin Wolff (1977) disagrees completely, saying that the subject is not that of Edith Wharton's problems. Using the strong language of early first-phase feminists, Wolff addresses the author's anger produced from repressed childhood desires: The novel is "infused with the woman's outrage and the long-suppressed fury of the girl whose deepest instincts had been engulfed by guilt. The object of that fury is a society whose norms are not equal to the range of experience that its members feel. An insensitive, effete, corrupt society; a society that might, without humor, produce a magazine called *Success*; a society whose 'best' people have been frozen into stupefaction by the niceties of 'propriety'" (230). Wolff describes the tone of the novel as "martial, furious, and devastating," "perverse in its constant change," "difficult and disorienting," and preoccupied with energy and initiative. "Undine comes out of the West, from a state renowned for its tornadoes. . . . Her essence is energy" (242). Wolff interprets Undine as both villain and victim in that the blind passivity of old New Yorkers causes them to ignore destructive natural energy. Shari Benstock (1994), nearly twenty years later, agrees with Wolff that Wharton's "difficulties with *The Custom of the Country* had always turned on the question of energy" (283). Benstock points out the irony that as she completed the novel Edith

Wharton was "fatigued almost to illness" (283), yet Undine is one of her most energetic characters.

Elizabeth Ammons (1980) elaborates on Wolff's comments, regarding the novel as a tour de force, a great business novel with Undine, a "blithe New Woman" (99) approaching marriage as a simple economic contract. To Ammons, "*The Custom of the Country* can be read as conservative satire of the nouveaux-riches invaders" who threatened leisure-class values. "There is a primitivism about Wharton's image, and Undine's character in general, that roots this novel not only in Veblenesque socio-economics, but also in feminist anthropological assumptions popular at the turn of the century" (101). Because Ammons's interest is in creating a separate canon of American women writers, she compares *The Custom of the Country* to early popular women's novels to show how Undine "speculates in husbands just as husbands speculate in stocks" (121). Continuing emphasis on the historical context of marriage, divorce, and money at the turn of the nineteenth century, Alexandra Collins (1983) contends that before the Great War some women used marriage as a business career, that the novel is an example of the new society emerging from the Spraggs' Midwest and that Ralph and Undine's marriage becomes metaphorical for the "dangerous attempt in American society to join spirituality to materialism" (210). Ultimately the target of satire is American marriage customs. Edith Wharton values marriage as a stabilizing social institution, deplores divorce, especially frivolous divorce, and finds single women's lives difficult. Compare the single lives of Gertie Ferish and *The Bunner Sisters*, or Mrs. Manstey in "Mrs. Manstey's View," to that of Lawrence Selden in *The House of Mirth*.

Susan Wolstenholme (1985) elaborates on energy in terms of Henry Adams's metaphor of the virgin and the dynamo. Undine's energy comes from sexual power because she sublimates her sexual desires, which resurface in desire for money (98). She appears entirely innocent of sexuality, but her energy combined with that of Elmer Moffatt, a dynamo of industry, ultimately defeats de Chelles in spite of his ancient French culture.

The Spraggs' Midwestern town, "Opake," becomes an entry for a deconstruction exercise. Robert L. Caserio (1986) alleges that the book is divided against itself in formalist vs. mimetic polarities, that it reverses public and private oppositions, and that it functions by lying to the reader as well as by "fabricating" a novel imitative of George Eliot and Henry James. Picking up the economic thread, Mary Suzanne Schriber (1987) posits another type of deconstruction, pointing out that Wharton made the unusual observation that sex as barter may be of no value to a woman. She "may trade what is, to her, nothing in exchange for something. Undine's absolute sexual indifference deconstructs the culture's frame of sexual reference, rendering it meaningless" (177).

In 1994 and 1995 respectively, Elaine Showalter and Debra Ann MacComb return to the subjects of feminism, marriage as a business, divorce, and biographical matters. Like Ammons, Showalter demonstrates how the novel is about "the art of the deal," in particular the American deal, and finds the language of gender intriguing in that "Moffatt used life exactly as [Undine] would have used it in his place" (91). By this time Wharton had created a business of her words and inscribes in the novel her kinship with her native country (96). MacComb (1996) reminds readers that the double standard held that divorce was socially criminal for a woman, regardless of whom the courts blamed. Wharton shows how society created a product out of divorce. Just as advertisers create business by evolving techniques from providing product information to creating desire for what a product represents ,so did divorce and desire for "rotary remarriage" become a business. Wharton distances herself from modern divorce consumerism and preserves "creditability." Divorce for Edith Wharton herself was apparently a painful social wound that never healed, for Lewis reports that "Wharton's papers . . . included a packet labeled, in her own hand, 'For My Biographer,'" and that the packet consisted primarily of documentation about the reasons for her divorce (xi), finalized in the year this novel appeared.

Jenijoy La Belle (1988) draws on the Lacanian concept that the mirror image—gigantic, ornate hotel mirrors—creates identity for Undine who defines her personhood, her "self," in the image of the mirrored double. Men, on the other hand, use conversation as a means of self-definition and self-projection. In this way the mirror image becomes "the Other," as well as the audience (62). So Undine feels there is an other self "beyond the glass" (63). Also noting the subject of identity, but traveling in the direction of the "land of letters," Janet Goodwyn (1990) takes a metaphorically geographical approach: *The Custom of the Country* is concerned with how to incorporate women into the culture, but community participation in the real life of a culture is entirely missing from Undine's sense of identity, and the ancient French social structure is advanced as the model that values women (41–42).

Turning to the feminist theories of Luce Irigaray, Ellen Dupree (1990) argues that the novel is "profoundly feminist" (5) and that Undine exposes women's oppression in marriage by showing how far women need to go to overcome them (5). Wharton, she says, uses Undine's "pioneer blood" (CC 56) and her "'Western girl' to deconstruct the feminine ideal" (6), and to join the patriarchal discourse (10). The novel is "an attack on a woman who defies patriarchal authority and therefore self-destruction. . . . [It is] a creation of the patriarchy, and not, therefore . . . 'real.' (Here, Wharton's patriarchal culture and Irigaray's patriarchal discourse are exactly the same)" (11). Wharton uses Undine to provide a realist way to deconstruct male discourse and casts doubt on men's ability to define women (15). Continuing the feminist perspective, Katherine Joslin (1991) elaborates on the social geographical theme examined by Lubbock (1915), McDowell (1976), Goodwyn (1990), and several others to consider Undine as the "female pioneer" who hears the "call of the Atlantic." The plot, she believes, inverts that of *The House of Mirth*. It cannot end in tragedy because the heroine lacks tragic insight, and because of the irony that by the close Undine returns to the nouveaux-riches she had originally aspired to surpass.

Lev Raphael (1990), on the other hand, prefers to apply a new psychological-biographical theory by Dr. Sylvan Tomkins, by which he determines the degree of Wharton's "poisonous" embarrassments from her fiction. Because the object of indifference becomes "unimportant, unvaluable, even non-existent" (274), indifference is Undine's "chief nemesis." Nothing was more bitter to Undine than confessing that her powers might fail.

Candace Waid (1991) differs from those who regard *The Custom of the Country* as an advance in the feminist canon. Drawing on the Ralph Marvell subplot, she argues that at one level the novel is about unfinished books and about the failure of the American writer. It tells of the "death of a writer who moves from Whitman and a poem about banished gods to a plan for a book that treats men as insects, from romantic ideals about chivalry and godlike men to a bleak determinism. . . . Undine represents a fatally alluring [decorative] surface language" (131). But to Kathy Miller Hadley (1993) the novel is less about writing than "about power and illusions of power." In taking over the role of Undine's all-providing father, Ralph makes Undine the child and uses that appellation for her. By the end of the novel, Hadley feels that Undine is under the power of Moffatt, who forces her to divorce de Chelles and marry him, thereby destroying Undine's belief in her power over others (58).

To condense the critical history of *The Custom of the Country*, the earliest criticism discussed Undine's disagreeable character and questioned the novel's morality. Edith Wharton's name was again associated with that of Henry James. Following that, discussions focused on the novel's moral didacticism or lack thereof, sometimes mentioning divorce, and often drawing on *The House of Mirth* for comparison. However, the *Nation* intelligently noticed the author's knowledge of the historical background of rapid social change that could produce such a novel. Then for the next forty years the novel all but disappeared, until the New Critics of the fifties and sixties began to examine its structure, and biographers and others made note of Edith Wharton's life and its connection to the novel. Some thought that her French divorce from Edward Wharton in 1913, the year the novel appeared, was unlikely to have been a coincidence. In the seventies and eighties feminists began to study the novel as a satire, drawn up from female rage, on marriage and divorce as business contracts, sex as meaningless barter, and sexual energy transformed into money.

Finally, Ammons attempted to place it in the new canon of women's writing. In the eighties and nineties various "deconstructions" were attempted: of the novel itself, of Undine's identity, and of the novel's use of patriarchal discourse. Then as if short of ideas, critics circled back to the subjects of marriage for power, marriage as the "art of the deal," and female energy. Critics raised questions about whether the novel is about the woman writer or about art versus business. The language of gender, Undine's identity as created by reflections, mirrors, and the gaze of others, and Edith Wharton's biography all have been included in the critical conversation. Some interesting criticism reflects the historical changes in American economic and geographical movement. For instance, rather than moving west to confront the frontier, these characters (like the characters in *The Great Gatsby*) move east to chase quick riches, becoming nomads who build nothing, but destroy everything in their paths. Yet most intriguing questions remain unconsidered. What was Wharton's larger point in showing rootless Americans? What makes this stinging satire, to use Henry James's oxymoronic phrase, such a "fine asperity"?

In exact contrast to Undine's energy in *The Custom of the Country*, the mythology of passivity, particularly that of Sleeping Beauty, is held in common by *The House of Mirth* and *Summer*. Based on its sophisticated New York and European settings, *The Custom of the Country* is categorized more easily with *The House of Mirth* and *The Age of Innocence*, while critics consider *Summer* the companion piece to *Ethan Frome*. Both *Ethan Frome* and *Summer* take place in the Berkshire country of Massachusetts, and in common with most American novels, landscape enriches this superb small novel.

Works Consulted

Ammons, Elizabeth. *Edith Wharton's Argument with America*. Athens, GA: U Georgia P, 1980.

Bell, Millicent, ed. *The Cambridge Companion to Edith Wharton*. New York: Cambridge UP, 1995.

Benstock, Shari. *No Gifts from Chance: A Biography of Edith Wharton*. New York: Scribners, 1994.

Bloom, Harold, ed. *Modern Critical Views: Edith Wharton*. New York: Chelsea House P, 1986.

Boynton, Henry W. "Mrs. Wharton's Manners." Rev. of *The Custom of the Country* by Edith Wharton. *Nation* 97 (30 October 1913): 404–5.

Candella, Joseph. "The Domestic Orientation of American Novels: 1893–1913." *American Literary Realism* 13.1 (Spring 1980): 1–18.

Caserio, Robert L. "Edith Wharton and the Fiction of Public Commentary." *Western Humanities Review* 40.3 (Autumn 1986): 189–208.

Colby, F. M. "The Book of the Month." Rev. of *The Custom of the Country* by Edith Wharton. *North American Review* 199 (February 1914): 294–99.

Collins, Alexandra. "The *Noyade* of Marriage in Edith Wharton's *The Custom of the Country*." *English Studies in Canada* 9 (2 June 1983): 197–212.

Cooper, Frederic Taber. "*The Custom of the Country*." Rev. of *The Custom of the Country* by Edith Wharton. *Bookman* 38 (December 1913): 416–17.

"Critical Reviews of the Season's Latest Books." Rev. of *The Custom of the Country* by Edith Wharton. *New York Sun* (18 October 1913): 8.

"The Custom of the Country." Rev. of *The Custom of the Country* by Edith Wharton. *Nation* 96 (15 May 1913): 494–99.

"Customs of Two Countries." Rev. of *The Custom of the Country* by Edith Wharton. *Independent* 76 (13 November 1913): 313.

Dupree, Ellen. "Jamming the Machinery: Mimesis in *The Custom of the Country*." *American Literary Realism* 22.2 (Winter 1990): 5–16.

Edmonds, Mary K. "A Theatre With All the Lusters Blazing: Customs, Costumes, and Customers in *The Custom of the Country*." *American Literary Realism* 28.3 (Spring 1996): 1–18.

Erlich, Gloria C. *The Sexual Education of Edith Wharton*. Berkeley, CA: U of California P, 1992.

F. M. L., "Mrs. Wharton's Novel: *The Custom of the Country*, A Book Which Will Excite Much Discussion." Rev. of *The Custom of the Country* by Edith Wharton. *New York Times Review of Books* (19 October 1913): 557.

"Fiction." Rev. of *The Custom of the Country* by Edith Wharton. *Athenaeum* [England] 4490 (15 November 1913): 554.

Goodwyn, Janet. *Edith Wharton: Traveller in the Land of Letters.* New York: St. Martin's P, 1990.

Hadley, Kathy Miller. *In the Interstices of the Tale: Edith Wharton's Narrative Strategies.* New York: Peter Lang, 1993.

Howe, Irving, ed. *Edith Wharton.* New York: Prentice-Hall, 1962.

Huneker, James. "Three Disagreeable Girls." *Forum* 52 (November 1915): 765–76.

James, Henry. "The Younger Generation." *Times Literary Supplement* [England] (2 April 1914): 157.

Joslin, Katherine. *Women Writers: Edith Wharton.* New York: St. Martin's P, 1991.

La Belle, Jenijoy. *Herself Beheld: The Literature of the Looking Glass.* Ithaca, NY: Cornell UP, 1988. 61–63.

Lawson, Richard H. *Edith Wharton and German Literature.* Bonn: Grundmann, 1974.

Lewis, R. W. B. *Edith Wharton: A Biography.* New York: Harper & Row, 1975.

Lubbock, Percy. "The Novels of Edith Wharton." Rev. of *The Custom of the Country* by Edith Wharton. *Quarterly Review* 222 (January 1915): 182–201.

MacComb, Debra Ann. "New Wives for Old: Divorce and the Leisure-Class Marriage Market in Edith Wharton's *The Custom of the Country.*" *American Literature* 68.4 (December 1996): 765–97.

McDowell, Margaret B. *Edith Wharton.* Boston: G. K. Hall, 1976. Revised 1990.

Miller, James E., Jr. *Quests Surd and Absurd.* Chicago, IL: U Chicago P, 1968.

Millgate, Michael. "The Novelist and the Businessman: Henry James, Edith Wharton, and Frank Norris." 1959. Rpt. in *American Social Fiction from James to Norris.* New York: Barnes and Noble, 1964.

Morrow, Nancy. "Games and Conflict in Edith Wharton's *The Custom of the Country.*" *American Literary Realism* 17 (Spring 1984): 32–39.

Nevius, Blake. *Edith Wharton: A Study of Her Fiction.* 1951. Berkeley, CA: U of California P, 1961.

"Novels." Rev. of *The Custom of the Country* by Edith Wharton. *Saturday Review* [England] 116 (22 November 1913): 658–59.

Pierce, Rosemary Erickson. "Clare Van Degen in *The Custom of the Country*." *Studies in American Fiction* 17.1 (Spring 1989): 107–110.

Raphael, Lev. *Edith Wharton's Prisoners of Shame: A New Perspective on Her Neglected Fiction*. New York: St. Martin's P, 1991.

"Review of *The Custom of the Country*." Rev. of *The Custom of the Country* by Edith Wharton. *Bookman* [England] 45 (9 March 1914): 330.

Schriber, Mary Suzanne. *Gender and the Writer's Imagination: From Cooper to Wharton*. Lexington, KY: UP of Kentucky, 1987.

Showalter, Elaine. "*The Custom of the Country:* Spragg and the Art of the Deal." *The Cambridge Companion to Edith Wharton*. Ed. Millicent Bell. New York: Cambridge UP, 1995. 87–97.

Tintner, Adeline. "A Source from *Roderick Hudson* for the Title of *The Custom of the Country*." *American Notes and Queries* 1.4 (Fall 1977).

———. "Henry James's 'Julia Bride': A Source for Chapter Nine in Edith Wharton's *The Custom of the Country*." *Notes on Modern American Literature* 9 (1985): Note 16.

Tuttleton, James W., Kristin O. Lauer, and Margaret Murray. *Edith Wharton: The Contemporary Reviews*. New York: Cambridge UP, 1992.

Voloshin, Beverley R. "Exchange in Wharton's *The Custom of the Country*." *Pacific Coast Philology* 22.1–2 (November 1987): 88–104.

Waid, Candace. *Edith Wharton's Letters from the Underworld: Fictions of Women and Writing*. Chapel Hill, NC: U of North Carolina P, 1991.

Walton, Geoffrey. *Edith Wharton: A Critical Interpretation*. Rutherford: Fairleigh Dickinson UP, 1970.

Ward, Joseph A. "'The Amazing Hotel World' of James, Dreiser, and Wharton." *Leon Edel and Literary Art*. Ed. Lyall H. Powers. Ann Arbor, MI: UMI Research P, 1988. 151–60.

Wharton, Edith. *The Writing of Fiction*. New York: Appleton-Century, 1925.

Wolff, Cynthia Griffin. *A Feast of Words: The Triumph of Edith Wharton*. New York: Oxford UP, 1977.

Wolstenholme, Susan. "Edith Wharton's Gibson Girl: The Virgin, the Undine, and the Dynamo." *American Literary Realism* 18.1–2 (Spring-Autumn 1985): 92–106.

5: *Summer*—The Law of the Father

As with *The House of Mirth* and *Ethan Frome*, the line of critical progression for *Summer* has been fairly direct, and in pure numbers, the practitioners of feminist theory have produced the greatest amount of criticism. And while the conclusion of *Ethan Frome* creates a type of horror, so does *Summer* (1918) for many readers, though for different reasons. Allowing for the usual variations in theoretical approach and points of view, *Summer* has consistently elicited discussion on the same few topics. From the first reviews until the present, debate has centered on genre, structure, biographical implications, social, religious, and psychological issues, and comparisons to other authors. Consensus among modern critics, where consensus exists, most often centers around the novel as an expression of Edith Wharton's personal sexuality, about her effort to escape the devastation of the First World War, and about the novel's strong treatment of the victimization of women like Charity Royall.

As a child, Charity Royall had been rescued from a life of abject poverty on "The Mountain" and raised by lawyer Royall, at the request of a man he had convicted of manslaughter. While Royall never officially adopted Charity, an incident early in the novel acquires incestuous overtones. One evening Charity hears him at her bedroom door, asking to be let in. She stops him on the threshold declaring, "Well, I guess you made a mistake, then. This ain't your wife's room any longer" (S 29). Afterward, she demands that Royall establish a woman in the house. Charity also insists that he get her a job as a librarian so that she can eventually earn enough money to get away from the dying town of North Dormer. Royall complies.

One summer day an unfamiliar young man enters the library. He introduces himself as Lucius Harney, the cousin of an influential woman who lives nearby, and an architect looking for books about old houses. Although she cannot find the books, Charity becomes his guide to the derelict houses in the surrounding hills. He wishes to sketch them for his book. Lawyer Royall reacts positively to Harney's intelligence, but negatively to a romance between Charity and Harney. Still, the pair continues seeing one another in secret, meeting in an abandoned house in the hills. After clandestinely attending a Fourth of July celebration in Nettleton, they are embarrassed by an encounter with lawyer Royall, drunk and in the company of a local "ruined" woman rumored to have become a prostitute.

Soon afterward, Charity and Harney become intimate. A few weeks later after Charity faints at the village "Old Home Week" celebration, she suspects pregnancy. Not long after that, lawyer Royall discovers the couple at their trysting place and demands that Harney marry Charity. Harney immediately finds a reason to return to the city, leaving Charity alone and pregnant. Depressed and fearful of the reaction of Royall and the villagers, she runs away to the Mountain to locate her biological mother, but the minister, Mr. Miles, discovers her along the road. He had been "fetched" to conduct the funeral of the very woman Charity seeks. Charity attends the grim funeral, then insists on staying at the outlaw settlement. But Mr. Miles informs Mr. Royall, who comes for her. On the way home Royall detours to Nettleton, where he marries Charity to save her reputation.

Edith Wharton wrote that *Summer* had shocked her audience more than *Ethan Frome,* and readers will recall the stigma of unwed mother-hood in Edith Wharton's day. "Boys could be boys" but girls were "cheap" or "fallen." Since publishers were leery of the novel, it took Wharton some time to find one, and because of the prevailing attitude, some contemporary critics received *Summer* unfavorably. Francis Hackett in the *New Republic* (1917) finds a strong note of falseness in it: "There is no such thing as a catastrophe too trite to be worth reciting. It is only that Mrs. Wharton, always inclined to be sub-human, is much too callous in the uses to which she has put [Charity's] seduction" (CR 250). He regards the novel as a "moral shipwreck," an empty story, which "suggests too often the failings of a person [the author] who is capable of going slumming among souls" (CR 251). The *Boston Evening Transcript* (CR 252) deplores its lack of moral lessons, and further accuses Wharton of "spic[ing up] her story in order to stimulate . . . jaded appetites . . ." (CR 252–53). The *Review of Reviews* calls the characters two-dimensional and the plot "sordid" (CR 261). Although Edith Wharton and her friends laughingly referred to *Summer* as the "Hot Ethan," and in spite of the passions in *Summer*'s plot, Edith Wharton is somehow again accused of coldness and icy restraint.

Regardless of the charges of triteness and the usual implications that Edith Wharton knew little of New England, the novel also drew a great deal of praise. The *Springfield* [Massachusetts] *Republican,* located in the vicinity of the novel's setting, remarks that "parts of *Summer* . . . tend to shake [Edith Wharton's] reputation for coldness and lack of sympathy." But it concludes that while *Summer* is "brilliantly conceived," it portrays New England from the point of view of a "'literary,' even a romantic, visitor" (CR 255). The *New York Times Book Review* wrote that this story of sleepy village life is an escape from the Great War (CR 253). John Macy, writing for *Dial*, literally praises it to the skies: "The author understands [what is happening to the characters] and sitting omniscient and Olympian at the right hand side of Fate, contemplates their lives. . . . The combined power of impartial contemplation and sympathy makes the genius of Thomas Hardy and it makes the genius of Mrs. Wharton as it is found in *Ethan Frome* and *Summer*" (CR 256).

Even in this tale of a simple New England village, unlike anything Henry James ever wrote, Macy asks: "Was her knowledge of life at once cosmopolitan and class-provincial, like the outlook of Henry James?" (CR 256) In the *North American Review,* Lawrence Gilman (1917) compares Wharton to George Bernard Shaw: "Mrs. Wharton, wearing the most guileless and disarming expression in the world, has in this novel dared to portray an erotic interlude in which Girlhood is exhibited to the reading public as instinctively bent upon fulfilling what Mr. Shaw so long ago called 'the woman's need of the man to enable her to carry on Nature's most urgent work,'" but unlike Shaw, she "is not projecting a social Utopia: she is denoting a social condition" (CR 258).

Most notably, T. S. Eliot, writing anonymously for *The Egoist* in England (1919) and possibly alluding to Sarah Orne Jewett and Mary Wilkins Freeman, comments that the book deals "the death-blow to a kind of novel which has flourished in New England, the novel in which the wind whistles through the stunted firs and over the granite boulders into the white farmhouses where pale gaunt women sew rag carpets. Mrs. Wharton does the trick by a deliberate and consistent realism, by refraining from the slightest touch of irony. . . . This novel will certainly be considered 'disgusting' in America. . . . But it should add to Mrs. Wharton's reputation as a novelist the distinction of being the satirist's satirist" (CR 263).

Miserable Ever After?

Whether or not the conclusion of the novel is a happy one became important to a number of critics, who felt that the answer supported their opinions about the novel's genre. Is it a good thing that Royall rescues Charity, or does she become a prisoner under his "incestuous" power? According to some more recent writers, the novel's conclusion is happy because it saves Charity from the life of an outcast and prostitute. More often to feminists, however, the ending represents Charity's literal imprisonment in the red house and her psychological imprisonment in a permanent child-like state by a domineering old man, her freedom permanently lost to the demands of a father figure.

Other debates have centered more directly around genre. Is *Summer* a sentimental, tragic, realist, naturalist, regionalist, Gothic, or mythic novel? Is it a feminist *Bildungsroman* (novel of female initiation) or is it merely another cliché, the seduced and abandoned plot of the popular novel meant to teach a moral lesson? Does it treat religion and morality through Calvinism, Puritanism, fate or determinism, or is its most important focus social issues like poverty, unwed pregnancy, marriage, women's opportunities, the social limitations of personal freedom and inner desire, patriarchal rule, or eugenics? Does the novel actually address social issues, or are Edith Wharton's biographical experiences predominant—particularly sex and a need to escape her war charities and her reports from the Front?

Most critics who discuss the novel agree that biographical issues implied by it include the expression of Edith Wharton's personal sexuality, her reaction to the war, or both. They raise psychological issues about both the author and the protagonist, such as conflict, isolation, and father-daughter relationships. Some raise matters of plot structure, noting, for instance, that the plot moves from North Dormer and back, that Charity and Harney meet halfway between North Dormer and the Mountain, that the structure is architectural, that Charity and Royall are parallel characters, or that the story contrasts the artificial to the natural.

Authorial Influences

One notable theme in the critical literature is the comparison of Edith Wharton to other authors. Reviewers have already raised Thomas Hardy, Henry James, and George Bernard Shaw. Feminists have compared the author to George Eliot and the plot to those of Ellen Glasgow, Louisa May Alcott, Mary Wilkins Freeman, and in one case Maria Cummins, Susanna Rowson, Susan Warner, and Augusta Evans. These comparisons at least in part represent the feminist effort to "canonize" neglected female authors. In contrast, more recent critics have discovered features in common with William Wordsworth, Walt Whitman, and Herman Melville.

Generally, people consider *Summer* a good but minor novel among Edith Wharton's works. On the one hand, the relatively limited number of categories examined, and on the other, the wide variety of subjects addressed indicate that critics have detected substance in the novel. That Edith Wharton wrote *Summer*, as she said, "at a high pitch of creative joy" (BG 356), and that she listed it as among her personal favorites seem to support that view (Lewis 490).

The Genre Debate

Critics make cases for the novel belonging to specific genres such as realism. Arthur Hobson Quinn (1936), for instance, assuming that realism is the preferable genre, insists that the tale of Charity Royall is not a great novel, even though it is told with "unrelentless realism," because while great characters emerge from *Ethan Frome*, none emerge from *Summer*. Furthermore, characters "caught in the toils of moral weakness and inherited evil rarely . . . have made the material for a great novel" (565).

Auchincloss and Hamblen stray from the subject of genre to discuss Wharton's familiarity with New England. In 1961 Louis Auchincloss, summarizes another familiar critical outlook: some critics distrust Wharton's excursions into life among the poor as in *Ethan Frome*, "The Bunner Sisters," and *Summer*, seeing her only as the great lady from The Mount, peering at the needy from the back seat of her large "motor." Auchincloss doubts whether the book would have drawn such criticism had it been written under a pseudonym since people assumed that Wharton's keen observation was affected by her social status. *Summer* convinces less than *Ethan Frome* because "one feels her presence," while in *Ethan Frome* the narrator has been eliminated (36). Abigail Ann Hamblen (1965) disagrees with Auchincloss, contending that Wharton was too rich to understand her subject and that life is vicious. She finds an animal-like apathy toward intellectualism, and she concludes that Edith Wharton sees this culture as a laboratory.

Yet to Geoffrey Walton (1970) *Summer* is a remarkable tragicomedy whose main character, Charity, is not a rebel but a social outcast from an "uncompromisingly hostile" society. The outcome is "a terrible inevitability" (79). But Donald Phelps (1973) describes Wharton as exhibiting the supreme criterion of realism. "She has a Chekhov like aptitude for identifying people as, at once, figures in a landscape and human eminences in motion" (228–29).

Thirteen years passed after Phelps's essay with little or no critical comment, years during which feminist criticism became well established. John W. Crowley (1986) writes that Wharton purposely uses clichés to emphasize the patriarchal structure of the plot and that Charity's re-crossing Royall's threshold as his wife is not a positive step toward adulthood, as some critics have thought, but an entrapment in her childish identity. Margaret McDowell (1976/1991), in choosing a determinist genre, agrees with those who find the ending negative: "Charity's love affair in effect costs her human independence. . . . She has, so to speak, spent her life in one summer," for the cosmic forces of the mountain represent a fatalism stronger than the individual (78).

Cynthia Griffin Wolff (1977) finds several conflicts in *Summer:* "a confrontation with [Joseph Conrad's] secret sharer (that uncivilized, unsocialized self within); conflict between generations; the two ages of man; the primitive in North Africa; the war: all of these—themes, journeys and events—must be understood as a part of the preparation for this novel. And in the end, all were atomized in the furnace of [Wharton's] imagination, absorbed into the fictional whole: a story of Charity Royall" (271). In 1979, Wolff focuses on female sexuality as a powerful life-force in the genre of the *Bildungsroman.* Wharton, she says, deliberately sets up a universal situation—lovers in conflict with the generation of their elders—bound together in "furious rage" and isolated from the outside world. The issue contains not only achievement of adulthood by sexual initiation, but also the subject of personal freedom. Freedom denied is a "horror." Like most other readers, Wolff finds the conclusion pessimistic. Elizabeth Ammons (1980) calls *Summer* "Wharton's bluntest criticism of the patriarchal sexual economy. The final union between Charity and Royall is not merely depressing; it is sick" (133). She finds that their marriage is a paternalistic, unhealthy extension of the father-daughter relationship (137). Because her "wedding reminds [Charity] of her mother's funeral . . . [it] is one of the ugliest scenes in all of Wharton" (138).

Shortly thereafter, John W. Crowley (1982) offers what has since become a fairly standard feminist interpretation of *Summer.* Charity is a victim of "paternal assumptions about women" (86), a sex object, bought and paid for, manipulated by Royall, and doomed to incarceration forever in the red house. In the same vein, Linda Morante (1982) examines the imagery of *Summer* to weave a kind of "tapestry of wasteland" to show how images of nature and a culturally impoverished hill town in New England (247) reflect Charity's character, in particular her sense of desolation, deprivation, abandonment, isolation, and failure.

Seduced and Abandoned

Turning to structure without dropping the subject of genre, Nancy Walker (1983) suggests that Wharton shows realism behind the "seduced and abandoned" woman through "images of animals, prisons, seasonal cycles, and 'the Fall'" (107). She describes two patterns of movement, one out of the world of North Dormer and back, the second a movement of Charity closer to lawyer Royall, through three key conversations, the proposals, and exchanges between Charity and Royall. She notes that each of three worlds—The Mountain, North Dormer, and the larger world of Lucius Harney—is represented by a woman and that Charity moves away from the artificial toward the natural, represented by her marriage to Royall. To Walker, Charity is "the strongest moral force in . . . a novel of integrity and insight" (114).

Since the influence of Edith Wharton on Sinclair Lewis is well known, Robert L. Coard (1985) analyzes the genre of Edith Wharton's *Summer* by comparing it point by point to Sinclair Lewis's *Main Street*. The protagonists both have small-town origins, work as librarians, and have a romance with a much more sophisticated man. Both novels depend on seasons ending in autumn, both describe auto rides, long walks detailing contents of shop windows, the presence of knights and lodges, and both use descriptions of nature to "underscore the moods and fates of the chief characters" (518). Looking at the popular sentimental genre, Barbara White (1984) compares the plot to those of Maria Cummins's *The Lamplighter*, Susanna Rowson's *Charlotte Temple*, Augusta Evans's *St. Elmo*, Louisa May Alcott's *Little Women*, and Susan Warner's *Wide, Wide World*. She finds that Charity does not model the perfection of the sentimental heroine because the "texture" of the plot and the heroine's character dramatically oppose nineteenth-century examples (48). First, Charity's feelings are described in extremes of intensity, and second, although Charity is a librarian, she does not read, unlike other nineteenth-century heroines. Edith Wharton made use of the conventions of "women's fiction" in *Summer* by combining two perspectives and two standard plots, and by emphasizing feeling. As in the conventional "seduced and abandoned" plot, in the end Charity accepts wifely submission as her fate.

Continuing in the feminist "genre," Sandra Gilbert (1985) asks "What paradigms of female sexuality have strong female precursors passed on to other women writers?" (355) Where is the model for "psychosexual development"? To Gilbert, George Eliot fulfills the role of "literary mother," and like *Silas Marner*, *Summer* is a *Bildungsroman*, a "revisionary daughter-text," but also a novel of "renunciation and resignation" enacted under the [library's] Olympian bust of Minerva. The father-daughter incest paradigm "lies at the heart of female psychosexual development in patriarchal society" (377).

Among those who place *Summer* in or near the Gothic genre, Judith Fryer (1986), basing her argument on the story as an inversion of the Demeter-Persephone myth, describes the novel as "structured as a bit of dreamlike evanescence between the harsher reality of two night-mares," the Mountain and Royall's house (195). Charity's life with lawyer Royall is a type of hell in the underworld of houses that Wharton describes in *A Backward Glance* (referring to *Ethan Frome*) as "grim, morally and physically, places of insanity, incest and slow mental and moral starvation" (BG 294). Charity is excluded from the world of Lucius Harney and from the world of the Mountain, but the town represents chaos (itself a metaphor for the chaos of war) and trapped with Mr. Royall, Charity lives on silently (198–99).

Instead of using psychological paradigms, Carol Wershoven (1986) reads *Summer* as the story of two protagonists with parallel qualities who must learn to confront reality to become adults (5). Both Charity and Royall are outsiders with fantasies of escape. Charity dreams of deliverance through romantic love as does Royall, and his attempt to seduce Charity parodies Lucius Harney's. She adds a hopeful note to the conclusion: If Charity and Royall learn when to adapt and when to rebel, then they can create a marriage that is a community of adults.

Catherine E. Saunders (1986) compares *Summer* to Ellen Glasgow's *Barren Ground,* and to some extent to Hawthorne's *Scarlet Letter*—all "seduced and abandoned" plots. She argues that the rules of society that limit expression of individual desires are necessary to build civilization. *Summer's* structure contrasts the Mountain's outlaw community to "the harsh code of the village" (54), and Charity and Harney's affair takes place halfway between the town and the Mountain. But rebellion against society is not the answer, though Charity wants a community that recognizes the holiness of her experience, "not one that condemns nothing because it also holds nothing sacred" (55).

Like Wolff, Marilyn French (1987) uses strong feminist language. She believes that the major "horror" of the story is in its treatment of female sexuality by way of the abortionist, prostitution, and forced marriage, for "the female body as commodity" is "ugly." But she also feels that the cyclical, predictable pattern of seasons, mentioned by biographer Cynthia Griffin Wolff (1987), attempts to draw a parallel between Charity's drama and Edith Wharton's personal life. "Disguised, deflected, refracted through the prism of art," Wharton's current problems became the important issues of *Ethan Frome* and *Summer* (99–100). Wolff writes that Wharton was still trying to work out a last life issue: childish dependency as a main bond between a couple. She finds *Summer* an "inversion of *Ethan Frome*" and "a tale not of passivity and dependency, but of passion and self-assertion" (109). Ultimately, Wolff's argument arrives at the conclusion that one major insight of this novel is that love must have a social component to last, and even when dependency and desire are present, no marriage can be perfect (113).

Using a different approach, Peter Hays (1989) focuses on words, particularly "penetration," "knowing," and metaphors of the journey, the harvest, and other botanical images, to foreshadow, link, and adumbrate themes throughout *Summer*. These themes emphasize the *Bildungsroman* genre, the Sleeping Beauty myth, the sexual education of the initiate, and wisdom, thereby demonstrating Wharton's masterly verbal architecture. In an interesting sidelight, Christine Rose (1990) finds *Summer* rich in architectural imagery and detail and that in architecture a "summer" is a "large horizontal supporting beam or girder" (16).

To Janet Goodwyn (1990), *Summer* is about the "tragedy of isolation" from civilization (80) or "a form of sentimental decentralisation" (79). Because the industrial capacity of the nation is growing, towns like North Dormer are shrinking—in a small way a metaphor for the war damage Wharton watched in France—and *Summer* considers the problem of what constitutes civilization. As the relation of humans to the landscape deteriorates, so do the old houses and the library of North Dormer (77).

Kathleen Pfeiffer (1991) argues that the "critics' discomfort" with *Summer* stems from the novel's departure from the novel of manners. The "doubleness" of the novel, its genre and revelation of Wharton's attitudes toward America also create conflict. Charity believes in the American myth but is "denied the tools" to achieve success. The novel "reverberates with strong feminist anger" (152). As a "radically subversive text" (142) it "registers a revision of authorial attitude" (142). Charity begins the novel as independent, and because of her connection to the earth, she becomes a "new American heroine." This ends when Charity "fails" by abdicating her independence to marry lawyer Royall. Her loss of virginity "parallels the rape of the land" (150) and her emotional independence parallels the Fourth of July which, Pfeiffer feels, further reveals Wharton's revised perception of America. One conflict among critics is whether Charity is that "failed heroine" (144).

Returning to the theme that everything Wharton wrote contains a subtext about the woman as writer, Candace Waid (1991) explores Wharton's effort to discover the position of a woman writer. Using a pun on the word "compose," she notes how Charity tries to "compose" or "write" her mother's body (82). Despite Wharton's efforts to distance herself from Sarah Orne Jewett and Mary Wilkins Freeman in her introduction to *Ethan Frome*, Waid details the similarity between

Summer and the themes from *The Winning Lady and Others* by Freeman. One of the themes in common regards the young girl who tells her protector about a threatening father (100).

Lev Raphael (1991) notes a theme that involves Charity's shyness and shame at having been born among the outlaws of the Mountain. Charity likes Harney because he never deliberately stimulates her embarrassment and is himself a shy person, who in fact takes comfort in her shame. Raphael attempts to show how, through Charity's "movingly intimated" (300) sexuality, Wharton "conceptualized" her own sexuality through shame. In another type of psychological approach, Gloria Erlich (1992) characterizes the plot as "seeking Mother, marrying Daddy" (126), stressing the implied incestuous relationships. Charity lives in a morally symbolic landscape poised between the mountain and the town (lawlessness/mother vs. law/lawyer/father) but she is unable to find a flexible place between them.

Jean Frantz Blackall (1992) discusses how Wharton plays ingeniously with framing (124), using the narrative verbalization of other "mind stuff" (117) that Charity can only perceive in terms of pictures and generalized spatial imagery, in sum: "blurred images" (120). In *Summer*, narrative frame replaces the frames of mirrors and windows which gradually focus on Charity or on some central moment or character (121). Adding to Blackall's observations by pinpointing an additional set of symbols and imagery, Mollie Burleson (1993) argues for a series of inversions or "subversions" such as this: "When Mr. Royall . . . originally went up the Mountain, he brought [Charity] down, yet by bringing her down, he has brought her up, raised her from a child; raised her up to her present status. He has brought her down and in so doing brought her up so that for her, to come down from the Mountain was to come up in the world" (19). Burleson also emphasizes that at the conclusion, the mirror imagery in the hotel room ironically reflects the white purity of the marriage bed. She concludes, however, that the summer of Charity's year has been the winter of her soul.

Returning to the genre of naturalism, last discussed in regard to *Summer* by Loggins in 1931, Donna Campbell (1994) observes similarities to local color authors. Charity is a local color heroine thrust unceremoniously into a naturalist world. Wharton uses this satiric method to repudiate the local colorists with whom she did not wish to be associated. To accomplish that, "Wharton's strategy. . . . was to engage, transform, and finally dismiss both genres" (180).

Placing *Summer* in the Gothic genre rather than the naturalist, Kathy Fedorko (1995) finds Charity in the process of "coming-to-awareness" crucial to Wharton's Gothic. To confront "her relation to the maternal body . . . with all its connotations of power" and vulnerability means tapping the "secret center" of that "knowledge which is power" (70–71). Wharton's emphasis on the Mountain as Charity's home and the place where she finds her dead mother suggests that she was aware of the archetypal potency of the Mountain as a symbol of femaleness (78). Lawyer Royall becomes the "Gothic tyrant" whose rescue of Charity is merely another act of domination, and Charity's assertiveness dies as she becomes a "trapped Gothic heroine" (80–82). Like Fedorko, Jenni Dyman (1996), also associating *Summer* with the Gothic, briefly notes that biographically *Summer* reflects the deprivation of sexual expression that Edith Wharton must have felt during her war work in Paris. With the routine of hard work and without an opportunity for actual sexual expression, "Wharton lived with circumstances that predictably foster sexual fantasy" (94).

The Law of the Father

In yet another authorial parallel, Carol Singley (1995) discovers that in *Summer*, Wharton incorporated elements of Whitman's style and philosophy (149) as well as his sexual freedom. She finds *Summer*'s freedom checked by a sense of inevitability that impedes choice, determinism contending with transcendence (150). *Summer* attempts to shake off Calvinist influences and reach an Emersonian ideal — to find a religious or philosophical system that could transcend Christianity (161). Singley also notes that the critical readings of *Summer* have not reconciled disparate elements of the novel (150). Barbara Commins (1997) finds contradictory religious imagery indicating that in *Summer* Edith Wharton intentionally transgresses the religious ideas with which she was raised to lead the reader in a circle, "*forced* like Charity in the end, to return to the beginning, home" (21).

In an observation similar to Singley's about inevitability (118), Rhonda Skillern argues that Wharton "incorporated a language of resistance into *Summer*" (119). She offers a "multilayered analysis, one that draws from literary theory, gender studies, semiotics, and anthropology" to unearth "resisting voices and gestures" in the novel (119). She concludes that Charity is caught up in an "ascendancy of passivity," emerging with a "legal identity" based on rejecting the mother (133). Charity not only represents her submission to the "Law of the Father," but also her subversion of it. The couple has not yet consummated the marriage, and the now legitimate child "exposes the fictionality of that legitimacy and that unity" (134). In addition, Charity resists becoming an "object for display" by using her clothes money to redeem the brooch given to her by Harney, a final act of rebellion against Royall's law.

Focusing on implications of male dynamics rather than female, William E. Hummel (1996) uses a Marxist-deconstructionist method to address subversion. Using more of the dense language of "theory," he posits that Edith Wharton exposes lawyer Royall's "male weakness" in order to employ incest "as a trope not only to explore sexuality" in many ways, but also to "flaunt and subvert a variety of conventions. . ." (216–17). These include damaging Victorian mores, and Darwinian and Freudian "transcultural taboos." He posits that lawyer Royall first enlists, then dismisses, Lucius Harney, by using jealous male messages and authority to subvert Harney's claim on Charity, who represents his "symbolic capital." Royall also uses symbolic violence to set up a perpetual relationship with Charity. Hummel employs the theories of Pierre Bourdieu to suggest a "doxic" social structure that discloses the "ideological tenants, social aspirations, and diaphanous origins of Wharton's male characters" (232).

Like Carol Singley, Abby Werlock (1997) finds that Whitman's *Leaves of Grass* provides a key to reading *Summer* (246). She points out many sexual images, finding in them brilliant prose and a humorous echo of Whitman's blatant sexuality. In writing *Summer*, she believes, Edith Wharton "compounded, complicated, and transcended" (261) the line between poetry and prose.

Dale Bauer (1997), however, regards Charity as a bridge between "eugenic" and "dysgenic" commentators and a hybrid of both "communities" (27). She asks "whether Charity Royall inherits her birth mother's penchant for the lawless . . . 'herd'" or whether she acquires characteristics from her adoptive mother, Mrs. Royall, whom Charity describes as "sad and timid and weak" (29). Bauer uses the context of eugenics to disagree with Ammons's finding that the ending is "sick" (34). She believes that Edith Wharton "questions the assumptions about 'normal' American family life" (36). Charity, having inherited her mother's sexuality, "gipsy-looking" appearance (39) and poverty makes her "dysgenic" (genetically undesirable) (44). Her marriage to Royall is a demand that society "acknowledge and accommodate the hybrid and the anomalous" (46).

Authorial Influences

Most recently, Linda Cahir (1999) finds a theme in common with Melville's *Pierre* and "Bartleby the Scrivener" in that "what matters is how we navigate our way through life's jagged, unpredictable course" (140). But in Pfeiffer's phrase, "the critics' discomfort" with *Summer* continues to be evident in the wide variety of disparate readings.

Besides Whitman and Melville, critics have considered authorial influences of Nathaniel Hawthorne, Henry James, and Sinclair Lewis; popular female writers, Maria Cummins, Susanna Rowson, Augusta Evans, Louisa May Alcott, Susan Warner, Ellen Glasgow, Charlotte Perkins Gilman; British authors George Eliot and William Wordsworth; Europeans Gottfried Keller, Theodor Fontane, and Anton Chekhov.

No consensus has yet been reached about *Summer*'s genre. Critics have argued that it is realist, naturalist, tragicomic, feminist, determinist, Gothic, psychological, a *Bildungsroman,* a sentimental "seduced-and-abandoned" morality tale, and also subversive of any of these. Insofar as genre is important, and insofar as an author can be believed, Edith Wharton's description of her sources for *Summer* in *A Backward Glance* suggests realism. But some authors cannot always be believed and consequently the question remains open.

While early critics tried to link Wharton to James, recent critics have dropped the attempt, and in the context of *Summer* discuss Wharton's emotional frigidity. The alternate attitude is that Edith Wharton's passionate sexual biography is reflected in the novel. Some essays find Wharton writing the novel as an escape from the First World War. Others discuss imagery and structure, and some discover in *Summer* Wharton's religious attitudes and even some global attitudes toward all of America, "sea to shining sea."

And just as Edith Wharton moved from the New England of *Ethan Frome* to the sophisticated life of *The Custom of the Country,* she next moves from the New England of *Summer* back to the sophisticated life of *The Age of Innocence.*

Works Consulted

Auchincloss, Louis. *Pioneers & Caretakers: A Study of 9 American Novelists.* Minneapolis, MN: U of Minnesota P, 1961. 36.

Bauer, Dale M. *Edith Wharton's Brave New Politics.* Madison, WI: U of Wisconsin P, 1997. 28–51.

Blackall, Jean Frantz. "Charity at the Window: Narrative Technique in Edith Wharton's *Summer.*" *Edith Wharton: New Critical Essays.* Eds. Alfred Bendixen and Annette Zilversmit. New York: Garland, 1992. 115–26.

Burleson, Mollie L. "Edith Wharton's *Summer:* Through the Glass Darkly." *Studies in Weird Fiction* 13 (Summer 1993): 19–21.

Cahir, Linda Costanzo. *Solitude and Society in the Works of Herman Melville and Edith Wharton.* Westport, CT: Greenwood P, 1999. 134–41.

Campbell, Donna M. "Edith Wharton and the 'Authoresses': The Critique of Local Color in Wharton's Early Fiction." *Studies in American Fiction* 22.2 Autumn (1994): 169–83.

Coard, Robert L. "Edith Wharton's Influence on Sinclair Lewis." *Modern Fiction Studies* 31.3 (Autumn 1985): 511–27.

Commins, Barbara. "'Pecking at the Host': Transgressive Wharton." *Edith Wharton Review* 14.1 (Spring 1997): 18–21.

Crowley, John W. "The Unmastered Streak: Feminist Themes in Wharton's *Summer.*" *American Literary Realism 1870–1910* 15 (Spring 1982): 86–96.

Dyman, Jenni. *Lurking Feminism: The Ghost Stories of Edith Wharton.* New York: Peter Lang, 1996. 94.

Edgett, Edwin Francis. "Edith Wharton's Tale of Thwarted Love." *Boston Evening Transcript* (25 July 1917): II.6.

Elbert, Monika M. "The Politics of Maternality in *Summer.*" *Edith Wharton Review* 7.2 (Winter 1990): 4–9, 24.

Eliot, T. S. "Summer." Rev. of *Summer* by Edith Wharton. *The Egoist.* [England] (January 1919): 10.

Erlich, Gloria. *The Sexual Education of Edith Wharton.* Berkeley, CA: U of California P 1992.

Evans, Tamara. "Edith Wharton and Poetic Realism: An Impasse." *The German Quarterly* 65 (Summer-Fall 1992): 361–68.

Fedorko, Kathy. *Gender and the Gothic in the Fiction of Edith Wharton.* Tuscaloosa, AL: U of Alabama P, 1995.

French, Marilyn. Introduction. *Summer.* New York: Collier Books, 1987.

Fryer, Judith. *Felicitous Space: The Imaginative Structures of Edith Wharton and Willa Cather.* Chapel Hill, NC: U of North Carolina P, 1986. 193–99.

Gilbert, Sandra M. "Life's Empty Pack: Notes Toward a Literary Daughteronomy." *Critical Inquiry* 11.3 (March 1985): 355–84.

Gilman, Lawrence, "The Book of the Month: Mrs. Wharton Reverts to Shaw." Rev. of *Summer* by Edith Wharton. *North American Review* 206 (August 1917): 304–7.

Gimbel, Wendy. *Edith Wharton: Orphancy and Survival.* Landmark Dissertations in Women's Studies Series. Ed. Annette Baxter. New York: Praeger, 1984. 93–125.

Goodwyn, Janet. *Edith Wharton: Traveller in the Land of Letters.* New York: St. Martin's P, 1990.

H[ackett], F[rancis]. "Loading the Dice." Rev. of *Summer* by Edith Wharton. *New Republic* 11 (14 July 1917): 311–12.

Hamblen, Abigail Ann. "Edith Wharton's New England." *New England Quarterly* 38 (June 1965): 239–44.

Hays, Peter L. "Signs in *Summer*: Words and Metaphors." *Papers on Language and Literature* 25.1 (Winter 1989): 114–19.

Hummel, William E. "My 'Dull-Witted Enemy': Symbolic Violence and Abject Maleness in Edith Wharton's *Summer*." *Studies in American Fiction* 24.2 (Autumn 1996): 215–36.

Loggins, Vernon. "Edith Wharton." *I Hear America*. New York: Crowell, 1937.

Macy, John. "Edith Wharton." Rev. of *Summer* by Edith Wharton. *Dial* 63 (30 August 1917): 161–62.

McDowell, Margaret B. *Edith Wharton*. 1976. Boston: G. K. Hall, Revised 1991.

Millgate, Michael. "The Novelist and the Businessman: Henry James, Edith Wharton, and Frank Norris." *American Social Fiction from James to Norris*. New York: Barnes and Noble, 1964.

Morante, Linda. "The Desolation of Charity Royall: Imagery in Edith Wharton's *Summer*." *Colby Library Quarterly* 18.4 (December 1982): 241–48.

"Mrs. Wharton's Story of New England: *Summer* a Pleasing Romance of Village Life." Rev. of *Summer* by Edith Wharton. *New York Times Book Review* (8 July 1917): 253.

"Mrs. Wharton's *Summer*." Rev. of *Summer* by Edith Wharton. *Springfield* [Massachusetts] *Republican* (5 August 1917): Magazine section, 15.

Nevius, Blake. *Edith Wharton: A Study of Her Fiction*. 1953. Berkeley, CA: U of California P, 1961.

"Novels Whose Scenes Are Laid in New England." Rev. of *Summer* by Edith Wharton. *Review of Reviews* 56 (September 1917): 333.

Papke, Mary E. *Verging on the Abyss: The Social Fiction of Kate Chopin and Edith Wharton*. New York: Greenwood P, 1990. 131–34.

Phelps, Donald. "Edith Wharton and the Invisible." *Prose* 7 (Fall 1973): 227–45.

Pfeiffer, Kathleen. "*Summer* and its Critics' Discomfort." *Women's Studies* 20 (1991): 141–52.

Price, Alan. *The End of the Age of Innocence: Edith Wharton and the First World War*. New York: St. Martin's P, 1996.

Quinn, Arthur Hobson. *American Fiction: An Historical and Critical Survey*. 1936. New York: Appleton-Century, 1936. 550–81.

Raphael, Lev. *Edith Wharton's Prisoners of Shame: A New Perspective on Her Neglected Fiction*. New York: St. Martin's P, 1991. 289–300.

Rose, Christine. "*Summer*: The Double Sense of Wharton's Title." *American Notes and Queries* 3.1 (January 1990): 16–19.

Saunders, Catherine E. "Two Kinds of Revolt: *Summer, Barren Ground*, and their Literary Formats." *Writing the Margins: Edith Wharton, Ellen Glasgow, and the Literary Tradition of the Ruined Woman*. Cambridge, MA: Harvard UP, 1986. 51–64.

Singley, Carol J. *Edith Wharton: Matters of Mind and Spirit*. New York: Cambridge UP, 1995.

Skillern, Rhonda. "Becoming a 'Good Girl': Law, Language, and Ritual in Edith Wharton's *Summer*." *The Cambridge Companion to Edith Wharton*. Ed. Millicent Bell. New York: Cambridge UP, 1995. 117–36.

Steiner, Wendy. "The Causes of Effect: Edith Wharton and the Economics of Ekphrasis." *Poetics Today* 10.2 (Summer 1989): 279–97.

Waid, Candace. *Edith Wharton's Letters from the Underworld: Fictions of Women and Writing*. Chapel Hill, NC: U of North Carolina P, 1991.

Walker, Nancy. "'Seduced and Abandoned': Convention and Reality in Edith Wharton's *Summer*." *Studies in American Fiction* 11.1 (Spring 1983): 107–14.

Walton, Geoffrey. *Edith Wharton: A Critical Interpretation*. 1970. Rutherford: Fairleigh Dickinson UP, 1982. 89–97.

Werlock, Abby H. P. "Whitman, Wharton, and the Sexuality in *Summer*." *Speaking the Other Self: American Women Writers*. Ed. Jeanne Campbell Reesman. Athens, GA: U of Georgia P, 1997. 246–62.

Wershoven, Carol. "The Divided Conflict of Edith Wharton's *Summer*." *Colby Library Quarterly* 21.1 (March 1985): 5–10.

Wharton, Edith. *A Backward Glance*. New York: Appleton-Century, 1934. Rpt. New York: Scribners, 1985.

White, Barbara A. "Edith Wharton's *Summer* and 'Woman's Fiction.'" *Essays in Literature* 11.2 (Fall 1984): 223–35.

———. *Growing Up Female: Adolescent Girlhood in American Fiction*. Westport, CT: Greenwood P, 1985. 47–64.

Wolff, Cynthia Griffin. "Cold Ethan and 'Hot Ethan.'" *College Literature* 14.3 (Fall, 1987) Rpt. in *Edith Wharton: New Critical Essays*. Eds. Alfred Bendixen and Annette Zilversmit. New York: Garland, 1992. 97–114.

6: *The Age of Innocence*—A Buried Life

*T*HE *AGE OF INNOCENCE* has drawn a smorgasbord of critical comment on a number of topics, but considering its apparent importance, relatively few essays have been written about it compared to *The House of Mirth*. Certain patterns, seen in reviews of previous novels, emerge in the reviews of 1920. Critics generally admire Edith Wharton's craftsmanship and structure, including her subtle irony and descriptions of interiors. Henry James is frequently evoked, but comparisons to Jane Austen, also known for irony and restraint, are now added to those of William Makepeace Thackeray, whose name first arose relative to *The Custom of the Country*. In fact, critics make ongoing references to authors who seem to have influenced the novel. They still consider Wharton's masterful restraint "narrow," cold, and passionless, the most famous accusation coming from Katherine Mansfield: "Does Mrs. Wharton expect us to grow warm in a gallery where the temperature is so sparkingly [*sic*] cool? We are looking at portraits—are we not?" (292)

Two topics are new, however. The first compares the plot to drama (and sometimes portraits), which is especially relevant to the 1928 stage adaptation starring Katherine Cornell as Ellen Olenska because not only were several of Wharton's novels dramatized, but some critics have speculated that she wrote them with that possibility in mind. The second topic was raised by a prescient reviewer for the *Times Literary Supplement* [England] (1920) regarding the importance of the First World War as a dividing line for literature: "Since 1914 there has been no present day, in the old sense. Now we must know from the start whether we are dealing with the world before or during or since the war; any and every action must be precisely timed . . ." (CR 289).

The New York Times Book Review evokes Henry James a number of times: "Like her idol and master, Henry James, she is forever comparing America with Europe, to the latter's advantage" (CR 284); "The style of *The Age of Innocence* is filled with the 'silver correspondence' spoken of by Henry James" (CR 285); "Here is where Mrs. Wharton resembles Joseph Conrad and Henry James, for the love scenes in this book are fully worthy of those two men of genius" (CR 286). What matters is not whether the comparisons are positive or negative, but that James and Wharton's names linger together in readers' memories.

But the *Times* reviewer does recognize the novel as a "consummate work of art" (CR 285).

Modern critics have raised a potpourri of topics, most notably those focusing on the frustration and futility of Archer Newland's empty life caused by the weight of social inhibitions. Some have discussed unwritten laws and the prevalence of silence rather than communication. Others raise issues of Puritanism and morality, as well as the question of the novel as a *roman à clef*. When feminism became strong, questions of whether old New York was a matriarchy or patriarchy, the degree of May's nobility and of her empowerment, whether Ellen is the stereotypical temptress, and the Woman Question also became topics of critical discussion.

This historical novel of the 1870s opens at the opera during a performance of *Faust*. Newland Archer trains his opera glasses on his soon-to-be fiancée, May Welland, occupying a box with her mother, and notes with satisfaction that she holds the lilies he had sent her. He sees that they are joined by May's cousin, Ellen Olenska, the family "black sheep," whose gypsy-like aunt had raised her primarily in Europe, and dressed her in the "wrong" fashions, and even now, opera glasses everywhere deem her elegant blue empire dress too décolleté. She has escaped her abusive husband, a Polish Count, and has returned to New York to pursue a divorce. Newland finds her fascinating; the rest of old New York finds the Welland family's social protection of such an "immoral" woman most shocking.

Knowing that all opera glasses are trained in their direction, Newland joins the group in their box, and whispers to May that they must announce their engagement earlier than planned in order to cement the Archer family's social support for her cousin. The action becomes the first in a series of impulsive acts by which Newland traps himself in a predictable life. After he is asked by his family to talk Ellen out of the disgraceful divorce and succeeds, he falls in love with her, and his love for Ellen teaches him how limited his thinking has been. Then, carried on the wave of events he unthinkingly sets in motion, he marries May. He tries to establish an affair with Ellen, but May and the combined families of old New York frustrate them continually. Eventually, May gives a large dinner in honor of Ellen, a dinner everyone knows is meant to end her "affair" with Newland and expel her from New York. Newland decides to follow Ellen, but May stops him by announcing her pregnancy. A generation later, Newland is widowed with grown children. Newland's son, who knows that Ellen lives in Paris and has never remarried, insists that Newland accompany him to Europe. When the time comes to visit Ellen, Newland cannot make himself do it. He says she is more real to him in his memory.

When the Pulitzer Prize Committee rejected Sinclair Lewis's *Main Street* for political reasons and chose *The Age of Innocence*, positive reviews and early criticism began to establish Edith Wharton as the American "first lady of letters" for at least a short time. Two exceptions to the general praise include Vernon Parrington's notoriously effective scorn in "Our Literary Aristocrat," quoted in chapter 1, and the well-known author Katherine Mansfield's charge of cold, passionless prose (*Athenæum* [England]). Mansfield's review (1920) recognizes Wharton's craftsmanship, but excoriates the passivity of her characters. Completely forgotten is Undine Spragg's relentless energy.

Mansfield is pleased that the author delights in New York in the 1870s and in an irony and romance so skillfully balanced "that it seems more like play than work" (291). But she is also bothered by the stately, unruffled quality of the tone. She asks her often-quoted question, so odd after *Summer*: Is it vulgar "to entreat a little wildness, a dark place or two in the soul?" In contrast, Joseph Warren Beach (1932), writing primarily about technique, returns to the theme of morals and Jamesianism: "The irony, the satire breaks down, since the author has an air of subscribing, herself, to the moral code in question" (295). He continues, "in true James manner, the two persons are like players in some dark game" (298). He adds probably the first note about structure by mentioning that each chapter, almost without exception, contains one discriminated occasion, "the French ideal of a scene of drama," the "unity and compactness" of which is that "Newland Archer appears in every scene" (296).

Harry Hartwick (1934) prefers to ignore questions of passivity and darkness of soul, and focus on materialism, describing the novel as picturing "Manhattan's Mayfair of the Victorian period, with its mingling of decayed grandeur and upstart crows decked in peacock feathers, its prudery, its tribal codes, its passion for 'barricading' itself against 'the unpleasant,' and its lack of pity for the woman who 'stooped to folly'" (376).

A generation later, Louis O. Coxe (1955) begins the long lapsed critical conversation anew by denying that *The House of Mirth* is a better novel than *The Age of Innocence*. He points to Wharton's scenes of careful "juxtapositions" (156) and the "tissue of objects, places, attitudes, and desires" that reveal a "lost life of feeling" (157). For all his sacrifices, most critics would say that Newland Archer got nothing in return. But he has lived a "buried life," (158) something his son will never understand in spite of his new social freedoms. Coxe senses

Wharton saying that America needs to evolve a society that can say what it feels and begin to develop a sense of the past (159). America wastes its past, the greatest of its resources (161).

An expert analysis of "style" in the novel is provided by Viola Hopkins (1958) who claims that the "clue to Mrs. Wharton's aesthetic and cultural ideals," is order, but "order is arrived at dialectically through a dramatized conflict" between the individual and society (346). She suggests that Newland's point of view is unifying. Additionally, she notes the importance of the literary allusions, images such as pictures of "life-in-death" (355), "anthropological" images (354), and the "precipice, abyss, and vortex" (357). Edwin Moseley (1959) points out Faustian imagery, but calls it "weak," insisting on Wharton's "typically Jamesian manner" (157).

The 1960s for the most part feature New Critical readings of the novel. Blake Nevius (1961), using *A Backward Glance* as a preface to his essay, reads *The Age of Innocence* as a "recoil from the postwar world," noting its complaints against "failures of education and opportunity" (177). The novel records a minor revolution from simplicity to vulgarity, while excluding notice of the outside world and dreading innovation. The failures of the leisure class are greater than their positive values because they waste social resources. In contradiction, Wharton turns her irony against a system that neglected the leisure class, then "swallowed it whole" (181). Nevius also compares Wharton to Balzac in her attention to the minutiae of costume and setting, and to James's "The Beast in the Jungle" in that Newland Archer is, like John Marcher, the man "to whom nothing was ever to happen" (187). "Wildness may be lacking," but sensibility is not. Auchincloss, expanding on the concept somewhat (1962), speaks of a world that had "disappeared as completely as Atlantis or the lowest layer of Schliemann's Troy." He notes the "richness of color and detail" and the "dominion of the female," later calling it a matriarchal world. He also repeats Edmund Wilson's assertion that "Mrs. Wharton was not only the pioneer but the poet of interior decoration" (vi, vii).

Trapped and Doomed

In O'Connor, Louis Auchincloss (1965) states that Newland Archer's coming to awareness is that of a "creature trapped and doomed" (43), while for Ellen, "rules and regulations have . . . validity" (48–49). Newland had come to believe that marriage had the "dignity of a duty," without which "it became a mere battle of ugly appetites" (43). In his 1965 "Reader," Auchincloss echoes the general idea that the

"Novel [is] perfect in form . . . a glowing series of pictures of the times" (xiv), but also states that it was like Henry James's *The Ambassadors* on the opposite side of the Atlantic" (xiii).

James Tuttleton (1965) raises politics on whichever side of the Atlantic, agreeing with Irving Howe (1962) that Wharton is not a political reformer, and argues that Archer's friendship with Theodore Roosevelt is meant to express the same anomaly in Archer's nature as his sense of duty vs. his passion for Ellen. He recalls Wharton's affection for Roosevelt (one of her cousins), who died in 1919, the year she completed the novel.

Next, R. W. B. Lewis (1968, xii-xiii) points to Wharton's mastery of place to dramatize Newland Archer's futile attempt to find a ground where he and Ellen might move away from public into private space to communicate their love—to locate that "country," that "world" where the social and moral "categories" they wish to violate do not exist. Lillie B. Lamar notes in 1966 "errors on the family tree of the Mingott clan" (385). In 1968 she notes another error. Instead of the wedding prayers, Wharton used the funeral service from *The Book of Common Prayer* at the Archer wedding. But Killoran later (1996) suggests that the "error" was a deliberate allusion to Newland's buried life.

A buried life can well contain a Puritanical element. Puritanism is discussed by British critic Geoffrey Walton (1970), who also touches on the subjects of morality. To him it hints of Henry James's influence: Ellen Olenska is not a merely a copy of *The European's* Baroness Munster, though the novel relates to James's. Walton remarks how, with great detail of setting, Wharton presents her frequent theme of the individual against society, agreeing with Yvor Winters that it demonstrates an "ethical tradition more ancient than Calvinist Puritanism, though modified by it" (141). He also quotes Winters' defense of the depiction of a society whose outward forms were once based on a moral point of view: "Mrs. Wharton satirizes [morals]; but in the main they represent the concrete aspect of the abstract principles of behavior" (141). Both agree that the Puritanical aspect of the tradition of New York emerges more strongly in *The Age of Innocence* than in *The Custom of the Country* (137). Walton continues: it is hard to decide whether this represents a "vein of Puritan tradition" in the novel or a "temperamental compulsion" on the part of the author (146).

Also in 1970 John J. Murphy builds on Viola Hopkins's work in addressing "the novel as a structural achievement" reflective of the "rigidity and conventionality" of the time (1). He identifies and analyzes six units, showing how the structural balance of the novel underlines the theme of order. The conclusion makes a distinction between "form," which is superficial, and "order" which is sociological in its requirement for "consistency of action" (4). The structure of the novel reflects Newland Archer's building of his own trap.

Literary Influences

Among those who recognize "influences," Charles Clay Doyle (1971) identifies biblical imagery patterns, pointing out how floral and garden imagery paradoxically defines America as an Eden, but like Eden ("heaven," as Ellen Olenska calls old New York), it contains forbidden fruit and requires obedience from those who dwell there. He suggests that the "sterile and moribund" gardens are associated with May, while Ellen is associated "with images of unrestraint," as when she "scatters [flowers] about loosely, here and there" (22). He goes on to develop these images with Faustian and Miltonian references.

Writing in the larger context of a genre study of the American novel of manners, James Tuttleton (1972), the first important Wharton critic, hinting at the influence of Blake, contrasts May's "innocence" with Newland's "experience," and defends it as a novel that should be read as a "portrait of the age." Though this imperfectly developed culture was "marked by sexual hypocrisy, intellectual narrowness, civic irresponsibility, and class snobbery," it also "preserved dignity," sensitivity to feelings, an appreciation for beauty and a powerful feeling for the grandeur of the English language; as well as "an unshakable belief in the civilizing power of education"; a high social style; and to "personal rectitude in public life . . ." (129). The final chapter modifies the concept that Wharton's point was that romantic love is inhibited when social values are threatened. New York values are more deeply reflected in Ellen's comment "that under the dullness there are things so fine and sensitive and delicate that even those I most cared for in my other life look cheap in comparison" (132). Tuttleton concludes that the "memorial manner" and "old established traditions" still "enrich, deepen, and intensify the value of the individual's life" (133).

At the start of the new decade, Adeline Tintner (1980) once more raises the subject of Jamesian influence, giving specific examples of "echoes" of names, scenes, and other resemblances from a number of James's novels. But she suggests that rather than imitation, the purpose of these echoes was Wharton's tribute to her deceased friend, "one way of never letting him go again" (346).

World Views

The novel's themes also attract Irving Jacobson (1973). Beginning with psychologist Erik H. Erikson's concept that a society's extreme contrasts lead to a kind of "cultural schizophrenia," he draws on diverse supporting examples in American literature. Jacobson argues that the "hieroglyphic world" of old New York, "where the real thing was never said or done or even thought, but only represented by a set of arbitrary signs" (80), includes "cultural semantics," open to misperception. In the modern world of the last chapter, easy speech replaces silent innocence, and telephone communication signals the end of an inarticulate "genteel era." The negative consequences of the innocence theme— "boredom, loneliness, ignorance, evasion, and hypocrisy" (76)— outweigh the safety value of innocence because it leads to dishonesty, both verbal and nonverbal, since no one wants to hear anything "unpleasant." Newland cannot visit Ellen because he has no means of communicating in the newly developed open society she has always represented, except to say that he is "old-fashioned."

In the same way that Newland fails to communicate or interpret Ellen's "foreign" décor, he fails to interpret Ellen herself because his observations are filtered through a screen of custom, according to Gary Lindberg (1975). Archer must either disregard Ellen's system of understanding the world or disregard the New York system. Through the strain of Newland's conflict, Wharton indicts the complete network of New York manners, ironically measuring them against the potential of that very system, a complex social order that can create meaning in human life. Contrary to this social organization, the reader can discern individual divergence and growth.

Unlike those who find the novel cold, biographer R. W. B. Lewis (1975) assesses *The Age of Innocence* as "a minor masterpiece, one of Edith Wharton's three or four most elegant novels" (429), "a warmly accurate portrait of a vanished physical and social scene." Hinting at a *roman à clef*, he also finds the names of the characters "audibly close to those of their originals" (430). Lewis also remarks that Edith Wharton created Newland Archer and Ellen Olenska from the New York and European parts of herself (431). Wharton's second biographer, Cynthia Griffin Wolff, feels that Henry James, who died in 1916, was very much on Edith Wharton's mind as she wrote *The Age of Innocence*. Partly for that reason, she believes that Newland Archer's name is borrowed from Henry James's Isabel Archer in *The Portrait of a Lady*.

To Wolff, the novel is a *Bildungsroman*, even more so than *Summer*. Archer, representing Wharton, evolves from an "untried youth" to an admirable middle-aged man through his "ordeal by love." Her reading is based on Erikson's idea that self takes place "*in the core of the individual* and yet also in *the core of his communal culture.*" Growth "must proceed from an understanding of one's background—a coming to terms with one's past" (313, italics Wolff's). Ellen is the catalyst who teaches Newland acceptance of reality and dedication to "generativity." May, as Diana, is the divinity of fertility. All of Newland's traditions enforce bonds of kinship and familial affection, but he is "terrified" by "the finality of his acceptance of old New York" (326) so he turns to Ellen for escape. She, however, forces him to look at reality. At the novel's end, Newland, at peace, has evolved into a good citizen who understands himself. According to Wolff his going up to meet Ellen would have denied the value of his chosen life.

Meanwhile, using Edith Wharton's original manuscript, Alan Price (1996) supplements the work of Joseph Candido (1979). He notes that Candido "has examined the stylistic revisions Mrs. Wharton made in the galleys of *The Age of Innocence* in the Lilly Library." Price follows the interesting process of revision, finding the revisions "stylistic rather than substantive" (29). He documents in detail Wharton's extensive preparation for the writing of the novel, also mentioned by Lewis (1975). Comparing the evolution of the novel to Wharton's statements about her creative process in *A Backward Glance*, Price shows that Wharton's statement "should not be taken as an exact account of her creative method" (23) because she does much more than simply "watch and record" her characters and their fate: the "sheer amount of work" is unfathomable (30).

After Wolff's, another prominent feminist reading of *The Age of Innocence* was that of Elizabeth Ammons (1980), who decides that Ellen Olenska arouses sexual fear in Newland Archer and others because she "places in jeopardy the very security of 'civilization'" (143). Ammons argues that the so-called matriarchal structure of New York society headed by Mrs. Mingott is actually patriarchal because she defers to her son and lawyer. Henry van der Luyden actually represents the "highest authority" about morality and form (150). The novel's anthropological language makes it a kind of "laboratory study" of the "primitive attitudes that mold patriarchal aversion to the mature female" (144). In Wharton's society the ideal woman is the child-woman embodied by May, an idea created by men for women.

By 1982 Elizabeth Ammons views Edith Wharton as "an author of the first rank" (209). Here she finds Wharton attacking an entire tradition by creating May as "Wharton's rarefied version of the stereotype . . . always connected with white" (213) and cool virginity. She is

"Diana, virgin deity of the hunt . . . a forever virginal goddess of death," who is empty, yet represents a "pernicious ideal," an image of "America's Dream Girl" (214) and "a manufactured symbol of patriarchal authority" (216). May is contrasted to Ellen Olenska, an "exotic and passionate" (218) "wild child" like Pearl of Hawthorne's *The Scarlet Letter*. Through Ellen's original manner of self-presentation, including sexy dark red clothing, exotic décor, and the choice of artistic friends, she becomes an image of the artist who represents Wharton herself. Ammons argues that Edith Wharton wished to make a point of rejecting New York (220).

Lois Cuddy (1982) offers another analysis of Wharton's structure by using the device of plot triangles in *The Age of Innocence* and *Ethan Frome*. "The protagonists assume a key position in each triangle and are required to make a choice between the two other characters, each of whom usually represents an opposing value system. . . . The novel begins with the protagonist's belief in control and position at the apex but ends with that character at the nadir" (19). Furthermore, "Wharton's personal attitudes are . . . reflected in the evolution" of her work from *Ethan Frome* in which men manipulate women to *The Age of Innocence* in which women manipulate men (19).

Manners Reflect Morals

The subject of morality surfaces once again in John Kekes's "The Great Guide of Human Life" (1984). Beginning with Hume's statement that "custom [is] the great guide of human life" (236), and noting that custom is part of morality, he posits that "in an orderly society, values are most naturally expressed in the prevailing moral customs so the way to live according to the values is to live according to moral customs" (237). "The conflict between decency and happiness is illusory" (238). He develops the idea at length, concluding that the conflict is an illusion, that Ellen and Newland love and admire each other's (decent) characters and their sensibility to the morality and customs of their societies, but that love and admiration would disappear should they act against it. The error that underlies the reader's sympathy with the couple is that "our relation to our society is contingent and changeable and has little importance" (245), but actually both define themselves by New York moral conventions.

Centering on the character of May Welland, Gwendolyn Morgan (1987) joins Louis Coxe in arguing that May has been neglected by critics and generally stereotyped as the naive "martyred wife," but a close look reveals that May acts differently than Newland perceives.

Therefore, May becomes both noble and tragic, capable of rising above convention. Her fight to protect her marriage "can be viewed as an act of great love . . . true honor and nobility" (38). In chapter 33 of the novel, May inspects "the basket of Jacqueminot roses," a single passage taken almost verbatim from "Society as I Have Found It," a neglected monograph, by Ward McAllister (held by the New York Historical Society). From this monograph, Morgan draws additional conclusions about which characters in the novel were drawn from which real people (*roman à clef*). She feels strongly that Wharton must have known and read it, for even the maidenhair fern in the center of the long table and the placing of the Maillard bonbons in an openwork silver basket, as described in the novel, are defined by McAllister as mandatory for the "guest dinners."

Relating to language and the difficulty of communication, David Godfrey (1987), who examines how, in order to support the community as a whole, individuals are trained to use "cowardly" language, refusing to discuss divorce and other "unpleasant" matters. Ironically, he argues, this cowardice undermines the good of the social whole because it cannot function efficiently without full knowledge. Archer is an example of this "cowardice," while Ellen, from another culture, has not been debilitated by a language of evasion, and faces the truth. An essay by Blackall (1991), also focusing on oral communication, shows how the telegram or cable serves as a dramatic device of emphatic interruption. The intrusive voice of the sender serves to "create a moment of crisis or of reversal or of urgency" used to complicate the plot (164).

The nineties usher in an increase in book-length studies and special journal issues devoted to Edith Wharton, as well as collections of critical essays, most of which include readings of *The Age of Innocence*. One particularly interesting analysis (Goodwyn 1991) looks at the anthropology of the novel in a new way (a subject of increasing interest to critics, especially in the 1990s). Here, New York society becomes a "museum culture," in which people, manners, and customs are valued for their rarity, their topographical borders having been extinguished by the First World War.

In a feminist reading, Katherine Joslin (1991) interprets the novel as "about womanhood because the plot turns on the Woman Question (the term used at the turn of the nineteenth century for 'feminism') puzzled out by a male protagonist" (91). New York society is divided into material and quasi-intellectual groups united by the marriage of Newland and May. Ellen represents a third "Bohemian" group that entices Archer but also threatens him. In the end he is an "'armchair' feminist" (99) who wonders, "If a woman does not follow convention and her abilities and talents develop more in line with men, who *is* she?" (97) He analyzes the lopsided education that makes men and women unable to know one another, unable to be equals rather than owner and "slave." He senses, but never quite realizes, that "the social community of economically subjugated women" (103–4), which has found colorful ways around the social restrictions, has "generat[ed] a power of *its* own" (104). Joslin speculates that Newland "never really wanted comradeship with a woman at all" (106). He keeps his marriage socially distant, and Ellen's social context of art and passion is too threatening. Gloria Erlich (1992) agrees. However, Erlich, in the context of interpreting Wharton's psychology through her fiction, reads those passages to mean that "Newland's psychological conservatism is like that of Edith Wharton who . . . chose to live . . . and to associate . . . with . . . conservative avatars of outmoded gentility" (134). To strengthen her point she quotes Shari Benstock's comment (1986) that Wharton "dared not risk exposure to a rebellious and often risqué modernity" (134).

Evelyn A. Fracasso's close reading (1991) focuses on May who seems not the passive, clinging, "human doll" that many critics have believed. Wharton's "symbolic treatment of May's expressive eyes," shows that May has consistently been tough and tenacious, having depth of feeling and strength of character (48). Next Lev Raphael (1991) points out a number of situations when Newland or May cannot say aloud the reasons for their actions because of the risk of public embarrassment. For instance, "Newland's reasons for being [in the opera box] cannot be discussed because of 'the family dignity which both considered so high a virtue.'. . . But despite this outward display of 'solidarity,' Newland is afraid that Ellen will afterward be brought to the Opera ball" (307).

The subject of morality returns when Carol Singley (1995) argues, based on quotations copied into Edith Wharton's Commonplace Book, that she drew on Plato's *Symposium*, *Phaedrus*, and *The Republic* to "distinguish between the real and ideal," which is "consistent with [Wharton's] belief in the soul's immortality." This is manifested in *The Age of Innocence* when Newland Archer confuses "truth" with "taste" (for instance, in his choice of "sincere" Eastlake furniture), while Ellen, as Plato's "wise woman Diotima uses the Socratic dialectal method to teach him Platonic rather than romantic ideals." Nancy Bentley (1995), on the other hand, applies "taste" in the context of manners, examining modern anthropological studies against the novel's anthropological imagery to show how Wharton participated in creating an entire "science of manners." A new consciousness of culture allows her to critique and also preserve the late-nineteenth-century elite class, "a double strategy that finally serves to accommodate the very social changes that the class appeared to oppose" (49). Pamela Knights (1995) complements this reading with her argument that "without the shape, the social mold, there may be no self at all" (21), and that, as Bell states it, "consciousness is created by social typologies and conventional paradigms of behavior" (16). Knights remarks that *The Age of Innocence* asks us to explore questions of social process; the "books on Primitive Man," in contrast, "assure Archer of the hazardousness of women and the primacy of the patriarchal modern family" (22–23). All of this is communicated through the hieroglyphic code of dress, action or non-action, and gesture.

Knights' essay demonstrates the current trend of scholars looking through anthropological lenses at a wide variety of literature. *The Age of Innocence* invites such views because of Wharton's use of words like "tribe," "totem terrors," and other intriguing phrases to discuss family relationships, and because she was, in fact, well read in anthropology. Judith Fryer (1984/1997) combines the anthropological with the dramatic—themes originally mentioned in the early reviews: "Wharton knew a great deal about cultural anthropology; one learns from *A Backward Glance* that she had been reading Darwin, Huxley, Spencer, 'and various popular exponents of the great evolutionary movement.' She made skillful use particularly of *The Golden Bough* in analyzing her own former world in tribal terms and in traumatizing its rituals, from the performance of the Old New York audience attending the Opera. . . ." Fryer discusses the "stage-setting of adultery" and a "stage-setting for the other scenes" (212). In the novel's opening, Wharton provides two simultaneous performances (212), the one onstage as well as the drama among members of the audience. Fryer brings Henry James into the equation: The singer performing *Faust* is "Christine Nilsson, the opera singer of whom Henry James had written, 'What a pity she is not the heroine of a tale, and that I didn't make her!'" (213)

These, as well as anthropological and dramatic aspects of the novel seem to provide room for deeper investigation. Critics have covered issues of structure, characterization, communication, Puritanism, and morality. Edith Wharton's collection of ghost stories, the subject of the next chapter, has been the subject of recent interest that covers some of these same topics.

Works Consulted

"*The Age of Innocence.*" Rev. of *The Age of Innocence* by Edith Wharton. *Times Literary Supplement* [England] (25 November 1920): 775.

Ammons, Elizabeth. "Cool Diana and the Blood-Red Muse: Edith Wharton on Innocence and Art." Ed. Fritz Fleishmann, *American Novelists Revisited: Essays in Feminist Criticism.* Boston: G. K. Hall, 1982. 209–24.

Auchincloss, Louis. "Edith Wharton and Her New Yorks." *Edith Wharton: A Collection of Critical Essays.* Ed. Irving Howe. Englewood Cliffs, NJ: Prentice-Hall, 1962.

———. "Edith Wharton." *Seven Modern Novelists: An Introduction.* Ed. William Van O'Connor. Minneapolis, MN: U of Minnesota P, 1965. 11–45.

———, ed. *The Edith Wharton Reader.* New York: Scribners, 1965. ix–xvi.

Beach, Joseph Warren. *The Twentieth Century Novel: Studies in Technique.* New York: Century, 1932. 291–303.

Bentley, Nancy. *The Ethnography of Manners: Hawthorne, James, Wharton.* New York: Cambridge UP, 1995. 68–113.

Blackall, Jean Frantz. "The Intrusive Voice: Telegrams in *The House of Mirth* and the *Age of Innocence.*" *Women's Studies* 20.2 (1991): 163–68.

Candido, Joseph. "Edith Wharton's Final Alterations of *The Age of Innocence.*" *Studies in American Fiction* 6 (1979): 21–31.

Chandler, Marilyn R. *Dwelling in the Text: Houses in American Fiction.* Berkeley, CA: U of California P, 1991. 149–79.

Coxe, Louis O. "What Edith Wharton Saw in Innocence." *The New Republic* (June 27, 1955): 16–18. Rpt. in *Edith Wharton: A Collection of Critical Essays.* Ed. Irving Howe. Englewood Cliffs, NJ: Prentice-Hall, 1962. 155–61.

Cuddy, Lois A. "Triangles of Defeat and Liberation: The Quest for Power in Edith Wharton's Fiction." *Perspectives on Contemporary Literature* 8 (1982): 18–26.

Dooley, R. B. "A Footnote to Edith Wharton." *American Literature* 26.1 (March 1954): 78–85.

Doyle, Charles Clay. "Emblems of Innocence: Imagery Patterns in Wharton's *The Age of Innocence.*" *Xavier University Studies* 10.2 (1971): 19–25.

Erlich, Gloria C. *The Sexual Education of Edith Wharton.* Berkeley, CA: U of California P, 1992.

Fracasso, Evelyn E. "The Transparent Eyes of May Welland in Wharton's *The Age of Innocence.*" *Modern Language Studies* 21.4 (Fall 1991): 43–48.

Fryer, Judith. "Edith Wharton." *American Women Fiction Writers* 1900–1960. Vol. 3. Ed. Harold Bloom. Philadelphia, PA: Chelsea House, 1997. 212–13.

Godfrey, David. "'The Full and Elaborate Vocabulary of Evasion': The Language of Cowardice in Edith Wharton's Old New York." *Midwest Quarterly* 30.1 (Autumn 1988): 27–44.

Hartwick, Harry. *The Foreground of American Fiction.* New York: American Book Co. 1934. 369–75.

Hopkins, Viola. "The Ordering Style of *The Age of Innocence.*" *American Literature* 30.3 (November 1958): 345–57.

Jacobson, Irving. "Perception, Communication, and Growth as Correlative Themes in Edith Wharton's *The Age of Innocence.*" *Agora* 2.2 (1973): 68–82.

Joslin, Katherine. *Women Writers: Edith Wharton.* New York: St. Martin's P, 1991. 89–107.

Kekes, John. "The Great Guide of Human Life." *Philosophy and Literature* 8.2 (October 8, 1984): 236–49.

Killoran, Helen. *Edith Wharton: Art and Allusion.* Tuscaloosa, AL: U of Alabama P, 1996.

Knights, Pamela. "Forms of Disembodiment: The Social Subject in *The Age of Innocence.*" *The Cambridge Companion to Edith Wharton.* Ed. Millicent Bell. New York: Cambridge UP, 1995. 20–46.

Lamar, Lillie B. "Edith Wharton and the *Book of Common Prayer.*" *American Notes & Queries* 7 (November 1968): 38–39.

———. "Edith Wharton's Foreknowledge in *The Age of Innocence.*" *Texas Studies in Language and Literature* 8 (Fall 1966): 385–89.

Lewis, R. W. B. *Edith Wharton: A Biography.* New York: Harper & Row, 1975. 428–39.

———. Introduction. *The Age of Innocence* by Edith Wharton. New York: Scribners, 1968.

Lindberg, Gary H. *Edith Wharton and the Novel of Manners.* Charlottesville, VA: UP of Virginia. 128–37.

M[ansfield], K[atherine]. "Family Portraits." Rev. of *The Age of Innocence* by Edith Wharton. *Athenaeum* [England] 4728 (10 December 1920): 810–11. Rpt. in *Novels and Novelists.* New York: Knopf, 1930. 319–20.

Morgan, Gwendolyn. "The Unsung Heroine—A Study of May Welland in *The Age of Innocence.*" *Heroines of Popular Culture.* Ed. Pat Browne. Bowling Green, OH: Popular, 1987. 32–40.

Moseley, Edwin M. "*The Age of Innocence:* Edith Wharton's Weak *Faust.*" *College English* 21.3 (December 1959): 156–60.

Murphy, John J. "Filters, Portraits, and History's Mixed Bag: *A Lost Lady* and *The Age of Innocence.*" *Twentieth Century Literature* 38.4 (Winter 1992): 476–84.

———. "The Satiric Structure of Wharton's *The Age of Innocence.*" *Markham Review* 2.3 (May 1970): 1–4.

Nathan, Rhoda. "Ward McAllister: Beau Nash of *The Age of Innocence.*" *College Literature* 14.3 (1987): 276–84.

Nevius, Blake. *Edith Wharton: A Study of Her Fiction.* 1953. Berkeley, CA: U of California P, 1961. 174–94.

Parrington, Vernon L. Jr. "Our Literary Aristocrat." Rev. of *The Age of Innocence* by Edith Wharton. *Pacific Review* 2 (June 1921): 157–60.

Phelps, William Lyon. "As Mrs. Wharton Sees Us." *New York Times Book Review* (17 October 1920): 1, 11.

Pöder, Elfriede. "Concepts and Visions of 'The Other': The Place of 'Woman' in *The Age of Innocence, Melanctha*, and *Nightwood.*" *Women in Search of Literary Space.* Eds. Gudrun M. Grabher and Maureen Devine. Tübingen: Gunter Narr Verlag, 1992. 171–83.

Singley, Carol. *Edith Wharton: Matters of Mind and Spirit.* New York: Cambridge UP, 1995. 171–83.

Tintner, Adeline R. "Jamesian Structures in *The Age of Innocence* and Related Stories." *Twentieth Century Literature* 26 (1980): 332–47.

Tuttleton, James W. *The Novel of Manners in America.* Chapel Hill, NC: U of North Carolina P, 1972. 128–33.

———. "The President and the Lady: Edith Wharton and Theodore Roosevelt." *Bulletin of the New York Public Library* 69.1 (January 1965): 49–57.

Walton, Geoffrey. *Edith Wharton: A Critical Interpretation.* Rutherford: Fairleigh Dickinson UP, 1970. Revised 1982. 137–46.

Wharton, Edith. *A Backward Glance.* New York: Appleton-Century, 1934. Rpt. New York: Scribners, 1985.

Wolff, Cynthia Griffin. *A Feast of Words: The Triumph of Edith Wharton.* New York: Oxford UP, 1977. 310–34.

7: *Ghosts*—In Broad Daylight

VICTORIAN AND *FIN DE SIÈCLE* ghost stories often hide interesting issues that authors could not address openly because of contemporary mores. Topics such as incest, mental illness, drug addiction, sexual perversions and the like, can all serve as a basis for creating the chilling and eerie. Engagingly, in the last year of her life, Edith Wharton collected many of her ghost stories in *Ghosts* (1937): "The Lady's Maid's Bell" (1902), "Afterward" (1909), "The Triumph of Night" (1913), "Kerfol" (1916), "Miss Mary Pask" (1923), "Bewitched" (1925), "Mr. Jones" (1928), "Pomegranate Seed" (1929), "A Bottle of Perrier" (1926), and "All Souls" (1937). In addition, Wharton wrote one of her rare prefaces, stressing the presence of ghosts even in broad daylight, hidden under the clash and clatter of modern technology, but overlooked in the chaos. In fact, each of these stories takes place in daylight with the exception of "The Triumph of Night" in which the ghost appears in the artificial light of an evening meal.

Scribners reprinted the collection as *The Ghost Stories of Edith Wharton*, creating what might be called a ghost in the text. Someone replaced "A Bottle of Perrier" with "The Looking Glass" (1935). Consequently, "The Looking Glass" is regarded as one of the ghost tales. Most critics have focused on the tales in *The Ghost Stories of Edith Wharton* because of its availability, but Edith Wharton considered "A Bottle of Perrier" a ghost story. Some critics list other tales as among the ghost stories, particularly, "The Duchess at Prayer," "The House of the Dead Hand," "The Fullness of Life," "The Legend," and even *The Touchstone*. These stories are not considered here, because the collection that Edith Wharton personally chose seems of most interest.

"The Eyes" and "All Souls" vie for masterpiece status among pre-feminist reviewers and critics. Later, feminists would concentrate more on "The Lady's Maid's Bell" and "Pomegranate Seed." Since these are quiet stories that do not shock the eyes as they first skim the print, gasps and chills are held in abeyance until "Afterward," to borrow the title of one of Edith Wharton's stories.

Not surprisingly, then, the 1937 reviews stress the superb but quiet methods that cause the sense of the eerie to creep slowly upon the reader: "The author's outstanding qualities in the use of different methods of short story writing make this a fascinating selection to browse through in nocturnal hours" (*Commonweal*). Desmond Shawe-Taylor of the *New Statesman and Nation* notes that Wharton's "speech is naturally quiet and unhurried . . . while I cannot say I found [the stories] hair-raising, they have a half-eerie, half-cozy charm of their own. You begin to feel the silence around your chair" (CR 541).

The well-known novelist, Graham Greene, writing in the *Spectator* and less concerned about silence, describes the best ghost stories as containing a physical sense and a moral twist. He too insists on reducing Edith Wharton by evoking the name of Henry James: "Mrs. Wharton, following her master Henry James, is good at [moral sense. . . . But] Mrs. Wharton seems a little tame compared with [the horrors of ghost story writer] M. R. James" (CR 542).

Peculiar Green Faces

Nearly every specific story has drawn some attention, and each has been both praised and censured. "The Eyes" has probably attracted the largest share. An anonymous author in the *Times Literary Supplement* feels that "The Eyes," "The Lady's Maid's Bell," and "The Triumph of Night" are "fogged" so that the reader is uncertain what happened. "The best three stories, 'All Souls,' 'Miss Mary Pask,' and 'Bewitched,' are ghostless." He decides that Edith Wharton leaves "the reader to invent several endings and choose for himself" (CR 541). W. R. B. in the *Saturday Review* states that

> Some years ago . . . the reviewer heard a now well known American novelist give, as his contribution [to the telling of ghost stories] Edith Wharton's tale of the ghostly dogs in "Kerfol". . . . More recently Alexander Woollcott has chosen . . . "The Lady's Maid's Bell" for inclusion in his forthcoming *Second Reader*. . . . [But] the present reviewer thinks that "The Eyes," owing to its psychological significance, and "A Bottle of Perrier," because of its Arabian atmosphere . . . are superior. . . . If you like good ghost stories then, this is the book for you. . . . Maybe you will like best poor young Rainer in "The Triumph of Night". . . . And what is that peculiar green face looking over your shoulder? (CR 541–42)

Edith Wharton usually wrote about the everyday rather than about peculiar green faces. Perhaps because of this, only a smattering of commentary appeared before R. W. B. Lewis (1975) produced a review of the reprinted stories in the prestigious *Times Literary Supplement*. When Margaret McDowell (1976) wrote the first of several essays on the subject, the ghost stories, after nearly forty years, began to receive more serious consideration. Blake Nevius (1953) addresses only "The

Eyes," which he calls "one of the most remarkable of Edith Wharton's short tales," but "strangely neglected" (94) in anthologies and criticism. (Ironically, it has since become one of the most anthologized of the ghost stories.) He finds it a "Hawthornesque study of egoism" (99)—an interesting comment in the light of later critics finding it Poesque and Emersonian. Nevius remarks that the story unflatteringly analyzes a type necessarily prominent in the world of society and literature that Wharton inhabited, but that its "singleness and intensity of effect" created by symbolism helps explain why "The Eyes" impressively evokes "emotional and creative dilettantism" (97).

Critique of the ghost stories then rests for a decade until Patricia Plante (1963) repeats Greene's lament that Wharton's ghost stories are "a bit tame." However, she claims for "Bewitched," "Miss Mary Pask," and "All Souls" universal admiration, an assertion probably influenced by the *Times Literary Supplement* review of *Ghosts.* Five years later, R. W. B. Lewis notes in the introduction to his *Collected Short Stories* that most of Edith Wharton's ghost stories deal with marriage. But in fact, only five of the twelve do, and those do so in an atmosphere contradictorily passionate and violent, muted and remote. He believes that "Pomegranate Seed" contains mythic qualities, and that "Kerfol" may distance personal issues, longings, and resentments from Wharton's own marital experiences. Like Nevius, Lewis finds "The Eyes" an "immeasurably superior story" (xix).

Wounded Women

In a review of Lewis's then newly published biography of Edith Wharton, Julie L'Enfant (1976) claims to discover the Fullerton affair in "The Eyes," and quotes Lewis's comment that in this story Wharton used her "full creative intelligence" (404). Following L'Enfant, Lawson (1977) primarily reviews the plot of "The Eyes," noting accurately that in Edith Wharton's hands, the ghost genre often merges into the psychological horror story.

One of the most influential modern commentators on the subject of Edith Wharton's ghost stories has been Margaret McDowell, who was the first to draw attention to their value in her books and articles, though she has modified her opinions over time, most recently in 1991. Edith Wharton claims no moral lessons for her ghost stories, but McDowell, like Graham Greene, disagrees. As normally happens with rediscovered work, the era of its rediscovery affects the critical approach. In this case, the primary approaches combine feminist and psychological theories that stress uses and abuses of women, examine restrictions on women's activities such as writing, or make biographical speculations about the author. McDowell neatly summarizes the topics of discussion, focusing mostly on the sexual and marital:

> If any consistent pattern of conviction emerges from the stories [of the implications of marriage as seen through the eyes of a woman] . . . it is that each woman must decide for herself what is best in her own situation. When Wharton began writing, divorce in many parts of America spelled disgrace not only to the divorcée but to her relatives; yet divorce was commonplace only a few years later. Views on love affairs outside marriage changed much more slowly. . . . It is remarkable that in the 1890s and even at the turn of the century a woman from Wharton's conservative milieu could examine so vigorously and so searchingly issues related to divorce and to love, legal, or illicit. Certainly no American author before 1939 produced such penetrating studies of women who, instead of marrying, decide to risk social ostracism by contracting temporary alliances based on mutual trust and sexual desire. (82)

In a 1970 essay later incorporated into her volume for Twayne (1976, revised 1991) McDowell notes that some of the stories have their source in Hawthorne, and that in most of Wharton's stories the ghost has an "archetypal dimension," that it "hints at psychic dislocation," and "always conveys some inescapable symbolic truth." Summarizing each of the stories, she remarks that Edith Wharton "often made use of a single obsessive and obtrusive image to organize a given tale" (137), but that in some of the "lesser" stories, the technique "obtrudes at the expense of mental conflict." She does not specify the archetypal dimensions, psychic dislocations, inescapable symbolic truths, and obsessive images, however. In her most recent essay on the ghost stories, "Edith Wharton's Ghost Tales Reconsidered," McDowell (1992) stresses biographical contrasts between Wharton's "despair and ecstasy" (292), "repressed hopes and frustrations" (293), and between childhood and old age. "Perhaps the most common theme running through Wharton's late ghost stories is her warning not to forfeit the sanctity of one's still developing soul through worship of one's past, through nostalgia for a vanished society, or through grief for those who have died." Stories developing this central theme include "After Holbein," "Kerfol," "Mr. Jones," "Pomegranate Seed," "The Looking Glass," and "All Souls" (295).

While McDowell makes interesting comparisons between Edith Wharton's stories and those of Walter de la Mare, to whom the author dedicated her ghost stories, the assumptions of biographical revelations ("Sara Clayburn is, in part, the author's self-portrait" [309]) and the connections to Henry James are dubious, and McDowell provides only the most general data with which to support her contentions.

The ghostly tale "The Eyes" begins, as traditional, with a group of men telling ghost stories around the fire. The host, Andrew Culwin, tells about some dubious personal activities in his past. After each event, he experiences a terrifying vision of evil eyes staring at him from the dark. Again, critics attempt to attach a real person to the evil protagonist. In the introduction to his short story collection, Lewis states that Culwin projects Edith Wharton's "most buried feelings about Walter Berry" (supposed to have been her lover, the affair with Fullerton not yet having been discovered) as the "evil genius" (xx) in her life. R. W. B. Lewis addresses the subject once again in 1975 in a review of *The Ghost Stories of Edith Wharton*, in which he concentrates primarily on "The Eyes" and "All Souls." What he says of "The Eyes" is true of most, if not all, of the ghost stories: "A full accounting . . . would lead into abnormal and sexual psychology, intellectual and literary history, and even theology, and thus indicate a good deal of the sometimes fascinating complexity of the superior ghost story" (644).

A contemporary of Lewis's, Henry James's psychological biographer, Leon Edel (1982), concludes that "All Souls" resulted from the anxiety created by a combination of the author's fears about the disappearance of servants (since Edith Wharton had never fended for herself) and fear of death due to her threatening heart disease. On the other hand, Douglas Robillard (1984) adds to Dorothy Scarborough's early volume (1917). Scarborough categorized hundreds of ghost stories into groups, such as ghost stories featuring animals or ghost stories featuring doubles. Noting that the types of ghost stories Wharton wrote include "stories of protective ghosts, of malignant ghosts, of revenants from long-gone episodes of brutality, [and] of ghostly women who still exert a hold on husbands" (786), Robillard says that "'All Souls' suffers from not being resolved" (787), but that Wharton "has a keen sense of how the world of the spirit can impinge upon the mundane, and one of her effective contributions to the field is the reality of that world. There is virtually no attempt to play upon the emotions by any heightened use of language" (788).

Feminist Ghosts

Alan Gardner Smith (1980, rpt.1986) begins the deeper psychological readings by defining Wharton as a feminist whose ghost stories deliberately suppress the "sexual pathology of everyday life" (90), and by asserting that her technique creates even more horror than the usual "supernatural story." He analyzes "All Souls" in this light as a "haunting *by absence*" (91), while "Miss Mary Pask" concerns loneliness in entrapment. He suggests that Wharton adapts Freud's analysis of Hoffman's "Sandman" in "The Eyes."

Continuing with Freudian-feminist analyses, Virginia Blum (1987) traces the "theme of the seductive female ghost" (12) in "Miss Mary Pask," "Pomegranate Seed," and "Bewitched," contending that Wharton transforms them: "Miss Mary Pask" to *The House of Mirth*, "Bewitched" to *Ethan Frome*, and "Pomegranate Seed" to *Summer*. In *The Age of Innocence*, "Bewitched" becomes "a novel full of 'perpetual daughters'" (24), kept by society from growing into "frighteningly" sexual women like Ellen Olenska. On the other hand, Annette Zilversmit (1987) joins Leon Edel in reading "Pomegranate Seed" and "All Souls" as a reflection of both Wharton's internal fears and external social constriction. She adds that at the end of each story, the female protagonist finds herself "wedded to a mother figure" (300), the greatest possible horror to Edith Wharton who, Zilversmit says, desperately feared her own witch-like mother.

Psychological Ghosts

In 1989 Richard Lawson returns to Lewis's point that the stories present problematic orientations toward marriage, divorce, or a surviving spouse. Critics agree, he feels, that "All Souls" is one of Wharton's best, but that "The Eyes" is unquestionably her masterpiece. Thus he cements the idea that "All Souls" is almost as superior as "The Eyes," and that "Pomegranate Seed" provides food for speculation about psychological complexities. Again, nearly every critic assumes that some aspect of "Pomegranate Seed" represents an unresolved conflict in Edith Wharton's life. In early criticism of the ghost stories, "The Eyes" and "All Souls" vie for greatest masterpiece status, but feminists continue to be particularly fascinated by "Pomegranate Seed." They see the story to some extent as a direct metaphor for the myth of Persephone. Alfred Bendixen (1985) judges "Pomegranate Seed" a "superbly crafted story," a sophisticated study of love and marriage, which "emphasizes the fragility of human relationships in an uncertain world" (8), but he denies that women who depend on wedlock for their identity can be protected from sorrow and danger as they might hope. He asserts that the two Mrs. Ashbys are alter egos, not competitors as others have alleged. Symbolizing an all-powerful dominating love, the "ghost represents both Charlotte Ashby's fears and her desires" (8). In a related thought, Margaret P. Murray (1989) suggests that through the story Wharton solved her ambivalence about herself as a powerless woman versus an accomplished author. Murray believes that she applies Jungian psychology to a "displaced wife" theme in "Pomegranate Seed."

The story tells of a second wife, Charlotte, who returns to her house many evenings to discover a letter to her husband on the hall table. The distinctive qualities of the handwriting make clear to Charlotte that the letters are from Elsie, the dead first wife. The ghost is attempting to convince her former husband to join her in the Land of the Dead. Murray reminds readers that Wharton's title is taken from the myth of Persephone, goddess of fertility, captured and raped by Pluto and held in the underworld for six months of the year (winter) because, although prohibited from eating, she ate six pomegranate seeds. Murray argues that because of Elsie's association with Mother Earth, she also represents Aphrodite, goddess of love and queen of the underworld, who in myth may also appear as a harbinger of doom. The twelve months of Elsie's marriage to Ken, according to Murray, represent the twelve pomegranate seeds. Nine ghostly letters arrive, but the missing three letters/seeds represent the growing season. Ultimately, "Ken is the symbolic bagatelle awarded to the conquering power" (320). Gloria Erlich (1992) points out that Wharton used Ovid's version of the Persephone-Demeter story as the basis of "Pomegranate Seed," interpreting the six months of Persephone's residence in the underworld as a psychological metaphor for Wharton as a "prisoner in her husband's house"(43). However, Edith Wharton tended to set her stories in the writer's present—in this case 1929—although she often drew content from personal experiences of a decade earlier.

Next, Carol Singley and Elizabeth Sweeney (1993) apply feminism, Lacanian psychology, reader response, and biographical tools to "Pomegranate Seed" to show it as a parable of "women's ambivalence toward the power of reading and writing" (198). "Pomegranate Seed" presents an "anti-manifesto of female writing," according to Judy Hale Young (1996), for whom Edith Wharton's story is an "indictment of the woman writer who perpetuates the state of non-communication between women" (2). Gianfranca Balestra (1996), on the other hand, reads "Pomegranate Seed," as well as "All Souls," in the context of publishers who wish to supply explanatory conclusions. Ghost story conclusions depend on an inscrutable and "unexplained absence" in which "the rhetoric of the unsayable is deployed at its best, producing a text overlaid with blanks and defiantly unyielding to decoding attempts" (15). Wharton's reluctant compliance with publishers' requests for changes explains her endings, and thus weakens them. (As proof

Balestra quotes Wharton's acquiescent letters.) So, while a generally positive opinion of the ghost stories has prevailed, the vocabulary of appreciation has remained obscure and vague. To support general claims, critics either find that the characters in the tales represent the people in Edith Wharton's life or reveal her personal anxieties and desires.

Marxist Ghosts

Many critics of the nineties tend to examine the ghost stories globally. For instance, Monika Elbert (1991) looks over all of the stories with a Marxist slant. She concludes that ultimately the author "allows spiritual concerns to triumph over economic circumstances and suggests that there is a 'world elsewhere'. . . a Realism tinged with the [Emersonian] idealism of the American Renaissance" (51). Edith Wharton loathes the old order, remaining ambivalent about the master-servant relationship, yet fears the chaos of creating a new order. Furthermore, Wharton follows a Gothic American tradition, claiming a "double vision that encompasses binary oppositions and destroys traditional categories of thinking" (60).

Another Marxist-economic view is contributed by Ellen Powers Stengel, discussing "The Lady's Maid's Bell" (1990). To greatly simplify, in Marxist theory, two opposing ideas, a "thesis" and an "antithesis," travel through historical time. Eventually they meet and clash resulting in a "synthesis"—a new historical idea that results from the conflict. A new opposing idea develops and the process repeats. For example, Marx believes that motives and ideas are economic and held by both upper and lower classes. The two classes clash, and the result is a kind of middle class. Often a conflict results in war, but not necessarily. According to Stengel, Edith Wharton "posits the preternatural as the Great Extension of the servant/master relationship" (3) since she hired servants because where class systems exist, envy must also exist.

In "The Lady's Maid's Bell," Alice Hartley accepts the position of lady's maid at a country home where her predecessor, Emma, had passed away. There Alice sees the ghost of the former lady's maid, and believes that it wants her to help their sick mistress. The ghost manifests itself several times, the last time being when Alice's mistress collapses and dies of an apparent heart attack. Combining Marxist economic principles with Freudian, Jungian, and Lacanian psychological concepts, Stengel describes this tale as a revenant story in which a Marxist dialectical process demands a synthesis between the real and supernatural, conspiring to overcome the "desires of the text" (6).

Here the language of theory becomes difficult. Specifically, ghostly "trespasses textually displayed prompt a reading that with synchronic (that is, space-based) heuristics (that is, tools of analysis), measure the real as the thesis of a dialectical process and that diachronic (that is, time-based) heuristics clocks the unreal as the antithesis of that same dialectical process. The revenant story as a dialectical process then demands the synthesis, which a dialectically-based heuristic can provide" (3). In Stengel's reading, Alice, the lady's maid, psychologically regresses to the Freudian atavistic animistic stage, "unsurmounted" in her earlier life.

In this story, then, the Marxist clash occurs between analytical reality in the present and the unreal ghost of the past. This clash takes place in the language of the story in which Alice, who has never successfully passed through the first psychological stage of personality development, regresses to it because of her fatigue and fear. In that state of mind, she unconsciously wishes to become her mistress, to create a clash between her lower-class servant status and the status of her upper-class mistress.

Treating the ghost story as part of the larger category of the Gothic genre, Kathy Fedorko (1991) argues that in "The Lady's Maid's Bell" and *The House of Mirth*, the Gothic reveals the secret that "traditional society and the traditional home, with their traditional roles, are dangerous places for women" (81). Taking a different approach, Helen Killoran (1996) finds evidence in this story of multiple sexual perversions. These are misperceived by Alice because of a brain illness, and because of careful camouflage, non-accidental resemblances, mirror images, costumes, and other deliberate deceptions on the part of participants who wish to hide their activities.

Briefly, in "A Bottle of Perrier," Medford responds to an invitation from Almodham to visit his half-European, half-Arabian castle. When Medford arrives, Gosling, the butler, informs him that Almodham has left for an archeological expedition but will return soon. Medford decides to wait. When the butler serves dinner, he seems unusually horrified to learn that Medford cannot drink wine, for the Perrier has run out. A trade expedition is expected soon, but the well water is brackish. Medford simply tells Gosling to boil the water. As the wait continues, time loses meaning for Medford, who alternately sleeps and enjoys the desert scenery. Finally, he proposes to the stable groomsman that they go looking for Almodham. Gosling, however, precipitously halts the adventure. Medford eventually learns that Almodham had not allowed Gosling a vacation in a number of years. Because of that Gosling murdered him and dumped his body in the well. As the story ends,

Medford and Gosling face each other in the moonlight, anticipating a deadly fight.

Candace Waid (1991) directly examines sexual implications of "A Bottle of Perrier," which she feels contains suggestive imagery of both genitalia and a cannibalistic landscape. Through the passivity of the protagonist waiting for his host, Waid feels that the story depicts Wharton's fears about the dangers of stasis, and her "anxieties about the stagnation she associated with the place of women." Since the story has no female characters, Gosling takes the place of the female, a man-servant who "cannot escape from his feminine role" (184) in a story depicting the struggle between men and women.

In "Mr. Jones," Lady Jane Lynke inherits a country house called "The Bells," run by Mr. Jones, a man whom no one ever sees. In the process of learning about the history of the house, Lady Jane comes across an old letter from a woman isolated in the house because she was deaf and dumb, and because her husband constantly traveled. While they attempt to understand the meaning of all the papers, one of the servants is murdered, apparently by Mr. Jones.

Reading "Mr. Jones" with "Kerfol," Candace Waid (1991) finds that even the houses are "mute" and "silent." Words eventually suggest that the houses are written texts, with ancestresses reduced to "mute texts," blank pages written over and over with the same story. In Waid's design, "Kerfol" and "Mr. Jones," like other stories, dramatize the psychosexual struggle between men and women. She envisions the silent houses in both tales as "texts containing stories," though the ghosts are visible. The tales involve cruel husbands who keep their childless wives isolated and imprisoned in large, lonely houses. But the narrator of "Kerfol" "rewrites the text" (185). In the story, Anne, the young wife of Yves de Cornault, leads a lonely life while her husband travels on business. After she is seen giving a gift to Hervé de Lanrivain, her husband accuses her of unfaithfulness. He expresses his anger by threatening her and murdering the dogs she adopts as companions. Eventually, de Cornault is murdered. Authorities charge Anne with the crime and place her on trial, but Anne claims that the ghosts of her dead dogs killed her husband. After the trial, Anne's in-laws confine her to a tower as a madwoman. Waid comments that Kerfol's power derives from the "juxtaposition of the narrator's view of Anne de Cornault's speech and thoughts with the way that her words are apprehended by the listening authorities" (187). The authorities seem hostile, almost otherworldly, and translate everything into a male point of view, especially Yves de Cornault's. Anne becomes as silenced as the murdered pets in which she had sought solace. In 1993 Killoran uses a literary-historical approach, combined with an investigation of Wharton's literary allusions, to show that in "Kerfol," Anne is inadvertently caught up in the historic eighteenth century Jansenist-Jesuit split within the French Roman Catholic Church.

The ghosts of the stories from Wharton's middle period are usually protective, according to Barbara A. White (1991). Stories like "The House of the Dead Hand" and "Mr. Jones" deal with incest and guilty daughters "preyed upon by parasitic fathers who can never be locked out" (40). She points to the sexual significance of locks and keys in both stories, and finds a biographical connection since Jones was Edith Wharton's maiden name. "In all cases the power of the father surpasses that of the ghost" (69). She quotes Lewis's statement that the ghost stories "secrete a sizable portion of the erotic," and that "Wharton distanced sexual feelings by projecting them into various forms of fantasy. . . . [T]hus we should expect to find . . . frequent echoes of the incest situation in Wharton's ghostly tales" (68). Ghosts of this middle period concern economics and "reason versus intuition" (70), while the late stories concern revengeful servants, like those in "The Looking Glass" and "All Souls."

Gloria Erlich (1992) spends the most space on "All Souls," the last story Edith Wharton wrote before her death. In that story a vigorous widow, Sara Clayburn, lives alone in a large house called Whitegates. As explained by the anonymous narrator, one All Souls' Eve, Mrs. Clayburn returns from her usual walk to see a strange woman entering her home. Immediately afterward, she slips on the ice and injures her ankle. Her servants call a doctor and put her to bed for the night. In the morning she awakens to find the house without heat or electricity and deserted by the servants. After a slow, terrifying inspection of the house, she spends another night alone. This time, when she awakens, everything appears as usual and everyone denies that the lost day ever occurred. But the next year, when she sees the strange woman again, Sara Clayburn is terrified into near helplessness, and she flees to her cousin's apartment, never to return to Whitegates.

Wharton's biographers, Lewis and Wolff, agree that Edith Wharton had reached Eriksonian "integrity" by the end of her life. But Erlich contends that the terror and fear of helplessness depicted in "All Souls" indicates that the author could not sustain that state in the face of old age, illness, collapsing competence, deaths of friends, and the "terror of entering alone and uncomforted into the unknown" (170).

In one the few readings of "Afterward," Janet Ruth Heller (1993) insists that the story is not melodramatic, as others have implied. Instead it is "a psychological study about the emotional alienation of a husband and his wife" (18). "Afterward" gets its title from a quip in the story by Alida Stair, a friend of the Boynes, the protagonist American couple to whom she rents an old English country house. When Mary Boyne jokingly insists that a truly charming house must include a ghost, her friend answers, "Oh, there is one, of course, but you'll never know it. . . . not till afterward" (GS 49). According to Heller, the ghost is not related to the history of the old house as is traditional but represents marital estrangement. Ned is haunted by dishonest business dealings and by deceiving his wife about them. Mary's gradual realization of the truth numbs her and reduces her worship of her husband to tolerant affection. One day while Ned is working on the house, a shadowy figure approaches him, then disappears, but Ned's answers to Mary's inquiries are vague. When the figure returns, both disappear. Mary realizes—afterward—that she had seen the shadow of a ghost.

In quite a different story, "The Looking Glass," Sherrie Inness (1993) finds Mrs. Clingsland a victim of the complex economy of the "beauty system." Inness suggests that Mrs. Clingsland has defined her self-worth by her beauty, which is rapidly fading with age. In the story, Mrs. Atlee, a masseuse, tells her granddaughter about her client, Mrs. Clingsland, to whom she did a great wrong. When the mirror begins to reveal age, a younger man's silent attention lifts Mrs. Clingsland's spirits. Unfortunately, he goes down with the Titanic. Mrs. Clingsland falls prey to fortune tellers in her zeal for a message from her drowned lover. The uneducated Mrs. Atlee decides to save her from the fortunetellers by convincing a dying "ghost writer" to compose love letters from "the beyond." The letters never quite satisfy Mrs. Clingsland, but after the man dies, the semiliterate Mrs. Atlee finds the perfect letter under his bed.

Elizabeth Sweeney (1995) examines this story with respect to the woman as an object of the erotic male gaze. Mrs. Clingsland depends on recognition of her beauty by the male's desiring glance because she has never progressed beyond Lacan's childhood "mirror stage." She finds the ideal male gaze in the "man struck dumb" by her beauty: her drowned lover. Since beauty can be constituted only by the desiring "male gaze," Mrs. Clingsland's masseuse tries to help her by pretending to summon a revitalizing male gaze from beyond, but she cannot sustain the illusion. Sweeney further speculates that Wharton's frequent use of the word "reflect" may indicate her own narrative technique of using the "reflecting consciousness" of Mrs. Atlee.

Confined settings such as locked rooms, libraries, parlors, and variations of cold produce what, in her preface to *Ghosts*, Wharton termed the "thermometric chill." Evelyn E. Fracasso (1994) pairs early stories with late stories of the same theme, such as "The Lady's Maid's Bell" and "Mr. Jones," in which abusive husbands imprison and maltreat their wives; and "Afterward" with "Pomegranate Seed," to emphasize Wharton's technique of handling the imprisonment theme. In "Afterward" the ghost spirits the husband away once his "painful shortcomings" are revealed. In "Pomegranate Seed," the husband also disappears, presumably to join his first wife in the "underworld." To Fracasso, Edith Wharton's ghost stories alternate periods of terror and tranquillity until an "inescapable symbolic truth" reveals itself, serving either to allow the women to understand or, in some cases, to escape the prison of their fearsome ghosts. Martha Banta (1994) argues that Wharton repositions the Gothic in the modern world in stories such as "Afterward" (and *Ethan Frome*). Banta attempts to demonstrate that by placing the Boynes in the context of Walter Benjamin's studies of "Ethnographic Surrealism," changes in perceptions of reality occur when a character goes through a door or crosses a threshold. People learn "afterward" that they have experienced "disequilibriuim," a ghostly questioning of reality.

In terms of reality, "Miss Mary Pask" seems an odd story, which may be the reason it has attracted so little commentary. The story involves a bachelor visiting in Brittany, who recalls that the sister of a friend, Miss Mary Pask, lives nearby. So he drives through a foggy evening to visit her. As he arrives, he recalls a telegram announcing the woman's death. However, Miss Mary Pask appears, a wraith-like creature who pitifully begs him to stay and relieve her loneliness. Her pathetic entreaty also seems an appeal for a sexual liaison. This terrifies the narrator, who summarily bolts. Eventually he visits Mary's sister, Grace, and relays the story, only to learn that Mary had not died but had fallen into a trance. Suddenly, without explanation, the narrator dismisses all further interest in Miss Pask.

Jennice G. Thomas (1991) reads the story from a strong feminist point of view, based on a quotation from Mary Daly's *Gyn/Ecology:* "Faced with being spooked, Spinsters are learning to Spook/Speak back. . . . Tactically, Spooking means learning to refuse the seductive summons by the Passive Voices that call us into the state of Animated Death" (108). Thomas uses the Spook/Spinster idea to read the story as "Wharton's protest against a world in which women must be perceived as dead in order to escape masculine scorn and claim an empowering autonomy" (114). Miss Pask's choice of reclusive spinsterhood "spooks the patriarchy," forcing scornful masculinity to retreat, so she wins "empowering autonomy."

Fedorko (1995) argues that the narrator's dismissal of Miss Pask shows how he ultimately cannot accept femininity, ghostly or real. Fedorko believes that Wharton's general theme is men's fear of female sexuality. In "Bewitched," Fedorko argues that the narrator, Orrin Bosworth, is aware that the "forbidden mystery" of the ghost with whom Saul Rutledge is carrying on an affair involves the story of women's lives and the male power that restrains their female power. The threat of female sexuality is represented by the daughters of Sylvester Brand, murdered by "the powerful phallic revolver" (7).

Jenni Dyman (1996) draws upon Blake Nevius's phrase, "lurking feminism," as a theme for reading Wharton's collection (178). Dyman sees this theme as an expansion of Wharton's subject of "trapped sensibility" (xvi) and as a prediction of late-twentieth century thought patterns. Dyman feels that Wharton uses the ghost story to explore the status of gender roles, relationships, marriages, communication patterns, creativity, and sexuality. Wharton wrote within a male literary tradition, but relied on the extensive symbolism of the supernatural tradition. In doing so she found a rich idiom for subtextual expression of feminist concerns. Besides gender roles, among her concerns are society's restriction of the individual, and repressive and victimizing cultural codes including those regarding marriage. The consequences are the disasters of cruelty, violence and madness, problems with communication, distribution of power, and sexuality. Considering Wharton as writing "feminist themes," Dyman combines the "wild zone" of the Gothic with the "wild zone" of women's culture (4). Wharton achieves a "vision of the brutal domination of patriarchal and capitalistic codes in western cultures, the debilitating limitations of cultural gender identity, and the blindness and suffering of men and women, both victims of restrictive social conventions" (7). Dyman concludes that Wharton longs for a new social order (179). "Unfortunately, Wharton did not achieve 'rebirth of the psyche' for her characters or fully for herself, but she did express and embody hope for women in the appropriation of language and finding voice, expatriation, and independence," so that women might prosper by cooperation rather than competition. Her ghost stories "objectified her terrors . . . to exorcise her intuitions and fears," and they "endure as a testimony of her feminist sensibility" (180).

Edith Wharton's ghost stories certainly do—and will—endure. Of course, some must be better than others. "The Eyes" and "All Souls" seemed predominately the choice of reviewers and critics until the early eighties. Feminist scrutiny then turned primarily to "Pomegranate Seed" and "The Lady's Maid's Bell," and although attention to "All

Souls" never wavered, in quantity criticism appears less than the story warrants. The neglect of certain stories such as "Bewitched" and "The Triumph of Night" may have more to do with literary critical trends than the quality of the stories. Neither, for instance, provides much opportunity for critics to posit the author's anxiety about silenced or otherwise distressed or imprisoned womanhood, ambivalence about writing, mothers, money, or servants, about "patriarchal and capitalistic codes," or "cultural gender identity." These rustic stories, generally dismissed as "Hawthornian," present little upon which to base psychological or biographical assumptions, or even the "desire of the text" to create a new social order.

Finally, unstated assumptions concerning Edith Wharton's ideas about herself and others cast doubt even on otherwise superb critical essays, for it is important to consider that any feminist concepts Edith Wharton may have applied must be taken in the context of her times— possibly even the stage of life during which she wrote a particular work.

Works Consulted

B., W. R. "The New Books." Rev. of *Ghosts* by Edith Wharton. *Saturday Review* 17 (6 November 1937): 19.

Balestra, Gianfranca. "'For the Use of the Magazine Morons': Edith Wharton Rewrites the Tale of the Fantastic." *Studies in Short Fiction* 33.1 (Winter 1996): 13–25.

Banta, Martha. "The Ghostly Gothic of Wharton's Everyday World." *American Literary Realism* 27.1 (Fall 1994): 1–10.

Bendixen, Alfred. "Introduction." *Haunted Women: The Best Supernatural Tales by American Women Writers.* New York: Ungar, 1985.

Blum, Virginia L. "Edith Wharton's Erotic Other-World." *Literature and Psychology* 33.1 (1987): 12–29.

"Briefer Mention." Rev. of *Ghosts* by Edith Wharton. *Commonweal* 27 (5 November 1937): 55.

Daly, Mary. *Gyn/Ecology: The Metaethics of Radical Feminism.* Boston, MA: Beacon P. 1978.

Dyman, Jenni. *Lurking Feminism: The Ghost Stories of Edith Wharton.* New York: Peter Lang, 1996.

Edel, Leon. *Stuff of Sleep and Dreams: Experiments in Literary Psychology.* New York: Harper & Row, 1982. 36–41.

Elbert, Monika. "The Transcendental Economy of Wharton's Gothic Mansions." *American Transcendental Quarterly* 9.1 (March 1991): 51–61.

Erlich, Gloria C. *The Sexual Education of Edith Wharton.* Berkeley, CA: U of California P, 1992. 43, 48; 167–70.

Fedorko, Kathy A. "Edith Wharton's Haunted Fiction: 'The Lady's Maid's Bell' and *The House of Mirth.*" *Haunting the House of Fiction: Feminist Perspectives on Ghost Stories by American Women.* Eds. Lynette Carpenter and Wendy K. Kolmar. Knoxville, TN: U of Tennessee P, 1991. 80–107.

———. *The Gothic in the Fiction of Edith Wharton.* Tuscaloosa, AL: U of Alabama P, 1995.

Fracasso, Evelyn E. *Edith Wharton's Prisoners of Consciousness.* Westport: Greenwood P, 1994.

"Ghosts and Ghost Stories." Rev. of *Ghosts* by Edith Wharton. *Times Literary Supplement* [England] (6 November 1937): 823.

Greene, Graham. "Short Stories." Rev. of *Ghosts* by Edith Wharton. *Spectator* [England] 154 (24 December 1937): 1155.

Heller, Janet Ruth. "Ghosts and Marital Estrangement: An Analysis of 'Afterward.'" *Edith Wharton Review* 10.1 (Spring 1993): 18–19.

Inness, Sherrie A. "An Economy of Beauty: The Beauty System in 'The Looking Glass' and 'Permanent Wave.'" *Edith Wharton Review* 10.1 (Spring 1993): 7–11.

Killoran, Helen. "Pascal, Brontë, and 'Kerfol': The Horrors of a Foolish Quarrel" (misprinted as "Quartet"). *Edith Wharton Review* 10.1 (Spring 1993): 12–17.

———. "Sexuality and Abnormal Psychology in Edith Wharton's 'The Lady's Maid's Bell.'" *CEA Critic* 58.3 (Spring-Summer 1996): 41–49.

Lawson, Richard H. "Edith Wharton." *Dictionary of Literary Biography.* 78 *American Short Story Writers 1880–1910.* Detroit, MI: Bruccoli Clark, 1989. 308–23.

———. *Edith Wharton.* 1977. New York: Ungar, 1984.

L'Enfant, Julie. "Edith Wharton: Room With a View." *The Southern Review* 12.2 (April 1976): 398–406.

Lewis, R. W. B. "Introduction." *The Collected Short Stories of Edith Wharton.* New York: Scribners, 1968.

———. "Powers of Darkness." Rev. of *The Ghost Stories of Edith Wharton* by Edith Wharton. *Times Literary Supplement* (13 June 1975): 644.

McDowell, Margaret B. *Edith Wharton.* 1976. Boston: G. K. Hall. Revised 1991.

———. "Edith Wharton's Ghost Stories." *Criticism* 12 (1970): 133–52.

———. "Edith Wharton's Ghost Tales Reconsidered." *Edith Wharton: New Critical Essays.* Eds. Alfred Bendixen and Annette Zilversmit. New York: Garland, 1992. 291–314.

Murray, Margaret P. "The Gothic Arsenal of Edith Wharton." *Journal of Evolutionary Psychology* 10.2–3 (August 1989): 315–21.

Nevius, Blake. *Edith Wharton: A Study of her Fiction*. 1953. Berkeley, CA: U of California P, 1961. 94–98.

Plante, Patricia R. "Edith Wharton as a Short Story Writer." *Midwest Quarterly* 4 (Summer 1963): 363–70.

Robillard, Douglas. "Edith Wharton." *Supernatural Fiction Writers*. Vol. 2. Ed. E. F. Bleiler. New York: Scribners, 1984. 783–88.

Scarborough, Dorothy. *The Supernatural in Modern English Fiction*. New York: G. P. Putnam's Sons, 1917.

Shawe-Taylor, Desmond. "New Novels." Rev. of *Ghosts* by Edith Wharton. *New Statesman and Nation* n.s. 14 (6 November 1937): 758. Rpt. New York: Appleton, 1937.

Singley, Carol J. "Gothic Borrowings and Invocations in Edith Wharton's 'A Bottle of Perrier.'" *Edith Wharton: New Critical Essays*. Eds. Alfred Bendixen and Annette Zilversmit. New York: Garland, 1992. 271–90.

Singley, Carol J. and Susan Elizabeth Sweeney, eds. "Forbidden Reading and Ghostly Writing in Edith Wharton's 'Pomegranate Seed.'" *Anxious Power: Reading, Writing, and Ambivalence in Narrative by Women*. New York: State U of New York P, 1993. 197–217.

Smith, Allan Gardner. "Edith Wharton and the Ghost Story." *Gender and Literary Voice*. Ed. Janet Todd. New York: Holmes and Meier, 1980. 149–58. Rpt. *Modern Critical Reviews: Edith Wharton*. Ed. Harold Bloom. New York: Chelsea House, 1986. 89–97.

Stengel, Ellen Powers. "Edith Wharton Rings 'The Lady's Maid's Bell.'" *Edith Wharton Review* 7.1 (Spring 1990): 3–9.

Sweeney, Susan Elizabeth. "Mirror, Mirror, on the Wall: Gazing in Edith Wharton's 'Looking Glass.'" *Narrative* 3.2 (May 1995): 139–60.

Thomas, Jennice G. "Spook or Spinster? Edith Wharton's 'Miss Mary Pask.'" *Haunting the House of Fiction: Feminist Perspectives on Ghost Stories by American Women*. Eds. Lynette Carpenter and Wendy K. Kolmar. Knoxville, TN: U of Tennessee P, 1991.

Tuttleton, James W., Kristin O. Lauer and Margaret P. Murray. *Edith Wharton: The Contemporary Reviews*. New York: Cambridge UP, 1992.

Waid, Candace. *Edith Wharton's Letters from the Underworld: Fictions of Women and Writing*. Chapel Hill, NC: U of North Carolina P, 1991. 17–21, 177–92, 194–95, 228.

Wharton, Edith. *Ghosts*. New York: Appleton-Century, 1937.

———. *The Ghost Stories of Edith Wharton*. New York: Scribners, 1973.

White, Barbara A. *Edith Wharton: A Study of the Short Fiction.* New York: G. K. Hall, 1991.

Wilson-Jordan, Jacqueline S. "Telling the Story That Can't Be Told: Hartley's Role as Dis-Eased Narrator in 'The Lady's Maid's Bell.'" *Edith Wharton Review* 14.1 (Spring 1997): 12–17, 21.

Woollcott, Alexander. *Woollcott's Second Reader.* New York: Viking P, 1937.

Young, Judy. "The Repudiation of Sisterhood in Edith Wharton's 'Pomegranate Seed.'" *Studies in Short Fiction* 33 (1996): 1–11.

Zilversmit, Annette. "Edith Wharton's Last Ghosts." *College Literature* 14.3 (1987): 296–305.

———. "'All Souls': Wharton's Last Haunted House and Future Directions for Criticism." *Edith Wharton: New Critical Essays.* Eds. Alfred Bendixen and Annette Zilversmit. New York: Garland, 1992. 315–29.

8: Review—Further Sources

GIVEN THAT EDITH WHARTON did not begin publishing until her late thirties, her output was prolific. Her literary production comprised some forty-five books, including novels, collections of short stories, poetry, and reviews, translations, and books on interiors, gardens, travel and other non-fiction, including war correspondence. Because of space limitations, this volume has featured only the fiction that has aroused the most interest, but these include only three novels, two novellas (*Ethan Frome* and *Summer*), and one collection of short stories.

From the beginning Wharton's work was well received. Even those reviewers and critics who could not praise content, plot, or characters usually praised her impeccable structure and craftsmanship. After the advent of New Criticism in the forties critics had more verbal tools than those of emotion and opinion available with which to analyze what they read. They could discuss structure, imagery, alliteration, and other poetic techniques, making themselves generally understood. Whatever a person thinks of the New Criticism, whether it is "dead" or not, it works at least on that level.

The vocabulary of New Criticism further made possible the great leaps in critical energy that have since occurred. Because of the Second World War and the codicil to her will denying scholars access to her papers, criticism on Edith Wharton's writing was in abeyance during the height of the New Critical trend in the forties. Critics of the twenties preferred male psychological writing, and those of the thirties were largely still convinced of the diminishment of Wharton's skills. The forties was the period during which the *avante garde* used the New Criticism, though much criticism was retarded by the Second World War. But as Killoran's reading of "Xingu" suggests, Edith Wharton was already fully aware of New Criticism, although she might not have called it by that name. The fifties saw the beginning of a resurgence of Wharton criticism. For the most part, the social values in the universities in the sixties clashed with the values that Edith Wharton represented. The "new" feminists of the seventies began to reexamine Edith Wharton as a "woman writer." Since then, most criticism written about her incorporates feminism, but much has expanded into French philosophical, "grammatological," sociological, economic, anthropological, and other critical theories. Most theories study the society in which

Wharton wrote as its context and reads her work as an example of how the theory in question works in that culture.

But *The House of Mirth* has attracted more attention than any other work of Edith Wharton's fiction. During her lifetime, critics tended to compare much of her other work to it, but when the novel was reissued in paperback in 1962, it became easily available to students and teachers, so criticism increased greatly in spite of the political situation. Much of the subsequent criticism focused on genre. Critics seemed determined to define *The House of Mirth* as a combination of the novel of manners and naturalism, so at the time Edith Wharton was much compared to Theodore Dreiser. Later, feminist and Marxist economic criticism produced the most frequent readings of the novel, although almost every type of criticism has been attempted.

Like *The House of Mirth, Ethan Frome* has been declared a classic. At first critics assumed it to have been modeled on a Greek tragedy, but found it too grim and cruel to be successful in that way. It had no moral value according to Lionel Trilling, whose pronouncement alone was enough to remove it from the consideration of serious critics for many years. In addition, various early critics insisted that Edith Wharton had no knowledge of New England, the setting of *Ethan Frome* and *Summer*. Questions continue as to whether *Ethan Frome* qualifies as a "masterpiece," or as leftist social critique, how it is influenced by landscape (local color and regionalist), and how much the strict, Puritan minds of New Englanders might be evident in the novel. And as yet no one has found a credible reason for the story's ghost-like horror.

Just as Satan stole Milton's *Paradise Lost*, Undine's ambitious, ruthless, but glittering character stole the plot of *The Custom of the Country*. The subject of greed lends itself well to Marxist-economic approaches, and moral didacticism about social climbing and divorce often offered easy comparisons with *The House of Mirth*. Eventually the literary historical critics' discovery of the author's knowledge of the historical background of rapid social change that could produce such a novel alerted critics, or should have, to her broad knowledge of other subjects.

Edith Jones's French divorce from Edward Wharton in 1913, the year the novel appeared. Not likely a coincidence, it diverted readers' attention. Feminist and biographical critics especially have found much to draw upon in that. In the seventies and eighties feminists began to study the novel as a satire, as drawn from female rage, as about marriage and divorce as business contracts, sex as meaningless barter, and as about sexual energy transformed into money. In 1980 Elizabeth Ammons attempted to place it in the new canon of women's writing, and in the later eighties and nineties various "deconstructions" of Undine's identity, and of patriarchal discourse, were attempted. Topics have lately circled back to the subjects of marriage for power, the "art of the deal," the woman writer, and art versus business. But the amount of space occupied by theoretical analyses distorts the sense of the criticism, implying that all of the novel is about social issues, or the author's gender, or the language of gender, or psychological development under the repression of the patriarchy or reification. Little about history, psychology (other than the Lacanian sort), morals, or art has been studied. Yet some of the criticism does reflect the historical changes in American economic and geographical movement. Strikingly, however, many of Wharton's characters, rather than moving west to confront the frontier, move east to chase quick riches—nomads and conquerors who build nothing but destroy everything in pursuit of wealth. The entire topic of the rootless American throughout Wharton's fiction has never been explained satisfactorily.

Reviewers criticized Edith Wharton for writing only about the upper classes, and whether in response to that or not, she wrote *Ethan Frome* and *Summer*. Feminists find her personal contemporary sexual biography somehow reflected in *Summer* (1918), or decide that the novel reflects Edith Wharton's sexual initiation, though her sexual initiation occurred in her forties and Charity is young. However, like *Ethan Frome* and the ghost stories, *Summer* remains rich material for exploration, as does *The Age of Innocence*.

The huge family of old New York and Edith Wharton's use of words and phrases like "tribe" and "totem terrors" sprinkled throughout *The Age of Innocence* naturally invites anthropological criticism, but to what end has been somewhat fogged by obtuse language. The subjects of language and communication have drawn much consideration and the concepts of drama and stage settings have been addressed to some extent by Wolff and others.

Of Edith Wharton's ghost stories, "The Eyes" and "All Souls" were by far the first choice of reviewers and critics for the "best" of these stories. In the early eighties feminist scrutiny then turned primarily to "Pomegranate Seed" and "The Lady's Maid's Bell," while quiet respect for "All Souls" never wavered. The neglect of certain stories such as "Bewitched" and "The Triumph of Night" may have more to do with literary critical trends than the quality of these stories. Further, like *Ethan Frome* and *Summer*, they cannot remotely invite comparisons to Henry James.

A Last Word About Henry James

Naturally it's absurd to insist that Henry James *never* influenced Edith Wharton because certainty is impossible and examples like Adeline Tintner's add several shades of doubt. The primary objections here are to lack of logic and condemnation by association. For example, here is an offering from a book on American literature by Irene and Allen Cleaton (1937). "Always slightly missing greatness, save with *Ethan Frome*, [Edith Wharton] has contributed a distinguished shelf of books to American Literature—books that are always well-bred and which never fail to reveal her high admiration of Henry James . . ." (249). No explanation. The following quotation from Edward O'Brien (1923) performs similar sleight-of-hand: "Edith Wharton . . . [is] so far the most representative disciple [of the School of Henry James]. The distinction of her stories is as evident as their Arctic frigidity. She has assimilated every lesson that her master can teach except tenderness and ease, and in sheer craftsmanship it may even be held that she has occasionally surpassed him" (202–203). After discussing how Wharton's characters are dry and gray and never grow (no examples offered) he concludes that, "Mrs. Wharton has psychological as well as social standards, subtle insight into the causes behind appearances, faultless decorum, and a wide acquaintance with the masters of her art. . . .To sum up, her collected short stories form a superb *pastiche* of Henry James with little added" (205). He cites no support for his opinion.

Refreshingly, Lynne T. Hanley (1981) contrasts Henry James and Edith Wharton in a most illuminating manner. Referring primarily to the Lubbock edition of James's Letters and Wharton's *A Backward Glance*, she describes the inception of their friendship, and the flavor of the interaction between them that beams through the fun and drama of James's delightful letters. Her analysis begins with James's personal passivity contrasted to Wharton's personal activity, qualities of energy that emerge from their work:

> Fixed on the possibilities of freedom [James] overlooked, [Wharton] thought, the pressures of circumstance and history. . . . Passing time is a crucial force in Wharton's fiction, an essential motivation, while James suspends time in order to arrest the object of his attention. . . . Such extreme refinement of consciousness, Wharton believed, neglected "the desultoriness, the irregularity, of life caught in the act, and pressed still throbbing between the leaves of the book. . . ." She is the "glorious pendulum," he a "stopped clock." (147)

The essay shows how, consciously or not, James anticipated the elevation of science to which the New Critics reacted: "James's mathe-

matical analogies stress the primacy of logic and structure in his production of fictions. Aping the scientist, he observes, takes notes, then
selects . . . his postulate, 'life being all inclusion and confusion, and art
being all discrimination and selection'" (148). One way in which James
and Wharton *were* alike was in their logic and ability to create complex
patterns—in Wharton's case, some invisible. And critics have yet to appreciate Wharton's combined sense of literary history and order and
pattern-making, and how the fact of that pattern-making can reveal
hidden ideas that could change our impression of an author.

The James and anti-James camps of the twenties and thirties exer-
cised political agendas in making their comparisons. As Millicent Bell
puts it so colorfully, Edith Wharton "was used as a paddle with which
to spank [Henry James]" (4). Her 1965 *Edith Wharton and Henry
James: The Story of Their Friendship* should not be missed. Recent critics, however, have thankfully dropped the attempt to compare the two,
differences in prose style becoming more apparent as critics examine
their writing more objectively.

Yet there is an important, well-respected exception. Adeline Tintner
has written innumerable notes and essays comparing Edith Wharton to
Henry James, often finding in the texts of the novels or stories, places
where she feels that Edith Wharton has borrowed from him. To offer
one example, in "Wharton and James: Some Literary Give and Take,"
she discusses a number of short stories, in particular "The Angel at the
Grave," "The Recovery," "Copy," "The Moving Finger," and *The
Touchstone*. Tintner notes plot similarities between "The Birthplace" by
James and "The Angel at the Grave" by Wharton: both stories discuss a
person left in charge of the birthplace of a famous author. Tintner feels
James "rewrote the story 'in [his] own way'" (3). "The Recovery" was
based on James's "The Tree of Knowledge" and "borrowed, to redo
[Wharton's] way" (4), and so on with the other stories. She notes that
possibly "it was in both of them an appetency for devouring anything
which could further the machinery of their narratives" (5). In a recent
volume of essays (1999) Tintner finds the authors writing about one
another in fictional disguise, Edith Wharton borrowing James's structure in *The Age of Innocence*, both employing similar themes, such as
"bad" mothers and daughters, and Wharton taking some of her titles
from the texts of James's novels. Tintner has found too many such
items to dismiss them as mere coincidence—and indeed, she concludes
with the proposal that Edith Wharton and Henry James may have been
playing "a conscious game." Potentially she has struck upon the answer: Henry James and Edith Wharton, helpless against the critics,
could well have been playing jokes at their expense.

Neglected Fiction

Some of Wharton's fiction has been critically unmined for a number of reasons. Often this work has been dismissed on grounds that since it was best-selling fiction, it could not have much literary value. But Edith Wharton's novels were always best-sellers. Not only did the most obscure of her novels and stories sell well, but so did *The House of Mirth*. At least on the surface, that argument fails.

The Touchstone (1900), a work about which very little has been written, contains an eerie precognition. A woman who becomes a famous author sends love letters to a man who, well, *almost* loved her. The moral dilemma concerns his sale of the letters after her death to support his new wife. It seems almost as if Edith Wharton predicted her affair, ten years later, with Morton Fullerton, who refused to return her love letters in spite of repeated requests. Fullerton did not personally sell them but, as a writer himself, he most probably recognized their value. He left them to his son, who did sell them, making public the most private part of this private woman's life, the ultimate humiliation. To be fair, much exists in literary history upon which Wharton might have drawn for such a story. Indeed, Adeline Tintner might say that she was inspired by James's "The Aspern Papers," based on the history of the Shelley and Byron papers (Edel 337).

Unlike *The Touchstone*, the main difficulty with *The Valley of Decision* (1902) is its stiff, unemotional characters. Wharton's background research on eighteenth-century Italian literature, history, and geography, to say nothing of costume and interiors, was extensive and impeccable. For the most part, although the novel was received enthusiastically at the time, and sold reasonably well, it has since remained almost untouched. However, it is probably fertile ground for people with parallel interests in Edith Wharton and Italian literature and culture.

Another novella that has scarcely been touched is *Sanctuary* (1903). Kate Orme decides to marry a man who has what she believes to be an inherited character flaw, then devotes her life to protecting her son from developing or acting on this same flaw. The first reviewers found it anywhere from deeply moving to irritating for its presumably nonsensical philosophical phrases. *Madame de Treymes* (1907), on the other hand, was automatically assumed to have been too close a copy of Henry James's *Madame de Mauves*, but anyone who has read both will barely find superficial similarities. These "French" novels, like *The Valley of Decision*, invite examination by comparative literature specialists who have knowledge of French and Italian history, religion, and culture.

The Fruit of the Tree (1907) proved controversial on two main points. One point concerned its subject of euthanasia, which people found too disturbing. The other point of contention was the charge that Edith Wharton had not fully understood the process of manufacturing in the mills she describes, and consequently made a number of mistakes that created flaws in its realism. Lewis suggests that when Wharton toured the mills while preparing to write the novel, the noise was so great that she misunderstood or could not hear all that was described to her. Another novel, *The Reef* (1912), has troubled general readers and critics alike because of its frustratingly indeterminate ending, but it has drawn some critical efforts, a few of which have been mentioned here in other contexts.

The fact that war is a depressing topic may account for the dearth of interest in *The Marne* (1918) and *A Son at the Front* (1923). Contemporary responses included the wonder that Edith Wharton had bothered to write war stories after the flourish of the genre's popularity had waned. Another possibility is that modern readers tend to ignore the First World War as outdated. However the outdated, proud, and terrified parents featured in both stories act the same as modern proud and terrified parents sending sons and daughters to wars all over the world. Worth pursuing are Alan Price's readings of these and other war stories in the context of Edith Wharton's war work and her personal experiences with young friends and relatives fighting and dying in Europe. Several general essays dealing with three or more of the war stories have appeared, all good efforts, but their loneliness in the bibliographies strongly suggests future possibilities.

In contrast, *The Glimpses of the Moon* (1923) is considered featherweight popular fiction. However, as in *Sanctuary*, hints of philosophical issues could bear fruit for the alert critic. *Old New York* (1924), consisting of four novellas, has been largely ignored. Only a small book by Catherine M. Rae (1984) studies the complete set: "False Dawn," "The Old Maid," "The Spark," and "New Year's Day." The few critics who have written about *Old New York* have confined their work to one or another of the four parts, but Wharton must have meant it in some way to be read as a unit.

As to *The Mother's Recompense* (1925), early reviews were mixed but more positive than not. The novel was described as everything from the best story Wharton ever wrote, to a melodramatic failure, to a sympathetic study of people it is hard to like. Reviewers noted her detachment from what they called a soul tragedy, but more positive comments compared Edith Wharton not only to Henry James, but to Galsworthy. She was praised for consummate art; the novel was called both her best, and her best since *The House of Mirth*. Critics even compared Kate Clephane to Lily Bart. What stands out is that many of the early reviews read much like those of *Ethan Frome*. The novel is too tragic, a moral torture, something the reader must endure, and it goes to the height of tragedy and stays there for no apparent reason, making it too painful and too cruel. Some feminist literature has been devoted to it, but for the most part it falls into the "neglected" column.

Also neglected, *Twilight Sleep* (1927) has been dismissed as light fare in much the same category as *The Glimpses of the Moon*. To them it is a frivolous novel about frivolous people involved in the frivolous fads of the 1920s. Yet the problem in the story is so severe that the Manford family is on the verge of disintegration from affairs, drug use, child neglect, and other self-destructive behavior that the fads are designed to disguise. Most critics, though, have felt that Edith Wharton sold her artistic soul for cash, and that the novel was merely intended as a money-maker. But so were *The Age of Innocence* and *Ethan Frome*.

The Children (1928) focuses again on divorce, this time as it affects children who are separated from one and often both parents since the parents are away playing in the Riviera. They become step-children, having a complete melange of half-brothers and half-sisters as well as siblings unrelated by blood. A group of such children are discovered traveling alone by Martin Boyne, a friend of one of the parents, who becomes attached to them. He pledges to find a way for all of them to stay together in spite of their variously split families, and Edith Wharton creates a great deal of sympathy for Boyne's attachment to the eldest, a fifteen-year-old girl. A recent search of the MLA on-line bibliography produced no recent criticism on this novel, although a search through the indexes of books about Edith Wharton will reveal that several spend from a few paragraphs to a chapter on this and a few of the other novels mentioned here. The apparent assumption that these books are merely "drugstore novels" could be productively challenged. Granted, Edith Wharton's inheritance was small, and that the Great Depression and personal charities had depleted her funds. Still, if people were to assume that Edith Wharton had too much professional pride to release anything she thought artistically inferior, a block might be removed that would result in further interest in novels like *The Children* and *Twilight Sleep*.

Unlike them, *Hudson River Bracketed* (1929) and its sequel, *The Gods Arrive* (1932), have largely been dismissed as Edith Wharton's failed literary autobiography. Since the protagonist writer is male, various critics have taken an assortment of positions on gender confusion, but only one has addressed the extent to which the novels are a negative critique of American education. Once again, Edith Wharton chose a topic on the lips of almost every politician in almost every election. Her ability to choose timeless topics is only one of the many strengths of her work.

Early reviewers loved what might now be considered the most sentimental scene in *Hudson River Bracketed*, the death of Vance Weston's wife, Laura Lou. One of Wharton's points about Vance's marriage to Laura Lou was undoubtedly that it takes a child to marry one, a marker as to how much living, learning, and maturing Vance would need before he could possess the materials from which to create great literary art. On the other hand, in *The Gods Arrive*, when Vance begins to develop as an artist, some reviewers objected to the "boring" discussions of art and literature, those objections inadvertently revealing not only one reason Edith Wharton escaped to Europe, but a subject for the critic to explore.

All in all, much of interest remains to be discovered by the critic willing to venture from theoretical maps into personally charted territory. The *roman à clef* aspects of *The House of Mirth* and especially *The Age of Innocence* have been discussed, but no one has worked out the entire key. Religious and regionalist considerations are re-emerging, this time tied to feminist ideals. And since interdisciplinary dissertations are on the rise, readers may soon find interdisciplinary interpretations of Wharton's work in the journals.

Other Voices

Some short essays have appeared in the last ten years reviewing the criticism from one or another point of view, or suggesting future directions for Wharton scholarship. Katherine Joslin (1991) focuses her analysis of the critical writing on feminist criticism. Her essay includes a particularly full account of the reasons for treating the Lubbock biography with the caution due an unreliable author. (In fact, it supplements her informative earlier essay, "What Lubbock Didn't Say" [1984].) She emphasizes the complaints among early critics that Wharton was too pessimistic and that she "lacked the vocabulary of happiness," as Irving Howe put it in the introduction to his essay collection. Joslin further suspects that some of the negativity about Wharton was caused by prejudice against her advancing age. Further, she draws on Cynthia Ozick's essay to emphasize another early prejudice against women: the absurdity that women can write well only in times of emotional distress.

She also points out most strongly that since the revelations in the Lewis biography and later those contained in the Wharton-Fullerton love letters, "inquisitiveness about personal, especially sexual, matters characterizes much of the direction of biographical criticism in recent years" (134). What she does not say is that except where direct evidence exists, it may be time to put these largely subjective topics in perspective, the evidence that Edith Wharton experienced passion that she could apply to her writing having been well and voluminously made. Yet another prejudice against Edith Wharton, according to Joslin, was that "male critics have tended to see her as the best writer in a fairly fallow field of writers at the beginning of the twentieth century" (138), all of whom wrote in too narrow a range. Joslin implies that the view of Wharton as a modernist and the "battle line" over the control of the study of her work have been drawn by powerful men in the academic establishment.

Shari Benstock's introduction to the Bedford Critical Edition of *The House of Mirth* (1994) is strong in lesser-known European reviews and the backgrounds of modern critical theory. She categorizes biographies more broadly than most. The introduction presents critical essays in Marxism, deconstruction, psychology, and other theories, most with feminist assumptions. And Annette Zilversmit (1992) offers suggestions that should not be lightly dismissed. Primarily, she encourages new psychological readings of Edith Wharton's work: "I believe that Wharton criticism needs to move out of the house of feminist protest, where society is always male dominated and female suffering is mostly male inflicted, to . . . the wildness within, that world of nature our own deepest nature where men sense abandon and madness and women fear rejection and self-disgust" (326). "I am urging that we see Wharton . . . as a psychological novelist whose fictional portraits capture fragile, wounded, and doomed women" (327). She recommends also that Wharton's characters be understood not simply as representations of all women but as individuals "whose precarious self-esteem has erupted into narratives of flight and self-defeat" (326). She would like to reclaim their "buried texts, these alienated, tabooed, even most disagreeable desires and feelings and yield up through our critical writings full and complex portraits of the real women in Edith Wharton's oeuvre" (326). Furthermore, while some work has been done on the house as setting in Edith Wharton's writing, especially *The House of Mirth* and *The Age of Innocence*, Annette Zilversmit feels that we should look more closely: "[T]hink again of Wharton's American houses, particularly of the Mount and its fictional counterpart in 'All Souls,' Whitegates" (327).

Another well-known critic, Linda Wagner-Martin, in an essay on "Prospects for the Study of Edith Wharton" (1996), also discusses some of the literary criticism and offers directions for further study. For the most part she dismisses early criticism, beginning her considerations with studies written after the publication of the Lewis and Wolff biographies. Her recommendations about work yet to be accomplished are most useful to graduate students or scholars new to Wharton criticism. She sees the need for several volumes of "retrospective critical essays" like Millicent Bell's, but containing six or seven decades of work. She would like print or on-line catalogues of the manuscript collections at Yale; The Harry Ransom Research Library at the University of Texas, Austin; the Lilly Library of the University of Indiana, Bloomington; the Firestone and Houghton libraries at Princeton; the Pusey Library at Harvard, and the collection, mostly of Bernard Berenson's letters from Edith Wharton, at the Villa I Tatti in Florence, Italy. (Yale's Beinecke Library does offer a printed catalogue.) While Wagner-Martin admires the Lewis and Lewis edition of *The Letters of Edith Wharton*, it is necessarily limited. More collections of letters would be universally welcome.

Furthermore, Wagner-Martin prefers "studies of Wharton's work using theories such as the newest feminist, psychoanalytic, and language-based 'narratological'" readings. She characterizes much Wharton criticism as New Critical, describing it as "myopic," and recommends the use of "more diverse" approaches, more comparisons across novels, for example, and more comparisons and contrasts of characters across different works. Wagner-Martin feels that those critics who treat Edith Wharton as "one of the boys," or who identify her male characters with the author, are quite mistaken, for to her mind criticism should be more "woman-centered." She praises the work of three critics who have written "wide ranging" work looking at "social, philosophical and medical issues, using Bakhtinian readings," or using "philosophical and biological theories of reproduction and eugenics" and other broadly intellectually based work (6). She also urges discussions of Edith Wharton in terms of modernism and feminist archetypal theory and more investigation of travel and memoirs. She recommends more on the writing read as a woman's text, more on Wharton and the literary marketplace, more on manuscripts, manuscript revision, film, the unpublished work, and the history of publication including the serialized novels. She also describes Edith Wharton as "plagued by issues of class, race, and sexuality," leading a "life more often disguised than transparent" (11). Ultimately, Wagner-Martin prefers criticism on the cutting edge of broadly based theory.

The quantity of authorial influences, both classical and popular, noted throughout the wide-ranging criticism, suggests compellingly that something interesting is happening in the Wharton novel that has not been adequately defined. Or was Edith Wharton alluding to literary and popular authors just for the sake of allusion, as one early critic insisted? Opportunities for further productive critical analysis of these and other Wharton works must be innumerable.

Finally, critics too frequently begin their arguments with unstated assumptions concerning Edith Wharton's ideas about herself and others, casting shadows of illogic over otherwise brilliant critical essays. Assumptions about Wharton's "feminism" have gradually modified since the seventies, thanks to common-sense approaches such as that by Julie Olin-Ammentorp, who recognizes that any feminist concepts Edith Wharton may have applied must be taken in the context of the times in which she lived.

Basic Tools for Wharton Scholars

This volume has been written primarily for the graduate student studying Wharton, but also for the established critic wishing to add Edith Wharton to another repertoire. It should be helpful, then, to provide a guide to the most useful basic bibliographical tools. First, the bibliographies are indispensable. The dependable annotated volume by Kristin O. Lauer and Margaret P. Murray updates that by Marlene Springer (1976) and another by James W. Tuttleton (1983), although Tuttleton's annotated bibliography is worth perusing anyway, for its shrewd, often outspoken comments. Since the Lauer-Murray bibliography ends at 1989, the scholar must then refer to bibliographical essays by Alfred Bendixen and Clare Colquitt in *The Edith Wharton Review* listed in the Works Consulted for this chapter. These can, and must, be supplemented by the annual MLA Bibliography available both in print and on-line in library data bases.

The most important biographies are those by R. W. B. Lewis (1975) and Cynthia Griffin Wolff (1977), well supplemented by Shari Benstock's fine life (1994). Benstock takes a different viewpoint on several important matters, so that scholars should compare the ideas of all three before embarking on a project. For an understanding of the friendship between Edith Wharton and Henry James, the volume by Millicent Bell is indispensable and enjoyable reading. In addition, Alan Price's close look at Edith Wharton's war work is essential and guaranteed to leave readers breathless. Finally, the first and most slippery biography by Lubbock benefits from studies of his editing of original

letters and manuscripts held by the Beinecke Rare Book and Manuscript Library at Yale. While fascinating, it must never be trusted. The
collection of some four hundred of Edith Wharton's letters selected by
R. W. B. and Nancy Lewis more than rounds out the biographies. Because Henry James burned most of his incoming letters, Lyall Powers's
collection of the James-Wharton correspondence offers only eight letters and post cards from Edith Wharton to Henry James. The remainder of this substantial volume is devoted to letters by Henry James to
Edith Wharton.

Other indispensable research volumes include *Edith Wharton: The
Contemporary Reviews* by Tuttleton, Lauer, and Murray. The beautifully edited *Edith Wharton: The Uncollected Critical Writings* containing endless useful information by Frederick Wegener can be most
helpful. Certain essay collections fill in the background of the criticism.
The collection edited by Irving Howe, then that edited by Bendixen
and Zilversmit, followed by the heavily theoretical collection edited by
Harold Bloom plot the direction of criticism from the fifties through
the nineties.

Those able to travel will find the greatest resources at The Beinecke
Research Library at Yale, which holds an enormous collection of letters
and papers useful to scholars. The Lilly Library at Indiana University
owns the collection of letters and other writings from the years just
before and after Edith Wharton's death—including notes by Elisina
Tyler for a proposed biography. The Harry Ransom Research Library at
the University of Texas, Austin, contains the collection of Edith
Wharton's love letters to Morton Fullerton, and the Firestone Library
at Princeton University holds Edith Wharton's business correspondence. Finally, The New York Public Library is the first source for information on her contemporaries.

A general consistency, then, can be demonstrated in the reception
of Edith Wharton's work over the last century, during her lifetime, and
during the following decades, up to *The Age of Innocence* published in
1920. Most of the work by Edith Wharton produced after that date has
been more or less uniformly dismissed because of its popularity with
the general public. By now the idea that Henry James was any kind of
mentor or influence should be nullified. The one exception could be in
the case of the discovery of any games or jokes between Edith Wharton
and Henry James in their fiction. Ideas for future study of that possibility and others are, of course, mentioned above, but also they are
sprinkled throughout this volume. Books and essays by Shari Benstock,
Katherine Joslin, Annette Zilversmit, and Linda Wagner-Martin offer
other minds through which to filter some of these submissions, and the

thorough scholar will take advantage of their wisdom. Finally, beginners in Wharton studies should find the suggested reference sources of help. Nevertheless, nothing surpasses the generosity of other Wharton scholars as demonstrated at conferences, by e-mail and by contributions to Donna Campbell's website out of Gonzaga University. (Search "Edith Wharton Society.") In the same spirit, information and helpfulness has been the undivided goal of this work.

Works Consulted

Bell, Millicent. "Introduction: A Critical History." *The Cambridge Companion to Edith Wharton*. New York: Cambridge UP, 1995.

———. *Edith Wharton and Henry James: The Story of Their Friendship*. London: Peter Owen, 1965.

Bendixen, Alfred. "A Guide to Wharton Criticism, 1974–1983." *Edith Wharton Review* 2.2 (Fall 1985): 5, 88–89.

———. "Recent Wharton Studies: A Bibliographical Essay." *Edith Wharton Review* 3.2 (Fall 1986): 5, 8–9.

———. "Wharton Studies, 1986–1987: A Bibliographic Essay." *Edith Wharton Review* 5.1 (Spring, 1988): 18–22.

———. "The World of Wharton Criticism: A Bibliographic Essay." *Edith Wharton Review* 7.1 (Spring 1990): 18–22.

———. "New Directions in Wharton Criticism: A Bibliographic Essay." *Edith Wharton Review* 10.2 (Fall 1993): 20–24.

Bendixen, Alfred and Annette Zilversmit. *Edith Wharton: New Critical Essays*. New York: Garland, 1992.

Benstock, Shari. "A Critical History of *The House of Mirth*." *The House of Mirth by Edith Wharton*. Ed. Shari Benstock. Boston, MA: Bedford, 1994. 309–25.

———. *No Gifts From Chance: A Biography of Edith Wharton*. New York: Scribners, 1994.

Bloom, Harold, ed. *Modern Critical Views: Edith Wharton*. New York: Chelsea House: 1986.

Cleaton, Irene and Allen Cleaton. *Books & Battles: American Literature 1920–1930*. Boston, MA: Houghton Mifflin, 1937.

Colquitt, Claire. "Contradictory Possibilities: Wharton Scholarship 1992–1994." *Edith Wharton Review* 12.2 (Fall 1995): 37–41.

Edel, Leon. *Henry James: A Life*. New York: Harper & Row, 1985.

Hanley, Lynne T. "The Eagle and the Hen: Edith Wharton and Henry James." *Research Studies* 49.3 (September 1981): 143–53.

Howe, Irving, ed. *Edith Wharton: A Collection of Critical Essays.* Englewood Cliffs: Prentice-Hall, 1962.

Joslin, Katherine. *Women Writers: Edith Wharton.* New York: St. Martin's P, 1991. 128–50.

———. "What Lubbock Didn't Say." *Edith Wharton Review* 1.1 (Spring 1984): 6.

Kaye, Richard A. "Textual Hermeneutics and Belated Male Heroism: Edith Wharton's Revision of *The House of Mirth* and the Resistance to American Literary Naturalism." *Arizona Quarterly.* 52.3 (Autumn 1995): 87–115.

Killoran, Helen. "'Xingu': Edith Wharton Instructs Literary Critics." *Studies in American Humor* 3.3 (1996): 1–13.

Lauer, Kristin O. and Margaret P. Murray, eds. *Edith Wharton: An Annotated Secondary Bibliography.* New York: Garland, 1990.

Leitch, Vincent B. *American Literary Criticism from the 30s to the 80s.* New York: Columbia UP, 1988. 24–59.

Lewis, R. W. B. *Edith Wharton: A Biography.* New York: Harper & Row, 1975.

Lewis, R. W. B. and Nancy Lewis, eds. *The Letters of Edith Wharton.* New York: Scribners, 1988.

Lubbock, Percy. *Portrait of Edith Wharton.* New York: D. Appleton-Century, 1947.

O'Brien, Edward J. *The Advance of the American Short Story.* New York: Dodd, Mead, 1923.

Olin-Ammentorp, Julie. "Edith Wharton's Challenge to Feminist Criticism." *Studies in American Fiction* 16.2 (Autumn 1988): 237–44.

Ozick, Cynthia. "Justice (Again) to Edith Wharton." *Commentary* 62 (October 1976): 48–57.

Powers, Lyall H., ed. *Henry James and Edith Wharton. Letters: 1900–1915.* New York: Scribners, 1990.

Price, Alan. *The End of the Age of Innocence: Edith Wharton and the First World War.* New York: St. Martin's, 1996.

Rae, Catherine M. *Edith Wharton's New York Quartet.* Lanham, MD: UP of America, 1984.

Raphael, Lev. *Edith Wharton's Prisoners of Shame: A New Perspective on her Neglected Fiction.* New York: St. Martin's P, 1991.

Sensibar, Judith L. "Edith Wharton Reads the Bachelor Type: Her Critique of Modernism's Representative Man." *Edith Wharton: New Critical Essays.* Eds. Alfred Bendixen and Annette Zilversmit. New York: Garland P, 1992.

Springer, Marlene. *Edith Wharton and Kate Chopin: A Reference Guide.* Boston: G. K. Hall, 1976.

Tintner, Adeline. "Wharton and James: Some Literary Give and Take." *Edith Wharton Review.* 3.1 (Spring 1986): 3–4, 8.

———. *Edith Wharton in Context: Essays on Intertextuality.* Tuscaloosa, AL: U of Alabama P, 1999.

Tuttleton, James W. *American Women Writers: Bibliographical Essays.* Eds. Maurice Duke, Jackson R. Bryer, and M. Thomas. Westport: Greenwood P, 1983.

Tuttleton, James W., Kristin O. Lauer and Margaret P. Murray, eds. *Edith Wharton: The Contemporary Reviews.* New York: Cambridge UP, 1992.

Wagner-Martin, Linda. "Prospects for the Study of Edith Wharton." *Resources for American Literary Studies* 22.1 (1996): 1–15.

Waid, Candace. *Edith Wharton's Letters From the Underworld: Fictions of Women and Writing.* Chapel Hill, NC: U of North Carolina P, 1991.

Wegener, Frederick, ed. *Edith Wharton: The Uncollected Critical Writings.* Princeton, NJ: Princeton UP, 1996.

Werlock, Abby H. P. "Edith Wharton's Subtle Revenge?: Morton Fullerton and the Female Artist in *Hudson River Bracketed* and *The Gods Arrive*." *Edith Wharton: New Critical Essays.* Eds. Alfred Bendixen and Annette Zilversmit. New York: Garland P, 1992.

Wolff, Cynthia Griffin. *A Feast of Words: The Triumph of Edith Wharton.* New York: Oxford UP, 1977.

———. "Lily Bart and the Drama of Femininity." *American Literary History* 6.1 (Spring 1994): 71–87.

———. "Lily Bart and Masquerade Inscribed in the Female Mode." *Wretched Exotic: Edith Wharton in Europe.* Eds. Katherine Joslin and Alan Price. New York: Peter Lang, 1992. 259–94.

Zilversmit, Annette. "'All Souls': Wharton's Last Haunted House and Future Directions for Criticism." *Edith Wharton: New Critical Essays.* Eds. Alfred Bendixen and Annette Zilversmit. New York: Garland P, 1992.

Bibliography

Works by Edith Wharton

Fast and Loose: A Novelette by David Olivieri. (Juvenalia, c. 1870.) Ed. Viola Hopkins Winner. Charlotte, VA: UP of Virginia, 1977.

Verses. Newport: 1878. Privately printed. (Juvenalia)

"Mrs. Manstey's View." *Scribner's Magazine* 10 (July 1891): 117–22.

"The Fullness of Life." *Scribner's Magazine* 14 (December 1893): 699–704.

"That Good May Come." *Scribner's Magazine* 15 (May 1894): 629–42.

"The Lamp of Psyche." *Scribner's Magazine* 18 (October 1895): 418–28.

"The Valley of Childish Things, and Other Emblems." *The Century Magazine* 52 (July 1896): 467–69.

(with Ogden Codman Jr.) *The Decoration of Houses.* New York: Scribners, 1897.

The Greater Inclination. New York: Scribners, 1899.

"April Showers." *Youth's Companion* 74 (18 January 1900): 25–28.

"Friends." *Youth's Companion* 74 (23, 30 August 1900): 405–6; 417–18.

"The Line of Least Resistance." *Lippincott's* 66 (October 1900): 559–70.

The Touchstone. New York: Scribners, 1900. (English edition, *A Gift From the Grave.* London: John Murray, 1900.)

"The Blashfields' Italian Cities." *Bookman* 13 (August 1901): 563–64. Rev. of Edwin H. and Evangeline W. Blashfield, *Italian Cities.*

Crucial Instances. New York: Scribners, 1901.

"More Loves of an Englishwoman." *Bookman* 12 (February 1901): 562–63.

"Mrs. Fisk's performance in *Tess.*" Rev. of dramatization of Thomas Hardy's novel *Tess of the d'Urbervilles.* *New York Commercial Advertiser* (7 May 1902): 9.

Rev. of *Ulysses: A Drama* by Stephen Phillips. *Bookman* 15 (April 1902): 168–70.

"The Three Francescas." *North American Review* 175 (July 1902): 17–30.

The Valley of Decision. 2 Vols. New York: Scribners, 1902.

"Mr. Paul on the Poetry of Matthew Arnold." Rev. of Herbert W. Paul's *Matthew Arnold. Lamp* 26 (February 1903): 51–54.

Sanctuary. New York: Scribners, 1903.

"The Vice of Reading." *North American Review* 177 (October 1903): 513–21.

The Descent of Man and Other Stories. New York: Scribners, 1904.

"The House of the Dead Hand." *Atlantic Monthly* 94 (August 1904): 145–60.

Italian Villas and Their Gardens. New York: Century, 1904.

"The Letter." *Harper's Magazine* 108 (April 1904): 781–89.

The House of Mirth. New York: Scribners, 1905.

"The Introducers." *Ainslee's* 16 (December 1905): 139–48; (January 1906); 61–67.

Italian Backgrounds. New York: Scribners, 1905.

"Mr. Sturgis's 'Belchamber.'" Rev. of Howard Sturgis's *Belchamber. Bookman* 21 (May 1905): 307–10.

"The Hermit and the Wild Woman." *Scribner's Magazine* 39 (February 1906): 145–56.

The Fruit of the Tree. New York: Scribners, 1907.

Madame de Treymes. New York: Scribners, 1907.

"The Sonnets of Eugene Lee-Hamilton." Rev. of *The Sonnets of the Wingless Hours,* by Eugene Lee-Hamilton. *Bookman* 26 (November 1907): 251–53.

The Hermit and the Wild Woman and Other Stories. New York: Scribners, 1908.

A Motor-Flight Through France. New York: Scribners, 1908.

"*Les Metteurs en Scene.*" *Revue des Deux Mondes* 67 (October 1908): 692–708.

Artemis to Actaeon and Other Verse. New York: Scribners, 1909.

"George Cabot Lodge." *Scribner's Magazine* 47 (February 1910): 236–39.

Tales of Men and Ghosts. New York: Scribners, 1910.

Ethan Frome. New York: Scribners, 1911.

The Reef. New York: Appleton, 1912.

The Custom of the Country. New York: Scribners, 1913.

"Introduction." *A Village Romeo and Juliet,* by Gottfried Keller. Trans. by A. C. Bahlmann. New York: Scribners, 1914.

Fighting France from Dunkerque to Belfort. New York: Scribners, 1915.

"*Jean du Breuil de Saint-Germain.*" *Revue Hebdomadaire* 24 (15 May 1915): 351:61.

"My Work Among the Women Workers of Paris." *New York Times Magazine* 28 (November 1915): 1–2.

The Book of the Homeless (editor). New York: Scribners, 1916.

"Bunner Sisters." *Xingu and Other Stories.* New York: Scribners, 1916.

"The French (As Seen by an American)." *Scribner's Magazine* 62 (December 1917): 676–83.

Summer. New York: Appleton, 1917.

Edith Wharton's War Charities in France. Mrs. Wharton's General Report from 1914–1918 and Report of the New York Committee. Microfilm. NYPL.

The Marne. New York: Appleton, 1918.

French Ways and Their Meaning. New York: Appleton, 1919.

"Writing a War Story." *Woman's Home Companion* 45 (September 1919): 17–19.

The Age of Innocence. New York: Appleton, 1920.

"Henry James in His Letters." Rev. of *The Letters of Henry James.* Ed. Percy Lubbock. *Quarterly Review* 234 (July 1920): 188–202.

In Morocco. New York: Scribners, 1920.

The Glimpses of the Moon. New York: Appleton, 1922.

"The Great American Novel." *Yale Review* n.s. 16 (July 1922): 646–56.

"Preface." *Futility* by William Gerhardi. New York: Ouffield, 1922.

"Christmas Tinsel." *Delineator* 103 (December 1923): 11.

Old New York. New York: Appleton, 1924. (Boxed set including four volumes: *False Dawn, Old Maid, The Spark, New Year's Day.*)

The Mother's Recompense. New York: Appleton, 1925.

The Writing of Fiction. New York: Scribners, 1925.

Here and Beyond. New York: Appleton, 1926.

Twelve Poems. London: Medici Society, 1926.

Twilight Sleep. New York: Appleton, 1927.

The Children. New York: Appleton, 1928.

"William C. Brownell." *Scribner's Magazine* 84 (November 1928): 596–602.

Hudson River Bracketed. New York: Appleton, 1929.

"Visibility in Fiction." *Yale Review* n.s. 18 (March 1929): 480–88.

Certain People. New York: Appleton, 1930.

The Gods Arrive. New York: Appleton, 1932.

"The Writing of *Ethan Frome.*" *Colophon* 2.4 (September 1932): n.p.

Human Nature. New York: Appleton, 1933.

A Backward Glance. New York: Appleton-Century, 1934.

"Permanent Values in Fiction." *Saturday Review of Literature* 10 (7 April 1934): 603–4.

"Reconsideration of Proust." *Saturday Review of Literature* 11 (27 October 1934): 233–34.

"Tendencies in Modern Fiction." *Saturday Review of Literature* 10 (27 January 1934): 433–34.

"Preface." *Speak to the Earth: Wanderings and Reflections among Elephants and Mountains* by Vivianne de Watteville. London: Methuen, 1935.

"Foreword." *Benediction* by Claude Silve. Trans. Robert Norton. New York: Appleton-Century, 1936.

"Foreword." *Ethan Frome: A Dramatization of Edith Wharton's Novel* by Owen David and Donald Davis. New York: Scribners, 1936.

"*Souvenirs du Bourget d'Outre-mer.*" *Revue Hebdomadaire* 45 (21 June 1936): 266–86.

The World Over. New York: Appleton-Century, 1936.

Ghosts. New York: Appleton-Century, 1937.

The Buccaneers. New York: Appleton-Century, 1938.

"A Little Girl's New York." *Harper's Magazine* 176 (March 1938): 356–64.

Eternal Passion in English Poetry (editor with Robert Norton). New York: Appleton-Century, 1939.

Chronological List of Works Consulted

1890s

Barry, John D. "New York Letter." Rev. of *The Greater Inclination* by Edith Wharton. *Literary World* (1 April 1899): 105–6.

———. "New York Letter." Rev. of *The Greater Inclination* by Edith Wharton. *Literary World* (13 May 1899): 152–53.

"Review of *The Greater Inclination*." *Academy* 57 (8 July 1899): 40.

1900s

"Mrs. Wharton's Nativity: The Clever and Subtle Disciple of Henry James a Native of the American Metropolis." *Munsey's Magazine* 25 (June 1901): 435–36.

Mabie, Hamilton Wright. "Mr. Mabie's Literary Talks." Rev. of *The Valley of Decision*. *Ladies Home Journal* 19 (May 1902): 17.

The Berkshire Evening Eagle [Pittsfield, Mass.] 12 March 1904: 1+.

"Review of *The Descent of Man and Other Stories*" by Edith Wharton. *Independent* 56 (9 June 1904): 1334–35.

"The Abode of the Fool's Heart." Rev. of *The House of Mirth* by Edith Wharton. *Literary Digest* 31 (December 1905): 886.

Hale, E. E. Jr., "Mrs. Wharton's *The House of Mirth*." Rev. of *The House of Mirth* by Edith Wharton. *Bookman* 22 (December 1905): 364–66.

McArthur, James. "Books and Bookmen." Rev. of *The House of Mirth* by Edith Wharton. *Harper's Weekly*. 49 (2 December 1905): 1750.

"New Novels." Rev. of *The House of Mirth* by Edith Wharton. *Athenaeum* [England] (31 December 1905): 886.

"A Notable Novel." Rev. of *The House of Mirth* by Edith Wharton. *Outlook* 81 (21 October 1905): 404–6.

Boutell, Alice May. "A Burst of Enthusiasm." Rev. of *The House of Mirth* by Edith Wharton. *Critic* 48 (January 1906): 87–88.

Bourget, Paul. "Preface." *Chez les heureux du monde.* 1908 Trans. Charles Du Bos. *Edith Wharton Review* 8.1 (Spring 1991): 19–22.

Hawthorne, Hildegarde. *Women and Other Women: Essays in Wisdom.* New York: Duffield, 1908.

Sedgwick, Henry Dwight. *The New American Type and Other Essays.* Boston, MA: Houghton-Mifflin, 1908.

1910s

Cooper, Frederic Taber. "*Ethan Frome.*" Rev. of *Ethan Frome* by Edith Wharton. *Bookman* 34 (November 1911): 312.

"*Ethan Frome.*" Rev. of *Ethan Frome* by Edith Wharton. *Saturday Review* [England] 112 (18 November 1911): 650.

"Three Lives in Supreme Torture: Mrs. Wharton's *Ethan Frome:* A Cruel, Compelling, Haunting Story of New England." Rev. of *Ethan Frome* by Edith Wharton. *New York Times Book Review* (8 October 1911): 603.

"Review of *Ethan Frome* by Edith Wharton." *Bookman* [England] 41 (January 1912): 216.

Bjorkman, Edwin A. "The Greater Edith Wharton." *Voices of Tomorrow: Critical Studies of the New Spirit in Literature.* New York: Mitchel Kennerley, 1913.

Boynton, Henry W. "Mrs. Wharton's Manners." Rev. of *The Custom of the Country* by Edith Wharton. *Nation* 97 (30 October 1913): 404–5.

Cooper, Frederic Taber. "*The Custom of the Country.*" Rev. of *The Custom of the Country* by Edith Wharton. *Bookman* 38 (December 1913): 416–17.

"The Custom of Her Country." Rev. of *The Custom of the Country* by Edith Wharton. *Nation* 96 (15 May 1913): 494–99.

"Customs of Two Countries." Rev. of *The Custom of the Country* by Edith Wharton. *Independent* 76 (13 November 1913): 313.

"Critical Reviews of the Season's Latest Books." Rev. of *The Custom of the Country* by Edith Wharton. *New York Sun* (18 October 1913): 8.

F., L. M. "Mrs. Wharton's Novel: *The Custom of the Country,* a Book Which Will Excite Much Discussion." Rev. of *The Custom of the Country* by Edith Wharton. *New York Times Review of Books* (19 October 1913): 557.

"Fiction." Rev. of *The Custom of the Country* by Edith Wharton. *Athenaeum* [England] 4490 (15 November 1913): 554.

"Novels." Rev. of *The Custom of the Country* by Edith Wharton. *Saturday Review* [England] 116 (22 November 1913): 658–59.

Colby, F. M. "The Book of the Month." Rev. of *The Custom of the Country* by Edith Wharton. *North American Review* 199 (February 1914): 294–99.

James, Henry. "The Younger Generation." Rev. of *The Custom of the Country* by Edith Wharton. *Times Literary Supplement* [England] (2 April 1914): 157–58.

"Review of *The Custom of the Country.*" *Bookman* [England] 45 (9 March 1914): 330.

Huneker, James. "Three Disagreeable Girls." *Forum* 52 (November 1915): 765–76.

Lubbock, Percy. "The Novels of Edith Wharton." Rev. of *The Custom of the Country* by Edith Wharton. *Quarterly Review* 22 (January 1915): 182–201.

Sergeant, Elizabeth Shepley. "Idealized New England." Review of *Ethan Frome* by Edith Wharton. *The New Republic* 3 (May 8, 1915): 20–21.

Phelps, William Lyon. "The Advance of the English Novel, X." *Bookman* 43 (July 1916): 515–24. Rpt. *The Advance of the English Novel.* New York: Dodd Mead, 1916.

Edgett, Edwin Francis. "Edith Wharton's Tale of Thwarted Love." Rev. of *Summer* by Edith Wharton. Boston *Evening Transcript* (25 July 1917): II.6.

Gilman, Lawrence. "The Book of the Month: Mrs. Wharton Reverts to Shaw." Rev. of *Summer* by Edith Wharton. *North American Review* 206 (August 1917): 304–7.

H[ackett], F[rancis]. "Loading the Dice." Review of *Summer* by Edith Wharton. *New Republic* 11 (14 July 1917): 311–12.

Macy, John. "Edith Wharton." Rev. of *Summer* by Edith Wharton. *Dial* 63 (30 August 1917): 161–62.

"Mrs. Wharton's Story of New England: *Summer* a Pleasing Romance of Village Life." Rev. of *Summer* by Edith Wharton. *New York Times Book Review* (8 July 1917): 253.

"Mrs. Wharton's *Summer.*" Rev. of *Summer* by Edith Wharton. *Springfield* [Massachusetts] *Republican* (5 August 1917): 15.

"Novels Whose Scenes Are Laid in New England." Rev. of *Summer* by Edith Wharton. *Review of Reviews* 56 (September 1917): 333.

Scarborough, Dorothy. *The Supernatural in Modern English Fiction.* New York: G. P. Putnam's Sons, 1917.

Eliot, T. S. "Summer." Rev. of *Summer* by Edith Wharton. *The Egoist* [England] (January 1919): 10.

1920s

"The Age of Innocence." Rev. of *The Age of Innocence* by Edith Wharton. *Times Literary Supplement* [England] (25 November 1920): 775.

M[ansfield], K[atherine]. "Family Portraits." Rev. of *The Age of Innocence* by Edith Wharton. *Athenaeum* [England] 4728 (10 December 1920): 810–11. Rpt. in *Novels and Novelists.* New York: Knopf, 1930. 319–20.

Phelps, William Lyon. "As Mrs. Wharton Sees Us." Rev. of "*The Age of Innocence* by Edith Wharton." *New York Times Book Review* (17 October 1920): 1, 11.

Parrington, Vernon L. "Our Literary Aristocrat." *Pacific Review* 2 (June 1921): 157–60. Rpt. in *Main Currents in American Thought*. New York: Harcourt Brace and World, 1927.

Gerould, Katharine. "Mrs. Wharton's New *House of Mirth*." Rev. of *The Glimpses of the Moon*. *New York Times Book Review* (23 July 1922): 1, 2.

O'Brien, Edward J. *The Advance of the American Short Story*. New York: Dodd, Mead, 1923.

Van Doren, Carl. *Contemporary American Novelists 1900–1920*. New York: Macmillan, 1923.

Lovett, Robert Morss. *Edith Wharton*. New York: Robert M. McBride, 1925.

Michaud, Regis. *The American Novel To-Day: A Social and Psychological Study*. Boston, MA: Little, Brown, 1928.

Zeitlin, Jacob and Homer Woodbridge. *Stuart Pratt Sherman: Life and Letters*. 2 Vols. New York: Farrar & Rinehart, 1929.

1930s

Pattee, Fred Lewis. *The New American Literature 1890–1930*. New York: Century, 1930.

Blankenship, Russell. *American Literature as an Expression of the American Mind*. New York: Holt, 1931.

Knight, Grant C. *The Novel in English*. New York: Richard B. Smith, 1931.

Beach, Joseph Warren. *The Twentieth Century Novel: Studies in Technique*. New York: Appleton-Century-Crofts, 1932.

Lewissohn, Ludwig. *Expression in America*. New York: Harper & Bros., 1932.

Boas, Ralph Phillip, and Katherine Burton. *Social Backgrounds of American Literature*. Boston, MA: Little, Brown. 1933.

Hartwick, Harry. *The Foreground of American Fiction*. New York: American Book Co. 1934.

Hatcher, Harlan. *Creating the Modern American Novel*. New York: Farrar & Rinehart, 1935.

Lawrence, Margaret. *The School of Femininity*. New York: Stokes, 1936.

Quinn, Arthur Hobson. *American Fiction: An Historical and Critical Survey*. New York: Appleton-Century, 1936.

Ransom, John Crowe. "Characters and Character: A Note on Fiction." *The American Review* 6 (January 1936): 271–88.

Taylor, Walter Fuller. *History of American Letters*. Boston, MA: American Book Co., 1936.

B., W. R. "The New Books." Rev. of *Ghosts* by Edith Wharton. *Saturday Review* 17 (6 November 1937): 19.

"Briefer Mention." Rev. of *Ghosts* by Edith Wharton. *Commonweal* 27 (5 November 1937): 55.

Cleaton, Irene, and Allen Cleaton. *Books & Battles: American Literature 1920–1930*. Boston, MA: Houghton Mifflin, 1937.

"Ghosts and Ghost Stories." Rev. of *Ghosts* by Edith Wharton. *Times Literary Supplement* [England] (6 November 1937): 823.

Greene, Graham, "Short Stories." Rev. of *Ghosts* by Edith Wharton. *Spectator* [England] 154 (24 December 1937): 1155.

Loggins, Vernon. *I Hear America*. New York: Crowell, 1937.

Shawe-Taylor, Desmond. "New Novels." *New Statesman and Nation* n.s. 14 (6 November 1937): 758.

Woollcott, Alexander. *Woollcott's Second Reader*. New York: Viking P, 1937.

Leavis, Q. D. "Henry James's Heiress: The Importance of Edith Wharton." *Scrutiny* (December 1938). Rpt. in *Edith Wharton: A Collection of Critical Essays*. Ed. Irving Howe. Englewood Cliffs, NJ: Prentice-Hall, 1962.

Wilson, Edmund. "Justice to Edith Wharton." *New Republic* 95 (29 June 1938): 209–13. Rpt. in Edith Wharton: *A Collection of Critical Essays*. Ed. Irving Howe. Englewood Cliffs, NJ: Prentice-Hall, 1962.

1940s

Gray, James. *On Second Thought*. Minneapolis, MN: U of Minnesota P, 1946.

Lubbock, Percy. *Portrait of Edith Wharton*. New York: D. Appleton-Century, 1947.

Sedgwick, Ellery. "Introduction." *Atlantic Harvest*. Boston, MA: Little, Brown, 1947.

Winters, Yvor. *In Defense of Reason*. New York: Swallop P. and William Morrow, 1947.

Trilling, Diana. "*The House of Mirth* Revisited." *Harper's Bazaar* 81 (1947). Rpt. in *Edith Wharton: A Collection of Essays*. Ed. Irving Howe. Englewood Cliffs, NJ: Prentice-Hall, 1962.

1950s

Auchincloss, Louis. "Edith Wharton and Her New Yorks." *Partisan Review* 18 (July-August 1951) 411–19. Rpt. in *Reflections of a Jacobite*. Boston, MA: Houghton Mifflin, 1961.

Freemantle, Anne. "Edith Wharton: Values and Vulgarity." *Fifty Years of the American Novel: A Christian Appraisal.* Ed. H. C. Gardiner, S. J. New York: Scribners, 1951.

Nevius, Blake. "'Ethan Frome' and the Themes of Edith Wharton's Fiction." *The New England Quarterly Review* 24 (June 1951): 197–207.

———. *Edith Wharton: A Study of Her Fiction*. 1953. Berkeley, U of California P, 1961.

Thomas, J. D. "Marginalia on *Ethan Frome*." *American Literature* 27 (November 1953): 405–9.

Coxe, Louis O. "What Edith Wharton Saw in Innocence." Rev. of *The Age of Innocence* by Edith Wharton. *The New Republic* (June 27, 1955): 16–18.

Trilling, Lionel. "The Morality of Inertia." *Great Moral Dilemmas*, Ed. Robert MacIver. New York: Harper & Bros., 1956. Rpt. in Irving Howe, ed. *Edith Wharton: A Collection of Critical Essays*. Englewood Cliffs, NJ: Prentice-Hall, 1962.

Leach, Nancy. "New England in the Stories of Edith Wharton." *New England Quarterly* 30 (March 1957): 90–98.

Hopkins, Viola. "The Ordering Style of *The Age of Innocence*." *American Literature* 30.3 (November 1958): 345–57.

Moseley, Edwin M. "*The Age of Innocence*: Edith Wharton's Weak *Faust*." *College English* 21.3 (December 1959): 156–60.

1960s

Auchincloss, Louis. *Pioneers & Caretakers: A Study of 9 American Women Novelists*. Minneapolis, MN: U of Minnesota P, 1961.

Bernard, Kenneth. "Imagery and Symbolism in *Ethan Frome*." *College English* 23 (December 1961): 171–84.

Brennan, Joseph X. "*Ethan Frome*: Structure and Metaphor." *Modern Fiction Studies* 3 (Winter 1961): 347–56.

Hafley, James. "The Case Against *Ethan Frome*." *Fresco* 1 (1961): 194–201.

Bristol, Marie. "Life Among the Ungentle Genteel: Edith Wharton's *The House of Mirth* Revisited." *Western Humanities Review* 16.1 (Autumn 1962): 371–74.

Howe, Irving. "A Reading of *The House of Mirth.*" *Edith Wharton: A Collection of Critical Essays.* Ed. Irving Howe, 1962.

Kazin, Alfred. *Edith Wharton: A Collection of Critical Essays.* Ed. Irving Howe. Englewood Cliffs, NJ: Prentice-Hall, 1962.

Plante, Patricia R. "Edith Wharton as a Short Story Writer." *Midwest Quarterly* 4 (Summer 1963): 363–70.

Millgate, Michael. *American Social Fiction: James to Cozzens.* New York: Barnes and Noble, 1964.

Auchincloss, Louis, ed. *The Edith Wharton Reader.* New York: Scribners 1965.

Bell, Millicent. *Edith Wharton and Henry James: The Story of Their Friendship.* London: Peter Owen, 1965.

Hamblen, Abigail Ann. "Edith Wharton's New England." *New England Quarterly* 38 (June 1965): 239–44.

Tuttleton, James W. "The President and the Lady: Edith Wharton and Theodore Roosevelt." *Bulletin of the New York Public Library* 69.1 (January 1965): 49–57.

Friman, Anne. "Determinism and Point of View in *The House of Mirth.*" *Papers on Language and Literature* 2.2 (Spring 1966): 175–78.

Lamar, Lillie B. "Edith Wharton's Foreknowledge in *The Age of Innocence.*" *Texas Studies in Language and Literature* 8 (Fall 1966): 385–89.

Poirer, Richard. *A World Elsewhere.* New York: Oxford UP, 1966.

Tuttleton, James W. "Henry James and Edith Wharton: Fiction as the House of Fame." *Midcontinent American Studies Journal* 7.1 (Spring 1966): 25–36.

Lamar, Lillie B. "Edith Wharton and *The Book of Common Prayer.*" *American Notes & Queries* 7 (November 1968): 38–39.

Lewis, R. W. B. *The Collected Short Stories of Edith Wharton.* New York: Scribners, 1968.

———. "Introduction." *The Age of Innocence* by Edith Wharton. New York: Scribners, 1968.

Miller, James E., Jr. *Quests Surd and Absurd.* Chicago, IL: U Chicago P, 1968.

Pucknat, E. M., and S. B. Pucknat. "Edith Wharton and Gottfried Keller." *Comparative Literature* 21 (9 Summer 1969): 245–54.

1970s

Firestone, Shulamith. *The Dialectic of Sex: The Case for Feminist Revolution.* New York: William Morrow, 1970.

Greer, Germaine. *The Female Eunuch*. London: MacGibbon & Kee, 1970.

McDowell, Margaret B. "Edith Wharton's Ghost Stories." *Criticism* 12 (1970): 133–52.

Millet, Kate. *Sexual Politics*. 1969. New York: Avon, 1970.

Murphy, John J. "The Satiric Structure of Wharton's *The Age of Innocence*." *Markham Review* 2.3 (May 1970): 1–4.

O'Connor, William Van, ed. *Seven Modern Novelists*. 1970. London: Fairleigh Dickinson UP, 1982.

Walton, Geoffrey. *Edith Wharton: A Critical Interpretation*. 1970. Rutherford: Fairleigh Dickinson UP, 1982.

Doyle, Charles Clay. "Emblems of Innocence: Imagery Patterns in Wharton's *The Age of Innocence*." *Xavier University Studies* 10.2 (1971): 19–25.

Tuttleton, James W. *The Novel of Manners in America*. Chapel Hill, NC: U of North Carolina P, 1972.

Bloom, Harold. *The Anxiety of Influence: A Theory of Poetry*. New York: Oxford UP, 1973.

Jacobson, Irving. "Perception, Communication, and Growth as Correlative Themes in Edith Wharton's *The Age of Innocence*." *Agora* 2.2 (1973): 68–82.

McIlvaine, Robert. "Edith Wharton's American Beauty Rose." *American Studies* 7.2 (August 1973): 183–85.

Phelps, Donald. "Edith Wharton and the Invisible." *Prose* 7 (Fall 1973): 227–45.

Rowbotham, Sheila. *Hidden from History: 300 Years of Women's Oppression and the Fight Against It*. London: Pluto P, 1973.

———. *Women's Consciousness, Man's World*. London: Penguin, 1973.

Wharton, Edith. *The Ghost Stories of Edith Wharton*. New York: Scribners, 1973.

Lawson, Richard. *Edith Wharton and German Literature*. Bonn: Bouvier Verlag Herbert Grundmann, 1974.

McDowell, Margaret. "Viewing the Custom of her Country: Edith Wharton's Feminism." *Contemporary Literature* 15 (1974): 521–38.

Lewis, R. W. B. *Edith Wharton: A Biography*. New York: Harper & Row, 1975.

———. "Powers of Darkness." Rev. of *The Ghost Stories of Edith Wharton*. *Times Literary Supplement* [London] (13 June 1975): 644.

Lindberg, Gary H. *Edith Wharton and the Novel of Manners*. Charlottesville, VA: UP of Virginia, 1975.

L'Enfant, Julie. "Edith Wharton: Room With a View." *The Southern Review* 12.2 (April 1976): 398–406.

McDowell, Margaret B. *Edith Wharton*. 1976. Boston: G. K. Hall, Revised 1990.

Ozick, Cynthia. "Justice (Again) to Edith Wharton." *Commentary* 62 (October 1976): 48–57.

Springer, Marlene. *Edith Wharton and Kate Chopin: A Reference Guide*. Boston: G. K. Hall, 1976.

Eggenschwiler, David. "The Ordered Disorder of *Ethan Frome*." *Studies in the Novel* 9 (1977): 237–46.

Lawson, Richard H. *Edith Wharton*. New York: Ungar, 1977.

Tintner, Adeline. "A Source from *Roderick Hudson* for the Title of *The Custom of the Country*." *American Notes and Queries* 1.4 (Fall 1977).

Wolff, Cynthia Griffin. *A Feast of Words: The Triumph of Edith Wharton*. New York: Oxford UP, 1977.

Daly, Mary. *Gyn/Ecology: The Metaethics of Radical Feminism*. Boston, MA: Beacon, 1978.

Ammons, Elizabeth. "Edith Wharton's *Ethan Frome* and the Question of Meaning." *Studies in American Fiction* 7 (1979): 127–40.

Candido, Joseph. "Edith Wharton's Final Alterations of *The Age of Innocence*." *Studies in American Fiction* 6 (1979): 21–31.

Gilbert, Sandra M. and Susan Gubar. *The Madwoman in the Attic: The Woman Writer and the Nineteenth-Century Literary Imagination*. New Haven, CT: Yale UP, 1979.

1980s

Ammons, Elizabeth. *Edith Wharton's Argument with America*. Athens, GA: U of Georgia P, 1980.

Candella, Joseph. "The Domestic Orientation of American Novels: 1893–1913." *American Literary Realism* 13.1 (Spring 1980): 1–18.

Hays, Peter L. "Bearding the Lily: Wharton's Names." *American Notes & Queries* 18.5 (January 1980): 75–76.

Lidoff, Joan. "Another Sleeping Beauty: Narcissism in *The House of Mirth*." *American Quarterly* 32.5 (1980): 519–39. Rpt. in *American Realism*. Ed. Eric J. Sundquist. Baltimore, MD: Johns Hopkins UP, 1982.

Price, Alan. "Lily Bart and Carrie Meeber: Cultural Sisters." *American Literary Realism* 13.2 (Autumn 1980): 238–45.

Rich, Adrienne. "Compulsory Heterosexuality and Lesbian Existence." *Signs: Journal of Women in Society and Culture* 5.4 (1980). Rpt. in *Compulsory Heterosexuality and Lesbian Existence*. Denver, CO: Antelope, 1980.

Smith, Allan Gardner. "Edith Wharton and the Ghost Story." *Gender and Literary Voice*. Ed. Janet Todd. New York: Holmes and Meier, 1980.

Tintner, Adeline R. "Jamesian Structures in *The Age of Innocence* and Related Stories." *Twentieth Century Literature* 26 (1980): 332–47.

Hanley, Lynne T. "The Eagle and the Hen: Edith Wharton and Henry James." *Research Studies* 49.3 (September 1981): 143–53.

Link, Franz. "A Note on 'The Apparition of These Faces . . .' in *The House of Mirth* and 'In a Station at the Metro.'" *Paideuma* 10.2 (Fall 1981): 327.

Sagarin, Edward. "*Ethan Frome*: Atonement Endures Until Darkness Descends." *Raskolnikov and Others: Literary Images of Crime, Punishment, Redemption and Atonement*. Ed. Edward Sagarin. New York: St. Martin's P, 1981.

Ammons, Elizabeth. "Cool Diana and the Blood-Red Muse: Edith Wharton on Innocence and Art." *American Novelists Revisited: Essays in Feminist Criticism*. Ed. Fritz Fleishmann. Boston: G. K. Hall, 1982.

Collins, Alexandra. "The Art of Self-Perception in Virginia Woolf's *Mrs. Dalloway* and Edith Wharton's *The Reef*." *Atlantis* 7.2 (Spring 1982): 47–58.

Crowley, John W. "The Unmastered Streak: Feminist Themes in Wharton's *Summer*." *American Literary Realism* 1870–1910 15.1 (Spring 1982): 86–96.

Cuddy, Lois A. "Triangles of Defeat and Liberation: The Quest for Power in Edith Wharton's Fiction." *Contemporary Literature* 8 (1982): 18–26.

Dimock, Wai-chee. "Debasing Exchange: Edith Wharton's *The House of Mirth*." *PMLA* (October 1982): 738–92. Rpt. in *Modern Critical Views: Edith Wharton*. Ed. Harold Bloom. New York: Chelsea House, 1986.

Edel, Leon. *Stuff of Sleep and Dreams: Experiments in Literary Psychology*. New York: Harper & Row, 1982.

Morante, Linda. "The Desolation of Charity Royall: Imagery in Edith Wharton's *Summer*." *Colby Library Quarterly* 18.4 (December 1982): 241–48.

Tintner, Adeline R. "Two Novels of 'The Relatively Poor'": *New Grub Street* and *The House of Mirth*." *Notes on Modern American Literature* 6.2 (Autumn 1982): Item 12.

Bazin, Nancy Topping. "The Destruction of Lily Bart: Capitalism, Christianity, and Male Chauvinism." *Denver Quarterly* 17.4 (Winter 1983): 98–108.

Collins, Alexandra. "The *Noyade* of Marriage in Edith Wharton's *The Custom of the Country*." *English Studies in Canada* 9 (2 June 1983): 197–212.

Conn, Peter. *The Divided Mind: Ideology and Imagination in America, 1898–1917*. Cambridge: Cambridge UP, 1983.

Dessner, Lawrence. "Edith Wharton and the Problem of Form." *Forum* 24.3 (1983): 54–63.

Murad, Orlene. "Edith Wharton and *Ethan Frome*." *Modern Language Studies* 13 (Summer 1983): 90–103.

O'Neal, Michael J. "Point of View and Narrative Technique in the Fiction of Edith Wharton." *Style* 17.2 (Spring 1983): 270–89.

Rusch, Frederick S. "Reality and the Puritan Mind: Jonathan Edwards and *Ethan Frome*." *Journal of Evolutionary Psychology* 4.3–4 (1983): 238–47.

Schriber, Mary Suzanne. "Convention in the Fiction of Edith Wharton." *Studies in American Fiction* 11.2 (Autumn 1983): 189–201.

Tuttleton, James W. "Edith Wharton." *American Women Writers: Bibliographical Essays*. Eds. Maurice Duke, Jackson R. Bryer, and M. Thomas Inge. Westport, CT: Greenwood P, 1983.

Walker, Nancy. "'Seduced and Abandoned': Convention and Reality in Edith Wharton's *Summer*." *Studies in American Fiction* 11.1 (Spring 1983): 107–14.

Blackall, Jean Frantz. "The Sledding Accident in *Ethan Frome*." *Studies in Short Fiction* 21.2 (Spring 1984): 145–46.

Gimbel, Wendy. *Edith Wharton: Orphancy and Survival*. Landmark Dissertations in Women's Studies. Ed. Annette Baxter. New York: Praeger, 1984.

Joslin, Katherine. "What Lubbock Didn't Say." *Edith Wharton Review* 1.1 (Spring 1984): 6.

Karcher, Carolyn L. "Male Vision and Female Revision in James's *The Wings of the Dove* and Wharton's *The House of Mirth*." *Women's Studies* 10 (1984): 227–44.

Kekes, John. "The Great Guide of Human Life." *Philosophy and Literature* 8 (October 1984): 236–49.

Michelson, Bruce. "Edith Wharton's House Divided." *Studies in American Fiction* 12.2 (Autumn 1984): 199–215.

Morrow, Nancy. "Games and Conflict in Edith Wharton's *The Custom of the Country*." *American Literary Realism* 17 (Spring 1984): 32–39.

Radden, Jennifer. "Defining Self-Deception." *Dialogue: Canadian Philosophical Review* 23.1 (March 1984): 103–20.

Rae, Catherine M. *Edith Wharton's New York Quartet*. Lanham, MD: UP of America, 1984.

Robillard, Douglas. "Edith Wharton." *Supernatural Fiction Writers*. Ed. E. F. Bleiler. Vol. 2. New York: Scribners, 1984.

Stein, Allen F. "Edith Wharton: The Marriage of Entrapment." *After the Vows Were Spoken: Marriage in American Literary Realism*. Columbus: Ohio State UP, 1984.

White, Barbara A. "Edith Wharton's *Summer* and Woman's Fiction." *Essays in Literature* 11.2 (Fall 1984): 223–35.

Wolff, Cynthia Griffin. "Lily Bart and the Drama of Femininity." *American Literary History* 6.1 (Spring 1984): 71–87.

Bendixen, Alfred. "A Guide to Wharton Criticism, 1974–1983." *Edith Wharton Newsletter* 2.2 (Fall 1985): 1–8.

———. "Introduction." *Haunted Women: The Best Supernatural Tales by American Women Writers*. New York: Ungar, 1985.

Coard, Robert L. "Edith Wharton's Influence on Sinclair Lewis." *Modern Fiction Studies* 31.3 (Autumn 1985): 511–27.

Edel, Leon. *Henry James: A Life*. New York Harper & Row, 1985.

Gibson, Mary Ellis. "Edith Wharton and the Ethnography of Old New York." *Studies in American Fiction* 13.1 (Spring 1985): 57–69.

Gilbert, Sandra M. "Life's Empty Pack: Notes Toward a Literary Daughteronomy." *Critical Inquiry* 11.3 (March 1985): 355–84.

Hays, Peter. "Wharton's Splintered Realism." *Edith Wharton Newsletter*. 2.1 (Spring 1985): 6.

Koprince, Susan. "Edith Wharton's Hotels." *Massachusetts Studies in English* 10.1 (Spring 1985): 12–23.

Showalter, Elaine. "The Death of the Lady (Novelist): Wharton's *House of Mirth*." *Representations* 9 (Winter 1985): 133–49. Rpt. in *Edith Wharton: New Critical Essays*. Eds. Alfred Bendixen and Annette Zilversmit. New York: Garland, 1992.

Shulman, Robert. "Divided Selves and the Market Society: Politics and Psychology in *The House of Mirth*." *Perspectives on Contemporary Literature* 11 (1985): 10–19. Rpt. as "*The House of Mirth*: The Political Psychology of Capitalism." Robert Schulman, *Social Criticism and Nineteenth-Century American Fiction*. Columbia, MO: U of Missouri P, 1988.

Spacks, Patricia Meyer. *Gossip*. New York: Knopf, 1985.

Tintner, Adeline. "Henry James's 'Julia Bride': A Source for Chapter Nine in Edith Wharton's *The Custom of the Country*." *Notes on Modern American Literature* 9 (1985): Note 16.

Wershoven, Carol. "The Divided Conflict of Edith Wharton's *Summer*." *Colby Library Quarterly* 21.1 (March 1985): 5–10.

White, Barbara A. *Growing Up Female: Adolescent Girlhood in American Fiction*. Westport, CT: Greenwood P, 1985.

Wolstenholme, Susan. "Edith Wharton's Gibson Girl: The Virgin, the Undine, and the Dynamo." *American Literary Realism* 18.1–2 (Spring-Autumn 1985): 92–106.

Bendixen, Alfred. "Recent Wharton Studies: A Bibliographic Essay." *Edith Wharton Review* 3.2 (Fall 1986): 5–8, 9.

Bloom, Harold, ed. *Modern Critical Views*. New York: Chelsea House P, 1986.

Caserio, Robert L. "Edith Wharton and the Fiction of Public Commentary." *Western Humanities Review* 40.3 (Autumn 1986): 189–208.

Fryer, Judith. *Felicitous Space: The Imaginative Structures of Edith Wharton and Willa Cather*. Chapel Hill, NC: U of North Carolina P, 1986.

Hovey, R. B. "*Ethan Frome*: A Controversy About Modernizing It." *American Literary Realism* 19.1 (Fall 1986): 4–20.

Kaplan, Amy. "Edith Wharton's Profession of Authorship." *English Literary History* 53–2 (Summer 1986): 433–57.

Tintner, Adeline. "Wharton and James: Some Literary Give and Take." *Edith Wharton Review* 3.1 (Spring 1986): 3–4, 8.

Beaty, Robin. "Lilies that Fester: Sentimentality in *The House of Mirth*." *College Literature* 14.3 (Fall 1987): 263–75.

Blum, Virginia L. "Edith Wharton's Erotic Other-World." *Literature and Psychology* 33.1 (1987): 12–29.

Dixon, Roslyn. "Reflecting Vision in *The House of Mirth*." *Twentieth Century Literature* 33.2 (Summer 1987): 211–22.

French, Marilyn. "Introduction." *Summer*. New York: Collier Books, 1987.

Miller, Carol. "'Natural Magic': Irony as Unifying Strategy in *The House of Mirth*." *South Central Review* 4.1 (Spring 1987): 82–91.

Morgan, Gwendolyn. "The Unsung Heroine—A Study of May Welland in *The Age of Innocence*." *Heroines of Popular Culture*. Ed. Pat Browne. Bowling Green, OH: Popular, 1987.

Nathan, Rhoda. "Ward McAllister: Beau Nash of *The Age of Innocence*." *College Literature* 14.3 (1987): 276–84.

Restuccia, Frances L. "The Name of the Lily: Edith Wharton's Feminism(s)." *Contemporary Literature* 28.2 (Summer 1987): 223–38.

Saunders, Catherine E. *Writing the Margins: Edith Wharton, Ellen Glasgow and the Literary Tradition of the Ruined Woman*. Cambridge, MA: Harvard U, 1987.

Schriber, Mary Suzanne. *Gender and the Writer's Imagination: From Cooper to Wharton*. Lexington: UP of Kentucky, 1987.

Seltzer, Mark. "Statistical Persons." *Diacritics* 17.3 (Fall 1987): 82–98.

Voloshin, Beverley R. "Exchange in Wharton's *The Custom of the Country.*" *Pacific Coast Philology* 22.1–2 (November 1987): 88–104.

Wershoven, C. J. "*The Awakening* and *The House of Mirth*: Studies of Arrested Development." *American Literary Realism* 19.3 (Spring 1987): 27–41.

Wolff, Cynthia Griffin. "Cold Ethan and 'Hot Ethan.'" *College Literature* 14.3 (1987): 230–45.

Zilversmit, Annette. "Edith Wharton's Last Ghosts." *College Literature* 14.3 (1987): 296–305.

Bauer, Dale. *Feminist Dialogics: A Theory of Failed Community.* Albany, NY: State U of New York P, 1988.

Bendixen, Alfred. "Wharton Studies, 1986–1987: A Bibliographic Essay." *Edith Wharton Newsletter* 5.1 (Spring 1988): 5–8, 10.

Boydston, Jeanne. "Grave Endearing Traditions: Edith Wharton and the Domestic Novel." *Faith of a (Woman) Writer.* Eds. Alice Kessler-Harris and William McBrien. New York: Greenwood P, 1988.

Godfrey, David. "'The Full and Elaborate Vocabulary of Evasion': The Language of Cowardice in Edith Wharton's *Old New York.*" *Midwest Quarterly* 30.1 (Autumn 1988): 27–44.

Kaplan, Amy. "Crowded Spaces in *The House of Mirth.*" *The Social Construction of American Realism.* Chicago, IL: U Chicago P, 1988.

La Belle, Jenijoy. *Herself Beheld: The Literature of the Looking Glass.* Ithaca, NY: Cornell UP, 1988.

Lewis, R. W. B. and Nancy Lewis, eds. *The Letters of Edith Wharton.* New York: Scribners, 1988.

Olin-Ammentorp, Julie. "Edith Wharton's Challenge to Feminist Criticism." *Studies in American Fiction* 16.2 (Autumn 1988): 237–44.

Ward, Joseph A. "'The Amazing Hotel World' of James, Dreiser, and Wharton." *Leon Edel and Literary Art.* Ed. Lyall H. Powers. Ann Arbor, MI: UMI Research P, 1988.

Barnett, Louise K. "Language, Gender and Society in *The House of Mirth.*" *Connecticut Review* 11.2 (Summer 1989): 54–63.

Hays, Peter L. "Signs in *Summer*: Words and Metaphors." *Papers on Language and Literature* 25.1 (Winter 1989): 114–19.

Gilbert, Sandra M. and Susan Gubar. "Angel of Devastation: Edith Wharton on the Arts of the Enslaved." *No Man's Land: the Place of the Woman Writer in the Twentieth Century.* Vol. 2: *Sexchanges.* New Haven, CT: Yale UP, 1989.

Lawson, Richard H. "Edith Wharton." *Dictionary of Literary Biography* 78. *American Short Story Writers 1880–1910.* Detroit, MI: Bruccoli Clark, 1989.

Murray, Margaret P. "The Gothic Arsenal of Edith Wharton." *Journal of Evolutionary Psychology* 10.2–3 (August 1989): 315–21.

Quoyeser, Catherine. "The Antimodernist Unconscious: Genre and Ideology in *The House of Mirth.*" *Arizona Quarterly* 44.4 (Winter 1989): 55–79.

Steiner, Wendy. "The Causes of Effect: Edith Wharton and the Economics of Ekphrasis." *Poetics Today* 10.2 (Summer 1989): 279–97.

Tuttleton, James W. "The Feminist Takeover of Edith Wharton." *The New Criterion* (March 1989): 1–9.

1990s

Bendixen, Alfred. "The World of Wharton Criticism: A Bibliographic Essay." *Edith Wharton Review* 7.1 (Spring 1990): 18–22.

Benert, Annette Larson. "Geography of Gender in *The House of Mirth.*" *Studies in the Novel* 22.1 (Spring 1990): 26–42.

Dupree, Ellen. "Jamming the Machinery: Mimesis in *The Custom of the Country.*" *American Literary Realism* 22.2 (Winter 1990): 5–16.

Elbert, Monika M. "The Politics of Maternality in *Summer.*" *Edith Wharton Review* 7.2 (Winter 1990): 4–9, 24.

Goodwyn, Janet. *Edith Wharton: Traveller in the Land of Letters.* New York: St. Martin's P, 1990.

Lauer, Kristin O. and Margaret P. Murray, eds. *Edith Wharton: An Annotated Secondary Bibliography.* New York: Garland P, 1990.

Papke, Mary E. "Edith Wharton's Social Fiction." *Verging on the Abyss: The Social Fiction of Kate Chopin and Edith Wharton.* New York: Greenwood P, 1990.

Pierce, Rosemary Erickson. "Clare Van Degen in *The Custom of the Country.*" *Studies in American Fiction* 17.1 (Spring 1990): 107–110.

Powers, Lyall H., ed. *Henry James and Edith Wharton: Letters: 1900–1915.* New York: Scribners, 1990.

Rose, Christine. "*Summer:* The Double Sense of Wharton's Title." *American Notes and Queries* 3.1 (January 1990): 16–19.

Stengel, Ellen Powers. "Edith Wharton Rings 'The Lady's Maid's Bell.'" *Edith Wharton Review* 7.1 (Spring 1990): 3–9.

Wagner-Martin, Linda. *The House of Mirth: A Novel of Admonition.* Boston: G. K. Hall, 1990.

Abbott, Reginald. "'A Moment's Ornament': Wharton's Lily Bart and Art Nouveau." *Mosaic* 24.2 (Spring 1991): 73–91.

Blackall, Jean Frantz. "The Intrusive Voice: Telegrams in *The House of Mirth* and *The Age of Innocence*." *Women's Studies* 29 (1991): 163–68.

Chandler, Marilyn R. *Dwelling in the Text: Houses in American Fiction*. Berkeley, CA: U of California P, 1991.

Colquitt, Clare. "Succumbing to the 'Literary Style': Arrested Desire in *The House of Mirth*." *Women's Studies* 20.2 (1991): 153–62.

Dittmar, Linda. "When Privilege is No Protection: The Woman Artist in *Quicksand* and *The House of Mirth*." *Writing the Woman Artist: Essays in Poetics, Politics, and Portraiture*. Ed. Suzanne W. Jones. Philadelphia, PA: U of Pennsylvania P, 1991.

Elbert, Monika. "The Transcendental Economy of Wharton's Gothic Mansions." *American Transcendental Quarterly* 9.1 (March 1991): 51–61.

Fedorko, Kathy A. "Edith Wharton's Haunted Fiction: 'The Lady's Maid's Bell' and *The House of Mirth*." *Haunting the House of Fiction: Feminist Perspectives on Ghost Stories by American Women*. Eds. Lynette Carpenter and Wendy K. Kolmar. Knoxville, U of Tennessee P, 1991.

Fracasso, Evelyn E. "The Transparent Eyes of May Welland in Wharton's *The Age of Innocence*." *Modern Language Studies* 21.4 (Fall 1991): 43–48.

Hochman, Barbara. "The Rewards of Representation: Edith Wharton, Lily Bart and the Writer/Reader Interchange." *Novel: A Forum on Fiction* 24.2 (Winter 1991): 147–61.

Holbrook, David. *Edith Wharton and the Unsatisfactory Man*. New York: St. Martin's P, 1991.

Joslin, Katherine. "Edith Wharton and the Critics." *Women Writers: Edith Wharton*. New York: St. Martin's P, 1991. 128–50.

Orr, Elaine Neil. "Contractual Law, Relational Whisper: A Reading of Edith Wharton's *The House of Mirth*." *Modern Language Quarterly* 52.1 (March 1991): 53–70.

Pfeiffer, Kathleen. "*Summer* and its Critics' Discomfort." *Women's Studies* 20 (1991): 141–52.

Raphael, Lev. *Edith Wharton's Prisoners of Shame: A New Perspective on Her Neglected Fiction*. New York: St. Martin's P, 1991.

Thomas, Jennice G. "Spook or Spinster? Edith Wharton's 'Miss Mary Pask.'" *Haunting the House of Fiction: Feminist Perspectives on Ghost Stories by American Women*. Eds. Lynette Carpenter and Wendy K. Kolmar. Knoxville, TN: U of Tennessee P, 1991.

Waid, Candace. *Edith Wharton's Letters from the Underworld: Fictions of Women and Writing*. Chapel Hill, NC: U of North Carolina P, 1991.

White, Barbara A. *Edith Wharton: A Study of the Short Fiction*. New York: G. K. Hall, 1991.

Bendixen, Alfred and Annette Zilversmit, eds. *Edith Wharton: New Critical Essays*. New York: Garland, 1992.

Blackall, Jean Frantz. "Charity at the Window: Narrative Technique in Edith Wharton's *Summer*." *Edith Wharton: New Critical Essays*. Eds. Alfred Bendixen and Annette Zilversmit. New York: Garland, 1992.

———. "Imaginative Encounter: Edith Wharton and Emily Brontë." *Edith Wharton Review* 9.1 (Spring 1992): 9–11, 27.

Erlich, Gloria. *The Sexual Education of Edith Wharton*. Berkeley, CA: U of California P, 1992.

Evans, Tamara. "Edith Wharton and Poetic Realism: An Impasse." *The German Quarterly* 65 (Summer-Fall 1992): 361–68.

Fryer, Judith. "Reading Mrs. Lloyd." *Edith Wharton: New Critical Essays*. Eds. Alfred Bendixen and Annette Zilversmit. New York: Garland P, 1992.

Goldner, Ellen J. "The Lying Woman and the Cause of Social Anxiety: Interdependence and the Woman's Body in *The House of Mirth*." *Women's Studies* 21 (1992): 285–305.

McDowell, Margaret B. "Edith Wharton's Ghost Tales Reconsidered." *Edith Wharton: New Critical Essays*. Eds. Alfred Bendixen and Annette Zilversmit. New York: Garland, 1992.

Murphy, John J. "Filters, Portraits, and History's Mixed Bag: *A Lost Lady* and *The Age of Innocence*." *Twentieth Century Literature* 38.4 (Winter 1992): 476–84.

Pöder, Elfriede. "Concepts and Visions of 'The Other': The Place of 'Woman' in *The Age of Innocence*, *Melanctha*, and *Nightwood*." *Women in Search of Literary Space*. Eds. Gudrun M. Grabher and Maureen Devine. Tübingen: Gunter Narr Verlag, 1992. 171–83.

Riegel, Christian. "Rosedale and Anti-Semitism in *The House of Mirth*." *Studies in American Fiction* 20.2 (Autumn 1992): 219–24.

Sensibar, Judith L. "Edith Wharton Reads the Bachelor Type: Her Critique of Modernism's Representative Man." *Edith Wharton: New Critical Essays*. Eds. Alfred Bendixen and Annette Zilversmit. New York: Garland P, 1992.

Singley, Carol J. "Gothic Borrowings and Invocations in Edith Wharton's 'A Bottle of Perrier.'" *Edith Wharton: New Critical Essays*. Eds. Alfred Bendixen and Annette Zilversmit. New York: Garland, 1992.

Tuttleton, James W., Kristin O. Lauer, and Margaret P. Murray, eds. *Edith Wharton: The Contemporary Reviews*. New York: Cambridge UP, 1992.

Werlock, Abby H. P. "Edith Wharton's Subtle Revenge?: Morton Fullerton and the Female Artist in *Hudson River Bracketed* and *The Gods Arrive*." *Edith Wharton: New Critical Essays*. Eds. Alfred Bendixen and Annette Zilversmit. New York: Garland P, 1992.

Yeazell, Ruth Bernard. "The Conspicuous Wasting of Lily Bart." *English Literary History* 59.3 (Fall 1992): 713–34.

Zilversmit, Annette. "'All Souls': Wharton's Last Haunted House and Future Directions for Criticism." *Edith Wharton: New Critical Essays*. Eds. Alfred Bendixen and Annette Zilversmit. New York: Garland, 1992.

Bendixen, Alfred. "New Directions in Wharton Criticism: A Bibliographic Essay." *Edith Wharton Review* 10.2 (Fall 1993): 20–24.

Benstock, Shari. "'The Word Which Made all Clear': The Silent Close of *The House of Mirth*." *Famous Last Words: Changes in Gender and Narrative Closure*. Ed. Allison Booth. Charlottesville, VA: UP of Virginia, 1993.

Burleson, Mollie L. "Edith Wharton's *Summer*: Through the Glass Darkly." *Studies in Weird Fiction* 13 (Summer 1993): 19–21.

Gabler-Hover, Janet and Kathleen Plate. "*The House of Mirth* and Edith Wharton's 'Beyond!'" *Philological Quarterly* 72.3 (Summer 1993): 357–78.

Goldman, Irene C. "The *Perfect* Jew and *The House of Mirth*: A Study in Point of View." *Modern Language Studies* 23.2 (Spring 1993): 25–36.

Hadley, Kathy Miller. *In the Interstices of the Tale: Edith Wharton's Narrative Strategies*. New York: Peter Lang, 1993.

Heller, Janet Ruth. "Ghosts and Marital Estrangement: An Analysis of 'Afterward.'" *Edith Wharton Review* 10.1 (Spring 1993): 18–19.

Inness, Sherrie A. "An Economy of Beauty: The Beauty System in 'The Looking Glass' and 'Permanent Wave.'" *Edith Wharton Review* 10.1 (Spring 1993): 7–11.

Killoran, Helen. "Pascal, Brontë, and 'Kerfol': The Horrors of a Foolish Quarrel" (misprinted as "Quartet"). *Edith Wharton Review* 10.1 (Spring 1993): 12–17.

Marshall, Scott. "Edith Wharton, Kate Spenser, and *Ethan Frome*." *Edith Wharton Review* 10.1 (Spring 1993): 20–22.

Sapora, Carol Baker. "Female Doubling: The Other Lily Bart in Edith Wharton's *The House of Mirth*." *Papers on Language and Literature* 29.4 (Fall 1993): 371–94.

Singley, Carol J. and Susan Elizabeth Sweeney, eds. "Forbidden Reading and Ghostly Writing in Edith Wharton's 'Pomegranate Seed.'" *Anxious Power: Reading, Writing, and Ambivalence in Narrative by Women*. New York: State U of New York P, 1993.

Springer, Marlene. *Ethan Frome: A Nightmare of Need*. New York: G. K. Hall, 1993.

Wolff, Cynthia Griffin. "Lily Bart and the Masquerade Inscribed in the Female Mode." *Wretched Exotic: Edith Wharton in Europe*. Eds. Katherine Joslin and Alan Price. New York: Peter Lang, 1993.

Banta, Martha. "The Ghostly Gothic of Wharton's Everyday World." *American Literary Realism* 27.1 (Fall 1994): 1–10.

Benstock, Shari. "A Critical History of *The House of Mirth*." Edith Wharton: *The House of Mirth*, Ed. Shari Benstock. Boston, MA: Bedford, 1994.

———. *No Gifts from Chance: A Biography of Edith Wharton*. New York: Scribners, 1994.

———, ed. *The House of Mirth by Edith Wharton*. Boston Bedford, 1994.

Campbell, Donna M. "Edith Wharton and the 'Authoresses': The Critique of Local Color in Wharton's Early Fiction." *Studies in American Fiction* 22.2 (Autumn 1994): 169–83.

Fracasso, Evelyn E. *Edith Wharton's Prisoners of Consciousness*. Westport, CT: Greenwood P, 1994.

Hoeller, Hildegard. "'The Impossible Rosedale': Race and the Reading of Edith Wharton's *The House of Mirth*." *Studies in Jewish Literature* 13 (1994): 14–20.

Kaye, Richard A. "Literary Naturalism and the Passive Male: Edith Wharton's Revisions of *The House of Mirth*." *The Princeton University Library Chronicle* 56.1 (Autumn 1994): 46–72.

Mehaffy, Marilyn Maness. "Manipulating the Metaphors: *The House of Mirth* and 'the Volcanic Nether-Side' of Sexuality." *College Literature* 21.2 (June 1994): 47–62.

Norris, Margot. "Death by Speculation: Deconstructing *The House of Mirth*." *Edith Wharton: The House of Mirth*. Ed. Shari Benstock. Boston, MA: Bedford, 1994.

Robinson, Lillian S. "The Traffic in Women: A Cultural Critique of *The House of Mirth*." *Edith Wharton: The House of Mirth*. Ed. Shari Benstock. Boston, MA: Bedford, 1994.

Sullivan, Ellie Ragland. "The Daughter's Dilemma: Psychoanalytic Interpretation and Edith Wharton's *The House of Mirth*." *Edith Wharton: The House of Mirth*. Ed. Shari Benstock. Boston, MA: Bedford, 1994.

Bell, Millicent, ed. *The Cambridge Companion to Edith Wharton*. New York: Cambridge UP, 1995.

Bentley, Nancy. *The Ethnography of Manners: Hawthorne, James, Wharton*. New York: Cambridge UP, 1995.

Colquitt, Clare. "Contradictory Possibilities: Wharton Scholarship 1992–1994." *Edith Wharton Review* 12.2 (Fall 1995): 37–41.

Fedorko, Kathy. *Gender and the Gothic in the Fiction of Edith Wharton.* Tuscaloosa, AL: U of Alabama P, 1995.

Hochman, Barbara. "*The Awakening* and *The House of Mirth*: Plotting Experience and Experiencing Plot." *The Cambridge Companion to American Realism and Naturalism: Howells to London.* Ed. Donald Pizer. New York: Cambridge UP, 1995.

Howard, Maureen. "The Bachelor and the Baby: *The House of Mirth.*" *The Cambridge Companion to Edith Wharton.* Ed. Millicent Bell. New York: Cambridge UP, 1995.

Kaye, Richard A. "Textual Hermeneutics and Belated Male Heroism: Edith Wharton's Revisions of *The House of Mirth* and the Resistance to American Literary Naturalism." *Arizona Quarterly* 52.3 (Autumn 1995): 87–116.

Knights, Pamela. "Forms of Disembodiment: The Social Subject in *The Age of Innocence.*" *The Cambridge Companion to Edith Wharton.* Ed. Millicent Bell. New York: Cambridge UP, 1995.

Pizer, Donald. "The Naturalism of Edith Wharton's *The House of Mirth.*" *Twentieth Century Literature* 41.2 (June 1995): 241–48.

Showalter, Elaine. "*The Custom of the Country:* Spragg and the Art of the Deal." *The Cambridge Companion to Edith Wharton.* Ed. Millicent Bell. New York: Cambridge UP, 1995.

Singley, Carol J. *Edith Wharton: Matters of Mind and Spirit.* New York: Cambridge UP, 1995.

Skillern, Rhonda. "Becoming a 'Good Girl': Law, Language, and Ritual in Edith Wharton's *Summer.*" *The Cambridge Companion to Edith Wharton.* Ed. Millicent Bell. New York: Cambridge UP, 1995.

Sweeney, Susan Elizabeth. "Mirror, Mirror, on the Wall: Gazing in Edith Wharton's 'Looking Glass.'" *Narrative* 3.2 (May 1995): 139–60.

Balestra, Gianfranca. "'For the Use of the Magazine Morons': Edith Wharton Rewrites the Tale of the Fantastic." *Studies in Short Fiction* 33.1 (Winter 1996): 13–25.

Brooks, Kristina. "New Woman, Fallen Woman: The Crisis of Reputation in Turn-of-the-Century Novels by Pauline Hopkins and Edith Wharton." *Legacy* 13.2 (1996): 91–112.

Clubbe, John. "Interiors and the Interior Life in Edith Wharton's *The House of Mirth.*" *Studies in the Novel* 28.4 (Winter 1996): 542–64.

Dyman, Jenni. *Lurking Feminism: The Ghost Stories of Edith Wharton.* New York: Peter Lang, 1996.

Edmunds, Mary K. "A Theatre With All the Lusters Blazing: Customs, Costumes, and Customers in *The Custom of the Country*." *American Literary Realism* 28.3 (Spring 1996): 1–18.

Hummel, William E. "My 'Dull-Witted Enemy': Symbolic Violence and Abject Maleness in Edith Wharton's *Summer*." *Studies in American Fiction* 24.2 (Autumn 1996): 215–36.

Killoran, Helen. *Edith Wharton: Art and Allusion*. Tuscaloosa, AL: U of Alabama P, 1996.

———. "Sexuality and Abnormal Psychology in Edith Wharton's 'The Lady's Maid's Bell.'" *CEA Critic* 58.3 (Spring-Summer 1996): 41–49.

MacComb, Debra Ann. "New Wives for Old: Divorce and the Leisure-Class Marriage Market in Edith Wharton's *The Custom of the Country*." *American Literature* 68.4 (December 1996): 765–97.

MacMaster, Anne. "Virginia Woolf and the Female Moderns." *Virginia Woolf: Texts and Contexts*. Eds. Beth Rigel Daugherty and Eileen Barrett. Westerville, OH: Pace UP, 1996.

Merish, Lori. "Engendering Naturalism: Narrative Form and Commodity Spectacle in U.S. Naturalist Fiction." *Novel: A Forum on Fiction* 29.3 (Spring 1996): 319–45.

Price, Alan. *The End of the Age of Innocence: Edith Wharton and the First World War*. New York: St. Martin's, 1996.

Wagner-Martin, Linda. "Prospects for the Study of Edith Wharton." *Resources for American Literary Studies* 22.1 (1996): 1–15.

Waid, Candace. "Building *The House of Mirth*." *Biographies of Books: The Compositional Histories of Notable American Writings*. Eds. James Barbour and Tom Quirk. Columbia, MO: U of Missouri P, 1996.

Wegener, Frederick, ed. *Edith Wharton: The Uncollected Critical Writings*. Princeton, NJ: Princeton, UP, 1996.

Young, Judy. "The Repudiation of Sisterhood in Edith Wharton's 'Pomegranate Seed.'" *Studies in Short Fiction* 33 (1996): 1–11.

Bauer, Dale M. *Edith Wharton's Brave New Politics*. Madison, WI: U of Wisconsin P, 1997.

Commins, Barbara. "'Pecking at the Host': Transgressive Wharton." *Edith Wharton Review* 14.1 (Spring 1997): 18–21.

Connell, Eileen. "Edith Wharton Joins the Working Class: *The House of Mirth* and the New York City Working Girls' Clubs." *Women's Studies* 2.6 (1997): 557–604.

Fryer, Judith. "Edith Wharton." *American Women Fiction Writers 1900–1960*. Vol. 3. Ed. Harold Bloom. Philadelphia, PA: Chelsea House, 1997.

Gair, Chrisopher. "The Crumbling Structure of 'Appearances': Representation and Authenticity in *The House of Mirth* and *The Custom of the Country*." *Modern Fiction Studies* 43.2 (Summer 1997): 349–73.

Hutchinson, Stuart. "From *Daniel Deronda* to *The House of Mirth*." *Essays in Criticism* 47.4 (October 1997): 315–31.

Nettles, Elsa. *Language and Gender in American Fiction: Howells, James, Wharton and Cather*. Charlottesville, VA: UP of Virginia, 1997.

Orr, Elaine Neil, "Negotiation [*sic*] Our Text: The Search for Accommodations in Edith Wharton's *The House of Mirth*." *Subject to Negotiation: Reading Feminist Criticism and American Women's Fictions*. Charlottesville, VA: UP of Virginia, 1997.

Werlock, Abby H. P. "Whitman, Wharton, and the Sexuality in *Summer*." *Speaking the Other Self: American Women Writers*. Ed. Jeanne Campbell Reesman. Athens, GA: U of Georgia P, 1997.

Wilson-Jordan, Jacqueline S. "Telling the Story That Can't Be Told: Hartley's Role as Dis-Eased Narrator in 'The Lady's Maid's Bell.'" *Edith Wharton Review* 14.1 (Spring 1997): 12–17, 21.

Moddelmog, William E. "Disowning 'Personality': Privacy and Subjectivity in *The House of Mirth*." *American Literature* 70.2 (June 1998): 337–63.

Ouzgane, Lahoucine. "Mimesis and Moral Agency in Wharton's *The House of Mirth*." *Anthropoetics* 3.2 (Fall 1997/Winter 1998): 1–8.

Stange, Margit. "Edith Wharton and the Problem of the Woman Author." *Personal Property: Wives, White Slaves, and the Market in Women*. Baltimore, MD: Johns Hopkins UP, 1998.

Cahir, Linda Costanzo. *Solitude and Society in the Works of Herman Melville and Edith Wharton*. Westport, CT: Greenwood P, 1999.

Tintner, Adeline. *Edith Wharton in Context: Essays on Intertextuality*. Tuscaloosa, AL: U Alabama P, 1999.

2000s

Kassanoff, Jennie A. "Extinction, Taxidermy, *Tableaux Vivants*: Staging Race and Class in *The House of Mirth*." *PMLA* 115 (January 2000): 60–74.

Killoran, Helen. "Under the Granite Outcroppings of *Ethan Frome*." *Literary Imagination* 2.3 (Fall 2000): 32–34.

Index